The African presence

MANCHESTER
1824

Manchester University Press

The African presence

Representations of Africa in the construction of Britishness

Graham Harrison

Manchester University Press
Manchester and New York
distributed in the United States exclusively
by Palgrave Macmillan

Published by Manchester University Press
Oxford Road, Manchester M13 9NR, UK
and Room 400, 175 Fifth Avenue, New York, NY 10010, USA
www.manchesteruniversitypress.co.uk

Distributed in the United States exclusively by
Palgrave Macmillan, 175 Fifth Avenue, New York,
NY 10010, USA

Distributed in Canada exclusively by
UBC Press, University of British Columbia, 2029 West Mall,
Vancouver, BC, Canada V6T 1Z2

British Library Cataloguing-in-Publication Data
A catalogue record for this book is available from the British Library

Library of Congress Cataloging-in-Publication Data applied for

ISBN 978 0 7190 8885 8 hardback

First published 2013

The publisher has no responsibility for the persistence or accuracy of URLs for any external or third-party internet websites referred to in this book, and does not guarantee that any content on such websites is, or will remain, accurate or appropriate.

Edited and typeset
by Frances Hackeson Freelance Publishing Services, Brinscall, Lancs
Printed in Great Britain
by TJ International Ltd

Contents

Tables

Preface

Having carried out research in Africa since the mid-1990s, I have come to see two kinds of Africa. Firstly, the different experiences and encounters during research trips: the people met during efforts to carry out research, the hospitality, the strangers displaying a range of dispositions from restrained hostility to overwhelming friendliness; the travel experiences; the academic and intellectual conversations; the tropical environments; the architectures of formality and informality that busily comingle and so on. Secondly, the Africa presented to the general public in Britain: the poverty, disease, war and drought; the wildlife; the children, women, and men directly addressing the camera; the appeal, campaign, political moralities; and the solidarity.

This book is an attempt to make sense of the latter view. It does so by looking at Africa campaigns in Britain. The reader can judge the book on its merits. I would like to start with an initial note on campaign organisations from the point of view of personal subjectivity. At times, during interviews I encountered a palpable antagonism towards me as a researcher. The gist of this, I think, was that academics are tendentially critical (*mea culpa*!) and that it is a lot easier to write about what is wrong with campaigning rather than pragmatically address important development and social justice issues in difficult political environments. If my intuition of this antagonism is right (it was only once stated explicitly to me), then I think that they have a point.

Although I think it is more complicated than that. Writing this book has not been easy, but that is not really an interesting response to the issue. The more worrying possibility is that critical analysis of campaigning is actually politically 'regressive': it undermines what is essentially a good project – to work to reduce poverty and suffering. So, let me be a little confessional in the preface before the proper academic material rolls out in the chapters. I have been an occasionally active member of various campaign organisations since the early 1990s. Amongst other things, I was a member of the Mozambique

Angola Committee, was involved in anti-apartheid activism, joined Oxfam and worked for them as a volunteer in the Leeds Development Education Centre. I left Oxfam after receiving campaign material based on an invitation to chose your favourite celebrity advocate for a campaign. I joined the World Development Movement at about the same time.

I think that there is a great deal of value in being involved in Africa campaigning. I think that a great deal of campaigning has various positive effects on public deliberation and political processes. If this book reads as a critique then it is largely a reflection of the 'agonistic' nature of campaigning in Britain – the broader political context and history – rather than an essential wrongheadedness of Africa campaigning. Some campaigns are more agreeable to me than others: campaigns based on notions of social justice are, in my view, politically a great deal more attractive than charitable appeals. Africa campaigns are – like all political movements – fallible.

Acknowledgements

Thanks to the following for comments on parts of the book: Rita Abrahamsen, Daniel Brockington, Ray Bush, Henry Kippin, Nick Sireau, Joerg Wiegratz. I am grateful to the many campaign workers who gave time for interviews: Carolyn Culey, Martin Drewry, Alison Fenney, Sam Gurney, John Hilary, Amanda Horton-Mastin, Sarah Kline, Adrian Lovett, Kirsty McNeill, Emma Parry, Stephen Rand, Tom Sharman, Benedict Southworth, Glen Tarman, Steve Tibbett, and Romina Vegro.

In obscure but important ways, Paul Harris and John Sephton kept this project on track.

Many conversations with the artist and musician Professor Duncan Higgins helped immensely in formulating my ways of thinking about representation and sentiment.

As ever, it's all about Jane, Jack and Lydia.

Abbreviations

AAM	Anti-Apartheid Movement
AR	Annual Review (Oxfam)
BBA	British Biafra Association
BOND	British Overseas NGOs for Development
CAFOD	Catholic Agency for Overseas Development
CSO	Civil Society Organisation
CT	Coordination Team
DAT	Debt AIDS Trade Africa
EPLF	Eritrean People's Liberation Front
G-CAP	Global Coalition Against Poverty
IDAF	International Defence and Aid Fund
INGO	International Non-governmental Organisation
J2000	Jubilee 2000
JDC	Jubilee Debt Coalition
MPH	Make Poverty History
NGO	Non-governmental organisation
SCF	Save the Children Fund
TPLF	Tigrayan People's Liberation Front
UKAN	United Kingdom Aid Network
WoW	War on Want

1

Representing Africa

Introduction

This book is about the ways in which Africa[1] has been represented within British modernity. More specifically, it looks at the ways that Africa has been evoked within what one might broadly call development campaigning. More than any other part of the world, Africa has served as the spatial focus on development discussion in Britain, and campaign organisations have been the central agency in propounding images and arguments about Africa. They have done this purposefully in order to engage with the British public.

Of course, Africa campaign organisations have varied a great deal in terms of their institutional make-up. Furthermore, they have devised a wide diversity of representations of Africa. They have done so over a period of some 200 years, during which both British and African modernities have been in considerable flux. So, there is a great deal of complexity and change to take into account. Throughout, this book will endeavour to be cognisant of the historical sequencing, institutional complexity, and representational diversity that this context connotes.

But, the book does not aim to map out or describe the rolling out of different representations over time. It does aspire to develop core arguments that seem to tolerate the buffeting effects of historical caprice and political complexity. The main argument is that Africa campaigning has mainly (but never exclusively) been a 'conversation' about the moral nature of Britishness. In this sense, Africa campaigns are 'introverted': developing imagery and discourse *about* Africa addressed *to* Britons in which they tend to take centre-stage. As such, Africa campaigns and the representations of Africa that they have generated in all of their diversity have served to contribute to a process of the construction of British self-perception and even self-esteem.

The connection between Africa campaigning and British virtue is key here. Representations of Africa speak to a British national identity that is ordinal: quite simply that Britain does things about/to Africa. Campaigns have been based in an ontology in which the British state, NGO, or people exercise agency in regard to a variety of issues articulated by campaign organisations. The nature of African societies, sovereignties, or agency is markedly less figured, and in some cases campaigns base themselves very centrally on the representation of Africans as entirely devoid of agency.

The normative drive of the book is not simply to critique campaigns for their evacuation of agency from Africans individually or collectively. Rather, it is to identify the limitations that this approach contains within it. As the book progresses, it opens up campaign representation to new possibilities, although it shies away from specific recommendations or punditry.

The book interjects into an existing literature on various facets of Africa's representation in Britain and relatedly more generally within the West. Its scope and ambition is to offer something both more focused and more broad. The focus on campaign organisations provides an empirical focus; and the selection of a relatively long timeframe (from abolition until the present-day) allows us to identify the sinews of continuity and the tensions towards change in a way that is less evident in studies that look only at empire, colonialism, post-colonialism, or the globalised present-day.

A sense of perspective

This book explores the ways that Africa has been represented within British modernity. The core argument is that representations of Africa have played a role in the construction of British social identities. In this sense, the book aims to destabilise the common ontology of Africa being distant, Africa being 'done to' (Chabal, 1996), and Britain having some kind of timeless stability, a self-evident national coherence and power. This is not to argue that narratives of Africa's vulnerability are misplaced; it is simply to recognise that the explorations and exploitations, missions and colonisations, interventions and aid packages, all have repercussions on Britain as well as Africa.

The focus of the book is the interaction between two spaces: Africa and Britain. However, the notion that there is an aggregate continental space called 'Africa' is either too generalised or too banal a unit to work with. Africa's ontology in this book is more akin to a cognitive space than one marked by state boundaries or geology. As such, we do not need to concern ourselves so much with discerning *in fine* the distinctiveness of Africa *vis-à-vis* other continents, regions, or states. In Chapter 6, we will look at the ways that essentialisms about Africa have been produced and indeed how they have changed rather than moved towards a greater degree of certainty about the 'real' Africa.[2] In Chapter 7, we will argue that contemporary representations of Africa are in some ways less certain now than they have been previously.

Post-colonial approaches to the study of Africa and other parts of the world formerly subjected to European empire would readily agree with this anti-essentialist position, one in which places are seen cognitively and as constructions. Most famously, Edward Said (2005) has argued that modern European intellectualism has been constructed on an imagined 'other' that has essential properties of exoticism, emotion, and violence – all of the properties supposedly antithetical to post-Enlightenment Europe after the late 1700s. This is what Said called Eurocentrism.

But, it is striking that Said does not deal with Africa – even if he does draw on brief examples of European–Africa engagements.[3] There might be many reasons for this, but it does suggest that a purely ideational approach to the representation of the non-European is too permissive in the sense that it provides too broad a history and too broad a space to expect any researcher to provide adequate and inclusive coverage. And, in light of this point, it is also important to consider why it is *Africa* that is largely missing from Said's Orient. To be more specific, Africa is not absent from the book; rather, it is that it is not seen as analytically interesting. At least, that would be the ostensible conclusion to draw from the deployment of examples from the Maghreb, the Horn, and Southern Africa but a focus on the Middle and Far East to discern the contours of Orientalism as a way of thinking and seeing.

Might it be that the reason for the elision of Africa lies in some important empirical coordinates? In other words that Africa's tapestry of social organisation and its specific interactions with Europe are distinct, and distinct in ways that diverge from the direction that Said's argument moves in. Europe's encounters with Africa have been relatively late in Europe's broader imperial history. It is also the case that throughout the imperial age, the majority of Africa's space was characterised by relatively small kin-based agrarian communities accompanied by a small number of larger and more centralised kingdoms and trading cities mainly on the coast and along major trade routes.[4] This makes Africa's social history less amenable to the rival civilisations narrative that is present in a lot of historical sociology on Eurocentrism.

This might seem like a contradictory argument: both that there is no positivist-empirical and essential Africa that serves as a metric against which to consider representations of Africa but that there is 'something about Africa' that significantly affects the ways that it has been represented. But, this contradiction is more apparent than substantive. All we are doing here is recognising that Africa has its own historicity (Bayart, 1991; Coquery-Vidrovitch, 1988). That is, Africa has a reasonably coherent set of social and historical patterns that allow us to see it as a single *place*, but its *perception* as a single space is intrinsically a product of the ways that it has been represented. Furthermore, the notion of historicity usefully prohibits us from assuming that any material features of Africanness are immutable: rather, the point is that Africa is changing.

Indeed, all of the forms of representation explored in this book need to be understood historically: not simply as a sequence of representations but also as integrated into a broader set of interactions between Britain and Africa. These interactions will be outlined in Chapter 3. But, it is important to bear in mind that Africa's changing representation is not just a product of a changing Africa; it is also the product of a changing Britain. Indeed, it is one of the weak points of post-colonial studies generally that analyses pay far greater attention to the shifting, constructed, and indeterminate nature of the 'post-colony' but tend to leave Europe, the West, or Britain relatively understudied – almost an Archimedean point of view from core outwards to periphery.[5] The implication here – even if not intended – is that the core or metropole is not subjected to the historical caprice that other parts of the world are. Certainly in Said and those influenced by him, there is a premise that the West is a stable and modern space that then tries to 'contain' in fixed ways other spaces. If one assumes a unique stability to the West, there will always be a sense that no matter how much attention one pays to post-colonial societies and their agency, somehow the West remains dominant or pre-emptory because it does not change, or changes less significantly.[6]

But this is not so. This book will show how, in a specific area of interaction – the representation of Africa within British public space – British modernity was itself constructed, (re)asserted, and modified. And, that these constructions, assertions, and modifications were enacted through practices of Africa's representation. For all of the manifest inequalities between Britain and Africa that have defined the last 250 years, Africa and its representation have, in a sense, helped to produce British modernity: with some licence one can say that images of Africa have helped create modern British nationalism and that representations of Africa have always been at the heart of what passes for British national identity. Much of the rest of this book will demonstrate how this is so in regard to campaign organisations.

A sense of focus

If our interest is the way Africa has been represented within Britain, we quickly come to a difficulty. This is that the representation of Africa in Britain is extremely diverse and multiplex. This is so by various criteria. In terms of imagery, we would need to account of the romantic and scientific, the portrait and caricature, the illustration and the photograph. In terms of literature, we would have to cover the personal diary, the ethnography, the survey, the development appeal, and the storybook. In terms of artefacts we would be mainly concerned with the museum (Woods, 2008), but also the art exhibition, documentary, and the commodity. In terms of political debates, we would need to investigate the lobby, Parliament, civic movements, campaigns, and public intellectuals. With the rise of the media,[7] we would have to open up the discourses and imagery, the norms and values of reportage. In short, the representation of Africa in Britain has been a veritable semiotic industry, involving a range of institutions with a diversity of purposes and generating a raft of different images.[8] Accounting for this industry is beyond this author's abilities, and (more positively) there is some merit in gaining a sense of focus in order to be able to do something more than map and narrate the myriad ways in which Africa has been represented.

Thus, this book is specifically focused on Africa campaigns. What do we mean by Africa campaigns? In the first instance, we understand this institutionally: those organisations that have (a) engaged with and mobilised over some political issue whose provenance is African; (b) that have constituted themselves as publicly recognised organisations which have within their constitutions a concern with Africa; (c) that have made it one of their primary goals to mobilise a broader constituency within the British public around African issues; and (d) that have directed their mobilisational energies towards actions concerning the way that Britain relates to Africa.

Campaign organisations wear their politics on their sleeves. Campaigns usually focus around a single political demand: abolish slavery, independence now, fight apartheid, drop the debt, make poverty history. It would actually be more appropriate to coin each of these demands as exclamatory (abolish slavery!): there is an urgency in campaigns, a strong motivational norm which will be considered more analytically later. The point here is to register the high presence of the political in contrast to other forms of representation. There is some excellent research on the representation of Africa in fiction, art, advertisements, and exhibitions (Coombes, 1994; Crais and Scully, 2009; Koivunen, 2009; Landau and Kaspin, 2002; Ryan, 1997), but in all of this literature the political content of representation requires a certain kind of implied analysis: drawing out heuristically the implicit political codes or norms.

Keeping with this broader picture for now, it is something of a truism to state that Africa's general representation in Britain has by and large been marked by admixtures of racism and arrogance. Indeed, it would be a more interesting approach to invert the burden of proof and ask where the non racist/imperial representations were or are in this respect.[9] But, as already argued in the previous section, if there are continuities in Africa's representation in Britain, they are hardly pristine. While it would be difficult to make a case that representation has ever escaped from a general set of Britain/Africa dyads established in the late seventeenth century as a set of 'negative tropes' (Comaroff and Comaroff, 1997: 689), based in 'manichean allegories' (JanMohamed, 1985) such as light/dark (Achebe, 1977; Brantlinger, 1985; Jarosz, 1992), presence/absence, agency/passive, modern/traditional, orderly/chaotic, normal/exotic, (Crozier, 2007) developed/undeveloped and so on,[10] it would also be difficult to maintain that these dyads are unflinching historical codes that tell us everything about representational form. In other words, we have some rough guides here, not co-ordinates. This book is as interested in the ways Britishness has changed as it is in the ways Africa's representation has changed.

What makes campaigns unique is that they occupy a particular political terrain. This terrain is both oppositional and conforming. Campaigns are necessarily adversarial: they require an object to focus on and push against. Campaigns are dynamic and prospective in a way that other cultural and political articulations of Africa are not. All campaign representations have a purpose (or many purposes), but only campaigns have both such an explicitly political and motile purpose – hence the exclamation marks, the sense of urgency, the will to mobilise. It is this feature that makes campaigns especially interesting as a means through which the British public is invoked. Britain's public space has been drawn upon by campaign organisations, and also to some extent *created through* campaigns themselves.

There is, however, a fairly specific kind of adversariality within Africa campaigns. As will be shown in a more conceptual way a little later, Africa campaigns have tended to serve as an 'immanent critique' of Britain's relations with Africa. Put plainly, Africa campaigns have mainly criticised aspects of Britain's involvement in Africa but within a context that does not problematise involvement per se. Campaigns entreat the British government to be 'better' in its interventions: to be more altruistic, more civilised, more humanitarian. These motivations themselves are not questioned, even if campaigns criticise their weakness in practice or their contested nature as a result of commercial pressures. Again, we will put this feature into some sort of conceptual framework a little later on.

Africa campaigns have changed a great deal in terms of their institutional form. We will come to make a description of Africa campaigns as a campaign tradition, and it is important to note early and clearly that this tradition does not connect to a specific institutional form. Campaigns can be broad and embedded in various institutions, more or less formalised (abolition); they can be focused on one single organisation (the anti-apartheid Movement), or they can be coalitions of like-minded organisations with or without apex leadership (compare Jubilee 2000 and Make Poverty History).

The campaigns selected here are those that have drawn large amounts of public attention. If the focus is on representation, then this makes good sense. However, it does generate some weak spots in the historiography. This is most obvious in regard to campaigns to promote 'civilised' colonialism (e.g. the Fabian Colonial Bureau) and advocacy for Independence (Movement for Colonial Freedom). These will be mentioned in passing but do not constitute focuses in the book. To include these campaign organisations would in effect be to tell stories about lobbying and ideological debate which, although extremely interesting, do not generate much material on representation.

Furthermore, campaign organisations do not always have clearly defined boundaries. Of course, we need to maintain a proper focus on the features outlined earlier in this chapter from (a) to (d). But – precisely because of the emergence of new institutional forms – campaigns have merged and transformed somewhat. The key shift here can be loosely correlated with the period of Independence in the 1960s. It is at this point that development NGOs took off as agents involving themselves in the British public space (Smillie, 1995, Wallace, Chapman, and Bornstein, 1999).[11] These NGOs – Oxfam, Save the Children, CAFOD, Christian Aid, War on Want, Action Aid and so on – emerged as strong Africa campaigners. These NGOs based themselves in a permanent membership, engagement in African issues,[12] and an engagement with the British government. But they are also (with the exception of War on Want) charities. And, herein lies the blurring. NGOs contain within them three institutional imperatives: to campaign, to raise money through charitable appeals, and to execute development work. On one level, these three tasks work well together: they all fit within a meta-norm of humanitarian concern for Africans in poverty. On a more detailed level, the charitable appeal and the campaign have produced a tense cohabitation of representations which are both mutually supporting – in that they maintain an NGO's public profile and resources, and mutually antagonistic – in that they produce contrasting notions of African life and agency (nfp Synergy, no date; Norrell, no date: 15). This tension and its playing out will be returned to throughout the book. The point for now is methodological: that throughout the book, we will allow a degree of 'greyness' between the modern NGO charitable and campaign appeal.

Concepts

The African presence

The notion of the African presence serves here as the main focusing concept. Its value derives from its hermeneutic properties rather than its scientific precision. The term was originally used to announce a political movement in post-war France, driven by radical intellectuals and focused around a journal of political debate. The *Présence Africaine* aimed, as V. Y. Mudimbe put it, to 'incarnate the voice of a silenced Africa' within French public culture (1992: xviii).[13] The *Présence Africaine* served as an intellectual and political agenda to articulate and assert a 'rival modernity' against the decolonising heartland, based in notions of negritude, African nationalism, and socialism. We take from this a sense of interpolated cultural expression – the interjection of African political aesthetics into the West; but we must necessarily make some adjustments.

We take the African presence in the UK to be a constitutively *mediated* phenomenon. There is no stable and definitive 'Africa' or African voice;[14] nor does Africa have an essential property that makes it entirely distinct from other places. And, many 'incarnations' of the African presence do not come directly – rather they are brought into British culture, curated and mediated by politicians, the media, and campaigners amongst others. The presence of Africa in Britain – like any other cultural intermingling – is an outcome of practices of representation which are themselves intrinsically mediations. This means that, unlike the original francophone project (which involved African and Caribbean intellectuals), the African presence here has no necessarily radical impetus; indeed, the African presence in British national culture has been largely a result of the ways that British agencies have 'domesticated' Africa into Britain (Mudimbe, 1988: 67) and done so within an imperialist and post-imperialist context. Domestication involves representing Africa as 'at once different, yet soothingly so' in that the act of domestication involves an affirmation of British national culture and inferiority or lack elsewhere (Kim, 2002: 145).[15] John Lonsdale puts it perfectly: the 'popular media constructs Africa as the hopeless, history-less "other", the dark antipodes to the purposeful, liberal – above all, *storied* – west' (Lonsdale, 2005: 2, emphasis in original). The 'storying' is the representational mediation performed by British agencies of one kind or another. This is an important point not only because it significantly attenuates any radical potential of the African presence; it also orients our line of enquiry throughout the book: how representations of Africa have served to consolidate national self-perceptions in Britain.

It is worth dwelling on the issue of domestication a little. This is not simply to aver to an 'importing' of some facet of African social life. Domestication in this sense is necessary but not sufficient to get at the crux of the African presence: it provides a bundle of raw materials (images, arguments, and narratives) with which Africa is represented in Britain. But, domestication also means *making* domestic. More specifically, it means making an aspect of Africa 'legible', rendering it in a national vernacular, making it resonate with some aspect of national public political and normative discourse. Herein lies the *re*presentation, the mediation. It is precisely here that the African presence is about both Africa and Britain. Campaign organisations have served as key institutional mediators of the Africa presence.

It is also worth recognising how diverse the African presence is in Britain. In a sense, Africa has always been with Britain: British political modernity has within it an African 'sinew', woven through the work of Africans in Britain, explorers,[16] humanitarians, novelists, missionaries, colonials, ethnographers, traders, journalists, aid personnel, celebrities ... and of course academic researchers. It is striking that this broad genre of representation has been by and large carried out by White British people. The presence of Africans, African-Caribbeans or Black British people in Africa's representation has been limited and scattered – located mainly within some abolitionist and anti-apartheid narratives (Fryer, 2010: 31–32).

Framing campaigns

How might we analyse the Africa campaign tradition? There are many ways that one might proceed with this question, but certainly one of the most proximate and potentially insightful concepts to use is frame analysis. The notion of framing is commonly used in social movement studies to draw attention to the ways in which movements perceive of political issues and also how movements develop solidarity and adversarial cultures or cultures of contention (Tarrow, 1998). Framing draws our attention towards the 'shared assumptions and meanings [that] shape the interpretation of events' within a movement (Oliver and Johnston, 2000: 37).

Frame analysis has been adopted and adapted[17] by those interested in social movements. Research into social movements has generally moved from a series of materialistic and rational choice approaches towards an interest in identity, norms, and emotions. The key issue is how a collectivity can create a common identity and a common adversary or 'other', what is generally known as collective action framing. Framing refers us to the ways in which a social movement sees itself, its members, society, and its adversaries. The notion of framing works as a simple metaphor: of drawing a boundary around something, in the case of social movements through discourse, practices of social movement membership, and a range of identifications (language, dress, song, etc.).[18] In essence, framing is about the *representation* of a social movement, an issue, and an adversary.

But the notion of the frame is perhaps a little too beguiling: it is almost a metaphor rather than a concept in which issues, perceptions, struggles, and norms can be 'framed' in some sense. Framing comes close to meaning everything and nothing, or at least different things to different people. Looking at the research that develops relatively detailed conceptualisations of framing, the work of David Snow is particularly useful for our purposes. Snow and his collaborators' work is oriented towards a concept of framing as a means to develop collective action, and herein lies a useful triad: diagnostic, prognostic, and motivational frames (Snow and Benford, 1992).

These three kinds of frames are essentially about the way connections are established between an issue, commonly held values, and action. Diagnostic frames pose a problem, issue, or injustice. The content of the diagnostic can vary from something fairly reformist (which is how the Africa campaign tradition tends to articulate it) to something more robustly based in injustice, 'a mode of interpretation that defines the actions of an authority system as unjust and simultaneously legitimates noncompliance' (Snow et al. 1986: 466) which seems more appropriate to direct action protests. Within diagnostic framing, the connection between a problem and the attribution of blame is pivotal because it feeds into the other two frames (Snow and Benford, 1988: 200). This book will suggest that Africa campaigns have tended to articulate diagnostic frames that are strong on problem identification but weak on blame/attribution.

Prognostic frames set out a means through which to engage with or address a problem. This involves both identifying solutions and more action-oriented 'strategies, tactics, and targets' (Snow and Benford, 1988: 201). As the next section will demonstrate, diagnostic and prognostic framing work very closely together: the problem and its solution are effectively articulated as a unity. For a campaign organisation, the posing of a problem only makes sense as a component of a solution. Like diagnostic frames, prognostic frames can vary a great deal in the scope of their ambition and radical potential. Moderate prognostics would require reforms, incremental change, or technical solutions; more radical prognostics tend to engage in more systematic analysis, perhaps about the nature of capitalism, imperialism, or the state system.

Motivational frames evoke norms and values to appeal to people to act. This frame is the *raison d'être* for the previous two because the singular purpose of a campaign is to mobilise. Motivational frames, as the name implies, are rich in norms and emotive appeals: this framing asserts a campaign identity. Motivational frames can be articulated in a variety of ways. Motivation might evoke 'thin' norms that connect many people, or 'thick' norms that generate a stronger sense of identity and adversarialism. Motivation might be based in outrage, enjoyment, affirmation, aesthetics, community, confession and so on. For our purposes – and to signal towards the next section – motivational framing can be broad, inclusive, and based on an evocation of a sense of moral virtue.

Propounding and connecting these three frames is the work of campaign groups. These three frames will be deployed in the next section, but there is an important adaptation taking place here because we are not concerned with social movement organisations strictly speaking. William Gamson – whose own three-way distinction between injustice, identity, and agency provides a match with Snow *et al.*'s three frames – makes the point that collective action frames in social movement studies are adversarial: "'we' stand in opposition or conflict to some 'they'" (Gamson, 1995: 101). Contrastingly, as argued earlier, Africa campaign organisations resemble more closely what Gamson calls 'aggregate frames' in which "'We' are the world, humankind, or ... all good citizens' (*ibid.*). This final phrase, *all good citizens*, cuts directly to the nature of the Africa campaign tradition's connections with British national identity, as will be seen in the next section. This distinction is important: Gamson amongst others has been centrally concerned with the driving mo- tivation of injustice within social movements, but in the aggregate framing, injustice is both weakened and not even necessary: if there is an injustice, the reasons or adversaries that constitute it are at best vaguely specified (consider the notion of poverty in this regard); and the mobilisation within an aggre- gate frame can be entirely non-conflictual (more in the spirit of a 'coming together'). But what, then, of the three frames and their ability to connect with an analysis of organisations that are not necessarily adversarial?

The answer to this question is necessarily hedged. In the first place, we must recognise the internal diversity of campaign organisations in which there are both very moderate 'median' engagements with the British public in which 'we' is as inclusive as possible; but there are also more clearly defined and radi- cal campaign organisations such as the World Development Movement and War on Want which are explicitly adversarial (Luetchford and Burns, 2003). Even Oxfam, commonly seen as the largest and generally moderate campaign organisation devises campaigns that are adversarial in areas such as arms trade and HIV/AIDS antiretrovirals.

In any case (and secondly), Africa campaigns *do* require a sense of adversar- ialism in order to construct a prognostic frame. This is commonly the British government. However, campaigns have to balance a political discourse of cri- tique *and* appeal in regard to how prognostic frames are articulated. It is one thing to appeal to the government's better nature – to assume that the gov- ernment has not acted on a specific issue because it was not aware of the facts for example – and another to highlight more directly how the government has been purposefully remiss perhaps because it serves certain elite interests. The point here is that Africa campaigns have tended to strike a balance that might be summarised as polite adversarialism in their prognostic frames, underpinned by motivational frames that assume that the government responds positively to the mobilisation of its citizens.

Finally, if we are discussing the issue of 'we' and 'them', it is worth noting that there is of course another 'them': Africans. Africa campaigning in Britain has been *on behalf* of Africans, however they are represented within campaign materials. This 'them' is not adversarial, but it nonetheless serves as a crucial component of campaign identity, one that also poses a broader 'we': that of the British nation as a whole. To borrow and adapt from Benedict Anderson's (1991) well-known aphorism: Africa campaigns imagine Britain through Africa; or more relevantly, in Mary Louise Pratt's phrase, Britain 'was constructed from the outside in as much as from the inside out' (Pratt, 1992: 6).[19]

Framing a campaign is, of course, all about trying to make a campaign successful. And here it is important to note something of a Janus quality to framing. In the main, framing analysis has been used to understand the ways that a community of campaigners makes sense of their activism. But frames must also reach out to a broader public culture, in some instances trying to appeal to people who have no familiarity with a cause. As Jasper and Poulsen (1995) argue, campaigns that aim to engage outwards (rather than frame a cause for an 'in group') tend to emphasise the diagnostic frame (problem setting) and represent that frame in a high-impact or 'shock' image. This is certainly the case in a lot of Africa campaigning.[20]

The Africa campaign tradition

Sidney Tarrow relays a common assumption within social movement studies well: that the 'best predictor of activism is past activism' (2005: 47). This section develops this aphorism in regard to Africa's representation through campaign organisations, and in doing so it discerns some key coordinates in the framing of those campaigns. The next section will briefly review the most salient campaign moments in the Africa campaign tradition, treating these campaigns as exemplars of this tradition. Before doing so, it is important to be clear on what we mean by tradition, and this requires two points of clarification.

Firstly, the notion of tradition is not used deterministically. There is no strict template within which campaigns (must) all fit. Rather, we use the notion of tradition in a more constructivist fashion: as a way of acknowledging that any campaign will likely reflect upon and draw on the imagery, norms, and practices of previous campaigns in order to bring their own campaign into the public sphere. Intuitively, one would expect that previous campaigns with a good measure of success would be likely to influence subsequent campaigns pretty strongly. Because campaigns occur in different periods, focused on different issues, each campaign can at most be a facsimile of any previous one, and campaigns may well also innovate and modify existing traditions of campaigning.

There is a considerable literature which develops a range of sophisticated ways of understanding political traditions and their dynamics, largely going under the rubric of historical institutionalism. Within this literature, perhaps the closest approach to ours is that developed by James Mahoney and Kathleen Thelen (2010). Mahoney and Thelen offer a number of useful metaphors to explain processes of change which are moderate and/or incremental rather than epochal and/or sudden. The one that seems most useful here is *layering*: where rules (and norms and practices) are introduced which then change the ways in which broader prevailing rules work (*ibid.*: 16). The metaphor has an affinity with geological phenomena; it seems to suggest a process of accretion in which new properties are added to an object which also change the general properties of the object itself.

Campaigns layer aspects of their own activities onto the tradition, affirming some aspects, rejecting some, and modifying others. The key reasons why we can still speak of a tradition – which must, after all, have some defining features which are reasonably robust – is that there is a certain kind of nationalism 'underdetermining' the layering of the campaign tradition: Christian, liberal, and humanitarian (Howe, 1993; Porter, 2008). This nationalism integrates our understanding of the African presence and the Africa campaign tradition as an example of this presence. The key point here, to state it plainly, is that campaign representations of Africa are principally evoking notions of Britishness – or more specifically *good* Britishness – over and above their efforts to represent Africa in ways that are detailed, faithful to issues of 'true' representation, or derived from the voices and cultural expressions of African societies. This is the 'we' that was earlier glossed as 'good citizens'; it is a nationalist collectivity that is evoked cordially against the 'they' of the British government and emotively in reference to the other 'they' of Africa/Africans.

Britishness is, of course, a much-debated thing. Discursively – and like all nationalisms – it is articulated through a bundle of norms and values. What is important for our purposes is to understand the ways in which Britishness has been expressed through the representation of Africa. 'Britishness' is no more definitive than 'Africanness': they are both unstable composites of evidence, generalisation, and fantasy. The particular facet of Britishness that is most salient for our purposes is Britain's experience as an imperial power.

If there is a constitutive facet of Britishness in relation to the African presence it is empire (Sherwood, 2001). Many historians have come to argue that modern Britishness[21] has always been articulated through a sense of imperial grandeur – the so-called 'new imperial history' school.[22] This grandeur has been based in tropes of mercantile expansion, military prowess, science, civilisation, liberalism, and religion. Indeed, the loss of empire after the Second World War up to the mid-1960s has been seen to have induced a post-imperial melancholia within British public culture (Gilroy, 2004).

The mutual constitution of ideas of Britishness and imperial mission both serves as the 'meta frame' for Africa campaigning, and it bequeaths a legacy to the African presence up to the present day. Although hardly straightforward, there is still an evocation of Britishness in contemporary Africa campaigning that reproduces the general imagery of a powerful Britain and a weak Africa in need of external intervention. This duality is most prominently reasserted after independence through the rise of famine appeals – indeed in the case of the Congo (1960–1961) and Biafra (1967–1969) appeals, the crisis imagery directly suggests that Independence from Britain (or Europe more generally) led to something atavistic and regressive in Africa.

But how does this broad orientation towards national grandeur, a tradition of Britain's victorious continuities, affect Africa campaigning more specifically? There are two key coordinates. In the first place, there is the association between Britishness, (protestant) Christianity, and charity/sympathy. Christian ethics provide a universalist sympathy[23] for distant others based in the virtues of helping those less fortunate than oneself.[24] In the case of Britain, from the late 1800s onwards, Anglican liberal politics comingled with Whiggish party politics as a key force in political modernisation (Brent, 1987).

Secondly, there is Britain's liberalism, articulated initially through 'pragmatic' thinking about civil society, order, and the market in writing by thinkers such as Adam Smith, J. S. Mill, Jeremy Bentham; and subsequently by politicians, campaign organisations, cultural producers, and the media (Mehta, 1999; Muthu, 2003; Pitts, 2005). Writers such as Muthu and Mehta differ in their views as to the relationship between liberalism and the imperial project – most certainly there has been a good deal of inconsistency between the notion of rights and the practice of colonisation (Jahn, 2005a, 2005b).[25] But, ideationally, liberalism's founding ontology of individual rights drove in large part a sense of Britain's national identity and relations with other parts of the world in ways that keyed in closely with Protestantism's own convictions that being a subject of God endowed one with moral choice and inalienable spiritual value (cf. Gray, 2008).

In regard to Africa campaigning, liberal norms – often in conjunction with religious norms – served to assert the notion of humanity and the possibility of Africa's place within this global imaginary. The qualifier 'possibility' bears emphasising. Both religious and liberal ideas were filtered through a third broad orientation which destabilised these universalisms: racism. Indeed, Africa's 'blackness' has been the leitmotif of the African presence in Britain, however the latter is valued. Both liberal and religious arguments in Britain relating to Africa have more or less explicitly[26] relied upon racialised political judgements.

This section has argued that an Africa campaign tradition can be identified within the culture of Britain as an imperial nation. More particularly, the norms of Christianity and liberalism – again very much associated with Britishness – have been evoked within Africa campaigns to attach British virtue to the diagnostics, prognostics, and motivations of campaigns. None of this has worked clearly and smoothly in reality, and the constant undertow of racism constantly works against universalisms. But, *mutatis mutandis*, this set of coordinates allows us to establish a working definition of an Africa campaign tradition.

The themes of this introductory chapter need further fleshing out. Chapter 3 will review the contours of the Britain/Africa encounter and the representations that this has generated. This will give a sense of the historical shifts that have taken place throughout the remit of this book. It will also help locate the specific case studies that follow within historical time. Chapter 4 then makes an introductory review of campaign organisations in order to discern the ways in which framings have been enacted. The point here is to show a certain (unstable) continuity generated by campaign layering. Chapters 5 and 6 take the Janus-like aspect of representation in more detail: looking in at 'Britishness' and then out at 'Africanness'. Chapter 5 shows how strong the liberal Christian humanitarianism is to the Africa campaign tradition, even as it has progressively secularised. Chapter 6 reveals the main shifts in representational work through a discussion of development campaigning, a phenomenon largely realised after the winning of African sovereignties. Chapters 7 and 8 also work in tandem, opening up the ways in which present-day representations and campaigns have both followed the campaign tradition but also opened up new spaces for the tradition's mutability. One can see this in the ways that campaigns have reconciled themselves to the increasing commoditisation of social life and also in the specific 'window' of the Year of Africa (2005). Chapter 9 ends the book with concluding reflections.

But before we explore all of these themes, Chapter 2 provides something of an intermission. This is necessary because looking at images of Africa is hardly straightforward – not only in regard to their complexity and content but also in terms of the emotions that they elicit (already alluded to above as 'shock'). Can anyone in Britain think of a part of the world that has proven so rich in images of suffering? Thus, the next chapter provides a reflection on the emotional issues raised in the witnessing of Africa imagery in Britain.

Notes

1   Throughout this book, 'Africa' refers to Africa south of the Sahara.
2   The complexities and difficulties of finding a 'real' Africa are explored in Howe, 1998.
3   Said's discussion of 'knowing the oriental' starts with more references to Africa than any other part of the world, but he proceeds incrementally to move eastwards and reflect on a concept of the Orient in which Africa does not figure (Said, 2005: 31ff.).
4   See Bayart, 1993; Vansina, 1991.
5   There is also relatively little research on how Africans see Britain or the West; and the extant research tends to be focused on the colonial period (Irobi, 2006).
6   This is hardly exclusive to post-colonial studies. In fact far more reified and rigid versions of the same vision have come from dependency theory and a great deal of International Relations theory as well.
7   A rigorous discourse review of the media is Brookes (1995). See also Crozier (2007) for some historical background and Mawdsley (2008) for something more contemporary although she reveals the persistence of familiar tropes.
8   A sense of the density and diversity of representation can be found by perusing: Anstey, 1962; Brantlinger, 1985; Coombes, 1994; Curtin, 1964 (especially Volume 1); Fulford and Kitson, 1998; Grant, 2005; Hall, 2002; Hammond and Jablow, 1977; Harrison and Palmer, 1986; Mayer, 2002; Nederveen Pieterse, 1992; Porter, 2008; Pratt, 1992; Ramamurthy, 2003; Robinson and Gallagher, 1961; van der Gaag and Nash, 1987; Ward, 2001; and Webster, 2005.
9   A well-written and stimulating start to an answer to this question would be Ferguson, 2004.
10 A reflection on these characterisations – especially Africa-as-absence – can be found in Mbembe, 2001. See also Brantlinger, 1985; Lonsdale, 2005.
11 The first major NGO campaign – tellingly described as a 'crusade' by the campaigners – was the Freedom from Hunger Campaign of the 1960s (Rootes and Saunders, no date: 4).
12 As we shall see in Chapter 4, the crisis in Biafra was a key moment for British 'Africa' NGOs.
13 There is also a slightly paraphrased coining of this phrase by Toni Morrison (1992) within the extended and distinct discussion of Africa's role in American public culture. Sertima (2007) and his colleagues understand the African presence in almost genotypical terms as much as cultural terms.
14 On the question of 'Africanness', see Appiah, 1993; Howe, 1998; Mudimbe, 1988.

15 I am stretching Kim's turn of phrase here – she provides a detailed analysis of racial imagery in the seventeenth century.

16 Some of whom became 'celebrities' when they returned to write and give speeches, notably David Livingstone and Henry Morton Stanley, but there was a train of less-known explorers who 'domesticated' Africa for a British public: Richard Buxton, James Grants, Samuel White Baker. On British exploration, see Curtin (1964: Chapters 5 and 6). The romantic exploration narrative was also propounded within literature such as Haggard's *King Solomon's Mines*.

17 Framing has also been used in psychology and media studies. See Goffman, 1986.

18 The connection of individual identities and values with a social movement is commonly known as frame alignment. See Snow, Burke Rochford, Worden, and Benford, 1986.

19 There is considerable debate about the extent and nature of Britain's 'extroverted' nationalism. For a comprehensive assembling of recent contributions to this debate, see Howe, 2010.

20 On shock and other emotions, see Chapter 2.

21 Britishness might sometimes seem like an awkward term. For much of the eighteenth and some of the nineteenth centuries, British national identity was rather protean. Indeed, the English roots of British empire have been expertly exposed by David Armitage (2002). Nevertheless, it is also striking how prominent the Scottish contribution to the British imperial project was from the mid-1800s, and how the Scottish Enlightenment provided key concepts of the market and social development to the imperial sense that Britain was uniquely modern/civilised. In this book, we take modern Britishness to be something that emerges roughly from the early eighteenth century onwards (Colley, 2005).

22 Key sources from a larger body of literature are: Hall, 2002; Hall and Rose, 2006; Wilson, 2003. An excellent compendium is Howe, 2009.

23 The next chapter will look more analytically at the role of emotions in representation.

24 A rather coruscating formulation of the role of pity in Christianity is Nietzsche, 2003.

25 More specifically on slavery and the 'Negro question', see Kohn and O'Neill, 2006.

26 Explicit racist language generally falls away during the twentieth century, but there also emerges a vocabulary of implicit racism which might rely on the contextual way in which a word like 'them' is used. On more general ideological racial othering within liberalism, see Amin, 2010; Wright Mills, 1997. On race and development, see Kothari, 2006.

2

Putting images into (e)motion: representing Africa through suffering

Africa, representation, and suffering

There is another sense in which Africa is difficult to see. To see Africa one must first see oneself. (Okri, 2009: 8)

Emotive images

On 13 May 2000, *The Economist* carried a front page image of a young Sierra Leonean man with a gun. The lead title on the page was 'Africa: the Hopeless Continent'. It provoked a strong response from African writers who despaired at the negative imagery and text. Previously, and equally infamously, writer Robert Kaplan on the front page of another mainstream American news magazine, the *Atlantic Monthly*, wrote of the 'The Coming Anarchy' (February 1994) in which Africa was presented as a continent descending into chaos, awash with mass suffering. From 1960 (initially as a result of the starvation experienced during the Congo's unstable decolonisation) the British mass media has disseminated images of famine in Africa to such an extent that the association of Africa with hunger on a mass scale is widespread and culturally familiar. So widespread is the association of Africa with mass suffering that this fundamental trope has become a familiar antagonist against which African writers battle to argue for other forms of representation. Consider the darkly sardonic tone of Binyavanga Wainaina giving advice to an imaginary writer: 'Never have a picture of a well-adjusted African on the cover of your book, or in it, unless that African has won the Nobel Prize. An AK-47, prominent ribs, naked breasts: use these.' (2005: no page)
He continues:

Among your characters you must always include The Starving African, who wanders the refugee camp nearly naked, and waits for the benevolence of the West. Her children have flies on their eyelids and pot bellies, and her breasts are flat and empty. She must look utterly helpless. She can have no past, no history; such diversions ruin the dramatic moment. Moans are good. She must never say anything about herself in the dialogue except to speak of her (unspeakable) suffering.

Wainaina's acerbic (but broadly accurate) narrative is a powerful critique against the canons of Africa's representation and within it the habitual reference to mass suffering. Since the 1960s, no other continent has been represented so singly as a place of mass suffering. 'The Starving African' (ironically capitalised by Wainaina to intimate its typological status) has become an embodiment of Africa in British public culture.

This book examines Africa's representation and specifically the way that campaign organisations have mobilised African causes. This chapter serves in a way as a prelude to the more empirical chapters. It is important not simply to assume that Africa's mass suffering (which is real enough) is a simple fact that can be related by campaign organisations to a beneficent public. This is the case most directly in terms of the particular characteristics of the famine image. Along with images of torture and murder, these images are the most disturbing that one can see (Sontag, 2004). This being the case, we should reflect on the emotional aspects of the famine image and try to connect these aspects with broader issues of representation.

During the writing of this book, I have been trying to track down a series of images from the 1988 famine in Sudan. The images are sequential and are taken in a food distribution centre. A tiny child sits by a bowl of grain by himself. A man walks up to the child. The man takes the grain from the child. The child looks up at the man.

This is my recollection of the images which I saw at least ten years ago, so in writing I have very likely created these images as much as described them. But the images are extant (somewhere), and they do directly transpose a real event into a sequence of images. And they had an impact on me. I have been careful to provide a minimal account of the photos in the above paragraph, but in recollecting them they become full of other kinds of content. I see the images with a pause between the man's approach and his taking the grain, as if considering the moral repercussions of his act of dispossession. I also see the child's gaze as complex and extremely upsetting: he (I think) conveys a realisation that he is going to die as a result of the loss of grain, a plea to the man, and most profoundly a complete sense of helplessness. Some or even all of these transactions might have happened. I also tend to see the man as a trader, a view influenced by writers in political economy who identified in

Sudan how famine allows opportunities to work markets, accumulate, and hoard (Bush, 1988; Keen, 1994).

As I recall the images, they upset me. This might seem self-evident to anyone who considers themselves to be humanitarian in moral orientation. Perhaps this is simply how 'good people' feel about this kind of image. This chapter explores how the cognitive, moral, and emotional reflexes provoked by images of suffering in Africa are profoundly political and that therefore – whatever one's views about human nature, traits of humanitarianism, and sympathy[1] – even the most direct connections between images of suffering and their emotional relays brings us to questions of power, identity, institutions, and history.

For now, we shall remain focused mainly on the emotive nature of imagery. The reasons for doing this are both *sui generis* and because they feed into the rest of the book. In regard to the former, it is important to recognise a premise about Africa's representation which is that it is often based on images of extreme suffering and that in the first instance – and with a resonance throughout any subsequent cognitive and reactive moments – these images produce a strong emotional reaction. The rest of this chapter will explore the ways in which we might describe these emotions before building a theoretical bridge between the apparently personal and confessional discourse of emotions (the way we feel) and the ways in which the emotional becomes *emotive*, that is, driving broader acts of valuing and political conviction.

Mapping compassion

To start at the beginning, there is sympathy: a complex emotional affinity with the sufferer. This sympathy can feel painful. The pain derives from a (weak) empathy for suffering. There is also a sense that – although the connections might be obscure – the suffering of the subject in an image is a negation of something broader, perhaps a more encompassing collectivity or identity. One might call this 'humanitarianism'. If we have any conviction that there is a universal human condition – even one pared down to very basic biological needs – then the denial of these 'basic needs' can be in some mediated sense recognised by distant others as a terrible thing. The sympathetic reaction is, then, a conspecific one. Furthermore, this reaction might be closely tied to a broader sympathy in which one does not simply 'feel' in some vicarious way the pain of others, but also 'feel for' that person, generating stronger acts of valuation which might in turn modify the nature of the agency of the viewer – say, to give to charity, pray, join a rally, or write. This painful and more expansive sympathy constituted my own emotional starting points.

I am sure of my sympathy in other ways but less *clear* about its sense. The Sudan child image outlined above is especially evocative. It has become increasingly difficult to witness images of children suffering since I became a parent, a banal point, but no less true for that, and a point that draws our attention to our own particular positionalities. In this sense emotional reactions to images render them dialogic; their reception is a result of an interaction between the content and the subjectivity of the viewer.

The Sudan famine image is also of a black child. Any white British person observing images of Africa who has an interest in reflecting on their emotional responses would do well to recognise the racialised and racist characteristics of British culture, even if these have softened as the age of empire becomes more distant.[2] I was exposed to racist representations of Africans from my early years: I can remember a teacher at primary school (I must have been between 5 and 10 years old) telling us – in the idiom of a storytelling homily – that God punished some humans for being bad by spraying them black, but because they were standing up with their hands against a surface, He missed the palms of their hands and soles of their feet which is why black people have lighter skin there.[3] We listened to the story as if it was a fairy tale, and I can't remember taking it seriously. But, why do I remember it when we were bombarded with so many other short stories that I don't remember? If I put it together with myriad other purportedly 'trivial' or banal racist socialisations, I can see how we were all being taught to think racially. We were all white children; the other class in our cohort had all of the British Asian children in it – an informal separation that I didn't question at the time.

The positionality of the viewer matters a great deal. Images of extreme suffering as a result of a basic lack of resources reflect back on how one sees oneself, especially if one's lifestyle is – to put it nicely – comfortable. Many people in Britain enjoy lives in which food is not the pursuit of metabolic sustenance but the pursuit of pleasure. Certainly the aestheticisation and sexualisation of food within the mass media would suggest so. The stark contrast between my lifeworld and that evoked in famine images generates a cognitive dissonance which – without getting into psychoanalytical theories – generates anger, powerlessness, and guilt. In one author's words, famine images produce a 'guilt-ridden Northern public' (Smillie, 1995: 136).[4]

For an academic who has an interest in history and especially the impacts and legacies of slavery and colonialism – and indeed an awareness of the imperialistic and racist content of so many images of Africa – the racist coding of British mainstream culture has become an entity to contest in some fashion. However, does this scholarly and political anti-racist sentiment rest opaquely on the racist foundations of my childhood? Do I perceive a special kind of tragedy in the Sudanese boy that is racially coded?

I have had conversations with like-minded people in the early 1990s about apartheid and in the 2000s about Zimbabwe in which, comfortably, we could share our concerns about the poor, oppressed, and subaltern. But I can also recall one person expressing a very critical view of South African singer Lucky Dube's wealth in the context of widespread poverty in post-apartheid South Africa, and others criticising the persistence of wealthy black businesspeople in Zimbabwe in the 2000s. At the time I assented to these views, but now I am less sure. Why should these social groups be condemned? There are capitalists throughout the world – tens of thousands of them – who make great wealth from the labour of the highly impoverished and proceed to hide and launder their money, install themselves in secure gated communities, and bend governments to their will. Is there an implicit sense that Africans *in particular* shouldn't pursue this social trajectory? If so, why? Might it be that African capitalists are not only violating the social-democratic norms of social equity and justice that most Western academics cleave to, but also that they are violating an equally Western and romantic vision of Africa as a body of noble suffering, as modest in means, as agrarian,[5] or simply as other? Or, do people dislike the raw acquisitiveness of 'black empowerment' in South Africa because it serves as an unforgiving mirror: a contemporary acting out of the ways in which capitalist classes try to forge their hegemony over states and other classes as they did in their various ways throughout Europe and America (the latter including the erasure of indigenous peoples along the way)? As I noted earlier, I am less sure how to agree with those who complain about Africa's nouveaux riches, but it has taken me some time to get to this point. This is circumstantial evidence of a personal and emotional sense of specifically African tragedy and suffering, filtered through representations of the famine image and the African elite neoliberal *wabenzi*.[6]

It gets more interesting. I might be able to discern a humanitarian fellow feeling, laced with less clearly defined emotions of parenthood; defined in some sense by my racialised socialisation as a white British person and my re-bellion against – or rejection of – it. But the premise of this reflection is that I can start to explain my feelings of compassion with reference to the suffering of others. How convincing is this way of framing the issue? Consider two sets of images: the Sudan famine in 1998 (mentioned earlier in this chapter) and the Biafran famine from 1967–1970.[7] These images are not contemporaneous. They are not part of an existing appeal which might deploy images in order to elicit donations under the claim that relief is extremely time-sensitive.

These are 'dead' images: images of the past.[8] They are also images of the dead; young people who will very likely not have made it to adulthood. The images have been purposefully taken to record – or witness – the last stages of life, the physical condition of those who will not live. The subjects of the photos are photographed and then forgotten outside of their image and its emotive impact. One might more aptly call sympathy for the dead a lament: a 'dreary and endless melancholy' (Smith, 2009: 17–18).[9] Perhaps a key part of the emotional pull of famine images is to mourn deaths that have likely taken place between the time the photos were taken and the time the viewer encounters them in a newspaper or on an NGO webpage. This kind of emotion – a deep sadness – is not a powerful prognostic framing. That is, it does not entreat us to 'do something' or even to feel like doing something. It makes us aware of the fragility of life and its ebbing away towards death. Famine victims experience a slow death and one in which they are forced to embody death itself, become increasingly skeletal. In those images of horror, *in extremis*, one is not sure if the camera has taken an image of a person living or dead.

If lamentation is the right word to encapsulate an aspect of the emotional response to famine images, then we need to recognise that it is, politically, a conservative emotion.[10] Infused with a certain kind of Christian sensibility – what Neiztsche (2003) angrily calls a religion of pity[11] – the lament is passive. A key icon in Christian visual representation is the mourning of Christ's death, depicted as a moment of grief, an end to things in which the mourners appear prostrate or even close to death themselves in the rapture of their grief. There is no suggestion here that the starving African child in Sudan or Ethiopia is analogous to Rubens' paintings of a dead Christ, but it seems reasonable to suggest a resonance: that images so awful of people so near to death create an emotion of lament which – for anyone exposed to a Christian culture which is based in a story that leads so powerfully to such a tragic and torturous death – is both emotionally familiar and culturally ingrained.

Images of extreme suffering contain this emotional tension – a feeling of humanitarian empathy and a feeling of lament. In this light, the Sudan images described from memory earlier in this chapter are rather unusual. They depict food *being taken* from somebody. Contrastingly, most famine images are non-relational. The best-known images here are of the starving Ethiopian child who was photographed isolated and dying by a group of photojournalists, the latter themselves photographed by another and revealing the contrived nature of the image and the setting-up of the child's isolation.[12] If one considers that access to food is a human right and that therefore famine is a mass rights violation – what De Waal (1997) famously calls a famine crime[13] – then these images of isolation are emotionally powerful in their ability to evoke a feeling of lament, but weak in their ability to present the social and political processes of dispossession, denial, and indifference that determine famine and its intensity. The sense of powerlessness embodied in the images of famine victims is emotionally transposed to the viewer. The image is a powerful but simple image of an approaching death. Contrastingly, in the Sudan images, one has to ask questions: Who is the man? Who gave the boy food? Why didn't someone stop this happening? In most famine images in which there is a single isolated victim, one feels despair. What questions might one ask?

This section has reviewed what might be called the basic coordinates of emotional response to images of suffering. These are sympathy and lament. It has also shown how in a very direct sense, images are personal. The way I 'receive' images is not only a story about the image but also about me. No image is received abstractly; cognitively it is viewed and categorised by each viewer. The work done in the conjoined acts of viewing and categorising is profoundly emotional and it requires us to explore further the kinds of emotional dynamics that often emerge in the representation of suffering.

Images and emotions

The speaking image

Jacques Ranciere (2009: 33) defines the image as both a representation and signification. The metaphor that people often use to analyse images that relates to Ranciere's definition is of images 'speaking'; a stylised way to think about the fact that images are always *communicative acts* ('a picture says a thousand words'). The previous sections outlined the cardinal ways in which images transmit, or evoke, emotional responses – of humanitarian sympathy, lamentation, and other emotions embedded in this author's (and everyone else's) social identity. None of this first blush of viewing takes place in an un-mediated fashion. This section starts to explore the ways in which we might broaden out the meaning of the 'text' of the image without losing sight of the image as a unique genre and indeed the central features of Africa's imagery in Britain.

Who can remain untouched by images of famine and death? Before the researcher's gaze – even if for the most fleeting of moments – the images of the starving child or the civil war victim are taken in emotionally. Although some writers have employed a language of emotions – compassion fatigue (Moeller, 1999; Sennett, 2004) or denial (Cohen, 2001), these writers employ these terms *analytically*. That is, they do not see compassion or denial as affective acts, as complex, or even as intrinsically important. Susie Linfield (2010) demonstrates how both *marxisant* and postmodern critical analyses of images of suffering rely on this anaesthetising sensibility which moves authors between critique and cynicism. For Linfield, in most analyses of images of suffering, there is no sense in which the images are in any way emotionally impacting on the writer, as he or she dutifully immerses themself in an archive of images and texts of suffering. Thus, in a sense, the emotive appears only in a sanitised form, as a conduit to broader points about public engagement or global norms.

The presence and absence of emotional terms (their iteration but only under conditions of analysis, neutrality, or displacement) is a paradox sustained within a broader post-structural intellectual field which both asserts the importance of subjectivity and especially the subjectivity of the author/researcher, but also bequeaths a Foucauldian (Platonic?) ontology and epistemology in which analytical deconstruction requires us to identify the nebulous workings of power through subjects by remaining disengaged.[14] In a sense, the author as subjective self is announced only to be quickly elided by a project to speak analytically and non-subjectively about history and power. This elision is not helped by a post-structuralist ontology in which the self is relegated to an analytical position of an instantiation of nebulous conduits of power.

Revealingly – and taking from Baudrillard (1981) – post-structuralism speaks of an *economy* of symbols: what clearer demonstration of this paradox than an interest in images and semiotics conjoined with that most scientific and purportedly value-neutral of the social sciences? The images themselves do not affect the author as viewer but are instead intellectually arranged into a representation of their logics, to sustain a discourse, to organise power or biopolitics. To feel that something is right or wrong, horrific, unbearable, or to despair is to make ideological statements that go against the post-structural sensibility of detachment.

The argument here is not to disavow the usefulness of Foucault or to argue that the production of images is not an act of power. But, in light of these points, it does seem important in some sense to reflect on the initial emotive import of imagery of death and suffering since this is always present and images are by definition only present when witnessed.

Images of suffering

Many prominent images of extreme human suffering have emerged from Africa, but the archive of images of suffering is much greater. Before (and continuing after) the camera, artists would represent wars that evoked their passions, outrage, and politics – witness Eugène Delacroix's *Scenes of the Massacres at Scio* relating to the Ottoman–Greek war of the 1820s. Perhaps most relevant for this book, the drawings of the *Brookes* slaving ship deck plans, packed with enslaved bodies, is a pertinent example on non-photographic suffering imagery, although there is also a body of drawings of the torture of slaves in the New World (Curry-Machado, 2004).

Photographically, the legacy of mass suffering and death is inextricable from the acts of destruction that produced them. The mass extermination of the Holocaust was also an extermination of evidence, leaving us a limited photographic archive (Didi-Huberman, 2008). The Red Terror of Stalin's purges has also left a very slender record of the millions killed, although the collapse of the Soviet Union has opened up photographic records of the imminently killed (Linfield, 2010). Since the First World War, images of death have come into the public purview, but in a fragmentary fashion, as a result of the nature of their production. War images are often taken under circumstances of danger; they are taken of specific events within war; and they are often heavily censored by states – especially states at war. The horror of war is often condensed into single images that have become iconic: the corpses left by mustard gas, the naked girl trying to escape the pain of Agent Orange, the emaciated Croat prisoner of war ... The bulk of death and suffering has taken place away from the camera or any kind of recording.[15]

The famine image

The core image of the African presence – at least since the late 1960s – has been the famine image. This genre of imagery has conformed to fairly obvious codes which have been touched upon in this chapter and will be returned to throughout the book. The famine image has been the representation of an infantilised, isolated, tragic subject in a near-death state. The image is definitively and extremely awful.

There are two general emotive motifs which are at the core of the famine image: shock and intimacy. The shock emotion is both immediate and powerful. The extreme nature of the famine image derives from the tortured state of the famine victim. It also might derive from the unexpectedness of the image when presented within the British public sphere. After all, those who live or work close to famine or war can readily become to some degree inured to extreme suffering as the testimonies and diaries of medical personnel, soldiers, and even *genocidaires* demonstrate (Hatzfield, 2006). Shock is partly about the nature of the image, but also its *unexpectedness*, its lack of context in terms of everyday life. This is an eloquent demonstration of how images are also texts, and that those texts are read in different ways. If the famine image 'speaks to' people in Britain, it does so in an abrupt and dramatic fashion. Indeed, images are produced in precisely this way. Consider the front cover of tabloid newspapers, for example *The Mirror* of 21 May 2002. In bold type: *Africa's dying again*; juxtaposed with a swollen-bellied child; the subtitle: *Shock report*.

The Mirror's front page is an iteration of a 'shock reportage' that goes back to the Biafra war.[16] The phrase 'Africa's dying again' is an explicit text for the image in which Africa is made corporeal – a single black body.[17] The page is designed explicitly to shock. But shock is by definition a transient emotion. And, in its wake it leaves a more complex emotional baggage. Shock images contain a tension between a rudely provoked humanitarianism and revulsion. Humanitarian sympathy has been discussed earlier and subsequent chapters will look at humanitarian campaigns. But, what about the more thorny notion that shock is at least in part revulsion? The common vernacular couplet 'shock-horror' is part of the emotional import of the famine image, presented unexpectedly into the public space. If the shock image speaks, it has a loud and unannounced voice, perhaps an unwelcome one. The shock image is not pleasant to look at and as a result, one reaction would be to regret seeing the image or to feel angry at being shocked in such a fashion. The notion of compassion fatigue – mooted by Clare Short during Operation Lifeline Sudan – suggests that people need to endure shocking images and arrive at an emotional disposition to donate money or engage with a campaign, and that too many 'shocks' leave people inured to famine imagery (Chouliaraki, 2006: 112–114; Moeller, 1999). One might also determine to avoid images because they seem 'offensive'. Is there also a sense, almost subliminal, in which unexpected exposure to the famine image produces a resentment or even anger at the image itself?

The emotional response of shock – not simply humanitarian but also based in revulsion – is again discussed in existing research but also again is stripped of the subjectivity itself. The key link here is the term pornography: the pornography of suffering, pornography of famine (Linfield, 2010; Manzo, 2006: 9–10; Moeller, 1999). This transposition alludes to the shocking nature of pornography and suggests (studies are rarely very explicit about this) that both pornography and famine imagery are gratuitous. They show us too much. They exploit victims. The images are acts of possession or an exertion of power over the subjects in the image. They 'expose something in human life that is as delicate and deeply personal as sexuality, that is, suffering' (Lissner, 1981: 23). In other ways the pornography allusion makes less sense, but there is one linking motif which is worth further reflection: intimacy.

Innocence and intimacy

The famine image is commonly a child and the child's body conveys a particular kind of text. Most obviously the child conveys innocence. In regard to political imagery, innocence is a powerful property; it tends to subsume critical appraisal. At first blush, the child image is apolitical. Conventionally, children do not have citizenship; they are the wards of adults who retain political agency. Beyond this, children are valued differently *because* of their lack of agency and their innocence. How can one critically assess messages conveyed by a child image without running the risk of opening up emotions of mean spiritedness, victimisation, or even violation?

But innocence is not innocent; innocence is *represented* and as such it is a product of constructive and symbolic effort. Furthermore, the reception of child images can only be mediated: received through an existing sense of aesthetics and values. The power of the child image is to convey innocence and in the process rely on powerful emotional relays and obscure equally powerful texts that enable the image. Innocence lends an image virtue; the subject of the image is in a sense beyond reproach because of his or her apolitical status, and the image claims a kind of enhanced impact as a result of its symbolic directness, its representation as an unmediated image.

The child famine image asserts it directness through the child's eyes. Very commonly, famine victims – and indeed images of African children more generally – look directly into the camera. This image persists despite a general awareness amongst campaign organisations that this gaze has all sorts of politically difficult repercussions as will be seen in Chapter 6. The direct gaze significantly enhances the emotive impact of the child image – it serves as the punctum of the image (Barthes, 2000). The gaze comes with text that is often explicitly written but otherwise encoded within the image: Can you look away? Can you ignore this? Can you help me? This gaze has proven to be the most prominent and emotively productive genre of representation of Africa and this gaze has served as the most crucial linkage between the widespread association of Africa with a plea for charity – a motif that will be returned to frequently in subsequent chapters.

The child's gaze and its emotive power is not simply a result of its directness, it is also a result of its intimacy. This is a salient distinguishing feature of the African image of suffering in comparison to other images of extreme suffering. The images of mass death that have emerged from genocides, the snatched and perilous images taken during conflict, the more uncertain or unstable images taken during pogroms, civil wars, and 'natural' disasters convey suffering in corporate form (with many subjects), in terrible contexts (within camps, facing a firing squad), or through the troubled capturing of images (from cover, on the run). The famine image and other child images are almost portraits. They involve photographers finding the appropriate child, organising a vista, perhaps placing a child in a certain way. The pictures are carefully taken, selected, and presented: carefully framed and cropped around the child's eyes, taken from above the child to enhance the sense of pleading. The images are arranged to convey a peculiar kind of intimacy which – as a device for charitable appeal – endeavours cognitively to place the viewer as close to the child and in a position which is vicariously parental. This can only be done by constructing an intimacy between the viewer and the child image.

The mediations of the child image derive from portrayals of innocence and their associated emotive power, and the emotional reactions to the child image are commonly admixtures of shock and intimacy. Recalling the comments above on lamentation, it is readily apparent that the innocent child in a near-death state might evoke both the shock of direct confrontation with innocent suffering and also lamentation. In the Christian genealogy, lamentation requires an innocent subject. It is emotionally far more complex to lament the death of a person who is not entirely virtuous; sadness for the death of a complex 'worldly' subject requires more explicit intellectual effort. In this sense, the child image has a unique moral value. But, the special value of a lamented innocent death is negated through the act of representation and specifically its iteration. Effectively, we are asked to lament the child's death image again and again: in Biafra, the Sahel, Ethiopia, Somalia, Cameroon ... To paraphrase *The Mirror's* phrase noted earlier in this chapter: Africa is dying again *and again*. The phrase Moeller coins is apposite here: 'trouble in Africa [as] ... routine disaster' (1999: 112). And herein lies a contradiction which leads researchers to speak of compassion fatigue: the child image is extremely emotionally upsetting and yet routine or even banal. As witnesses to the image, people are *expected* to feel a direct emotional reaction, people expect to see this template image when appeals are rolled out. The socialisation of the child image into British public culture contains this awkward cohabitation of normalisation and extremity.

The way people feel: biopolitics and emotion

Biopolitics and sentiment

Thus far, we have registered that African images – and especially the extreme suffering of childhood in the famine image – are in the first instance (and resoundingly thereafter) emotive. As has been suggested, these emotional components are not simply a 'natural' set of responses that we can categorise as pre- or non-political. They are, in many important ways, the motivational origins of the politics of representation. To anticipate the next chapter, this one will approach representation through a particular way of framing imagery that is based on a series of normative entreaties which rely on an emotional generative force. If representations of Africa have often been made in order to frame campaigns and charitable appeals, then the *active* nature of those frames must necessarily be premised on *emotions*; not simply sentiments but the *putting into motion* of sentiments, a political argument about why one's shock, lamentation, sympathy, etc. requires political engagement. This section serves as a stepping stone towards the subsequent analysis of framing. It will reflect upon and adapt the notion of biopolitics in order to start thinking about the ways in which the emotions of Africa imagery might be analysed.

Foucault's use of the term biopolitics is vague and evasive. He sometimes puts the term between the caveat quotation marks. Foucault's (2008) lectures on biopolitics (1978–1979) are not really about biopolitics but rather the rationalities of liberal political economy – something that he confesses to on page 185. These lectures are generally rather vague about dates and indeed even about places, beyond occasional distinctions between Britain and France. Foucault's definition of biopolitics in the course summary that accompanies the lectures runs as follows: 'the attempt, starting from the eighteenth century, to rationalise the problems posed to governmental practice by phenomena characteristic of a set of living beings forming a population: health, hygiene, birthrate, race ... ' (2008: 316).

Foucault has bequeathed a range of interpretations which are in themselves more substantive than his original notes on biopolitics. The starting point that Foucault establishes is of a transition to modernity, the assertion of sovereignty, and the ways in which governments use science (and especially medical science) to produce 'docile bodies' which are either healthy self-regulative agencies or medically categorised as in some sense morbid or deviant (Foucault, 1991).

The main way in which authors within political science have developed the term biopolitics is to make arguments about the ways in which states define those within a biopolitical community and those outwith whose lives are in some sense less valued. This work relates closest to Foucault's interest in modern state sovereignty, modern in the sense that internal[18] state sovereignty is asserted not only through force but through regulative processes which define a national community. The emergence of population surveys (census, medical records, etc.) and the development of some kind of infrastructure of medical, social, and educational provision define a 'healthy' national population – what Agamben (1998) characterises as *bios* – or social life. Outside of this exists the *zoe*, or bare existence of the non-national. Duffield (2007) makes a broader distinction between insured and uninsured life – which roughly maps the former onto the West and the latter onto Africa and other impoverished spaces – in the same vein.

Biopolitics has also been used to think about race – especially in regard to the ways in which Western intellectual cultures have developed racist models of polygenesis in order to medicalise the oppression of black peoples. For Ann Laura Stoler (1995), the racialisation and medicalisation of peoples served as a generative force of colonial endeavour. The biopolitical trope enabled a range of colonial texts which naturalised the wealth and poverty, the health and illness of different peoples.

Taken together these two developments in the concept of biopolitics are both powerful and relevant for this book. Biopolitics relies upon a separation of peoples between a collective 'pure' nation and diffuse externalised impure peoples, a distinction sometimes affirmed by (social) scientists, but also in cultural production in which white and black bodies were described, drawn, and dramatised (Macey, 2009). A great raft of literature on 'miscegeny', tropical disease, exotic indigence, and the peculiar national virility of Britain/Britons mainly in the late nineteenth century attests to this. To anticipate a little, we will return to this sense of national health and external pollution in our discussion of boycott politics in Chapter 7.

The insight of the term biopolitics is that it allows us to think about power in a more directly *embodied* fashion than many other theories of power. It suggests that power can be understood as existing within people, and especially within their biological processes. Foucault's work has, as a result, become well taken up within the biomedical sciences as well as the social sciences. But, there are some limitations in the ways in which biopolitics has been used which impinge on our intention to bring emotions into the ways Africa is represented through imagery.

Foucault's notes on biopolitics are largely concerned with the rise of modern states and sovereignty. This has rendered a lot of analysis of biopolitics state-centric. This has served well in analyses of state actions against terrorism (Morton and Bygrave, 2008; Dillon and Neal, 2008) but relates less effectively to the ways in which power has worked outside or in less strict connection to state power. This lacuna is quite important in an age when a great deal of research has suggested that the nature of state power has been changing in important ways and that sovereignty contains less solid institutional Weberian properties than it might have previously (Harrison, 2007). It is also a curious focus for a term that brings us to a most intimate sphere of political agency – the self – and one that is more remote (though not unconnected) from, say, institutions, ideologies, coercive apparatuses, and all of the other objects of the study of power that are clearly proximate to the state. Foucault's biopolitics seem to open up ways of seeing power that are non state-centric before foreclosing these openings with a focus on sovereignty.

Foucault's lectures on biopolitics were historically very provisional. He is happy to paint the rise of modernity in a very broad brush, and to condense together a range of different shifts in the way states and societies changed from the late 1600s to the 1980s, sometimes hopping over some changes while focusing on others. This book is interested in the period from the late 1700s, telescoping towards the present. It is worth noting here that Foucault's broad historical focus renders the notion of biopolitics provisional: open to varied historical specifications and focuses within which a concerted state-centrism may or may not make sense. The argument here is that biopolitics can be adapted to analyse the ways people feel about representations of Africa in a fashion that connects emotional dynamics to broader constructions of power which are not directly focused on sovereignty but also on issues of public engagement and norm construction.

How might this be done? Biopolitics has been employed largely as a kind of politicised life science. It has considered the medical categorisation of populations and the distinctions between life and death. In this way, insight-fully, we can identify the ways in which the truth claims and assertions of value-neutrality within the biomedical sciences are challenged and also how state power relies on the knowledges and institutions of biomedical sciences to control or order populations. So far so good; but this is only a fragment on how we might consider biopolitics. To develop an ontology of life proc-esses we might equally validly consider not only how people feel but also how people *feel*. The behaviour of selves, their self-regard and self-regulation, are biological and emotional.[19]

Biopolitics and the way that we feel

> Thoughts, feelings and actions may appear as the very fabric and constitution of the intimate self, but they are socially organised and managed in minute particulars. (Rose, 1990: 1)

In Agamben's discussion of the refugee as the embodiment of the separation between political rights and bare life, he speaks of the 'imploring eyes of the Rwandan child, whose photograph is shown to obtain money but who is now becoming more and more difficult to find alive' (1998: 133). This passage seems to relate closely to our discussion in this chapter: the direct intimacy of the famine image and the lamentatious sense of death that it conveys. This ref-erence comes during Agamben's discussion of biopolitics in which he affirms Foucault's sense of the term as oriented towards the biomedical distinctions between life, death, and the legal-medical distinctions between those who have citizenship and those who do not. But, emotively, there is more to be extrapolated than these broad categorisations. This is because the selves that are arguably created through citizenship (Agamben's *bios*) are neither entirely fixed by their constitutional status nor completed by their existence under the mantle of a sovereign state. Suggestively, we can say that the Rwanda image is not just a representation of a biopolitical separation between bare and politi-cal life; it is also an emotional resource to generate feelings of agency, power, association, and separation. It is these feelings – biopolitics as how we feel – that the rest of this chapter aims to set out.

'Feeling' is a difficult word to introduce. It is far from academic. Outside of psychology, feelings are difficult to fix in any analytical fashion. The notion of feeling is offered here strictly as a signposting in regard to biopolitics and the power of representation. It suggests that it is no longer sufficient simply to consider biopolitics in terms of the strictly medical – Foucault's 'health, hygiene, birthrate, race' – and it suggests that biopolitics is also about the feelings evoked by public representations of the stranger. Perhaps Foucault would have conceded some ground on this point, interested as he was in the power of spectacle and especially terror when performed by states (cf. Foucault, 1991). This kind of analysis of power is speaking directly about the evocation of fear, obedience, and desire in ways that move beyond bodily health and into the generation of shared feelings.

Emotional upheavals

The connections between imagery, feelings, and power seem only to have become more dense as time has gone by. Changes in communications technology, the rise of consumer societies, the mass media, and mass advertising have produced extremely powerful effects on public spaces and the meaning of citizenship[20] – to an extent that identities might have become inescapably produced through myriad symbolic mediations (de Zengotita, 2005). Furthermore, as Rose demonstrates, modernity has ushered in a wide range of 'techniques for managing our emotions' (1990: 3): therapeutic professions, educationalists, and so on. But, of course, the efflorescence of evocative representation and its regulation does not necessarily mean that we can say feelings have become more intense or have changed in certain ways. This is the problem with the term 'feelings': it is virtually impossible to encapsulate in any reliable way how 'we feel' without resorting to stylisations or behaviouralist proxies. For example, a person might feel entirely blasé about highly intimate imagery of starvation; or one might find the image so unbearable that one commits suicide. Furthermore, from a psychoanalytical viewpoint, a blasé emotional reaction might itself be a displacement of other deeper feelings of despair or empathy. Nevertheless, the emotional content of imagery is a central component of its political impact, and it is in this sense that representation becomes a dynamic terrain of power relations. The task at hand is to think about emotions in ways that do not rely on the myriad personal feelings of people but rather establish an intimate connection between the self and the world of images.

A related and extensive discussion is Martha Nussbaum's *Upheavals in Thought*. Nussbaum's adaptation of a neo-Stoic approach to emotions provides a very useful way of recognising that feelings might move our understanding of biopolitics away from the strictly medical, statist, and life-and-death towards something more focused on the internal (but hardly isolated) responses that people have to imagery and events (that is, their external world). Appropriately, Nussbaum brings us back to emotions: a way of thinking humanely about emotions and their repercussions on broader norms and sociabilities.

For Nussbaum, emotions 'should be understood as "geological upheavals of thought": as judgements in which people acknowledge the great importance, for their own flourishing, of things that they do not fully control – and acknowledge thereby their neediness before the world and its events' (2001: 90). This is a very dense definition. What Nussbaum is interested in is the ways in which people make value judgements both intellectually and emotionally, and that the latter 'upheaval' represents the reconciliation between a desire for well-being and a sense that the external world is beyond our control. Nussbaum's 'neediness' is the emotion of a desire for fulfilment (eudaimonism) present within myriad encounters with images and events. Well-being is not simply a utilitarian state, or even an egotistical one; rather, wellbeing is understood relationally. That is, the wellbeing of the self is in a profound sense an expression of its emotional stability, a stability that derives from a recognition that one's external environment (however defined or understood) is stable, recognisable, and right. Emotions are, therefore, socially infused.

Nussbaum uses her approach to analyse the nature of compassion: a 'painful emotion occasioned by the awareness of another person's undeserved misfortune' (Ibid.: 301). Unlike pity, compassion is an emotion that is based in 'thicker' judgements about the observed subject's misfortune and the observer's values of what it is to enjoy well-being. Nussbaum's understanding of compassion is – like the book more generally – founded in an optimism of the self: a meliorist sense of the subject as considerably reflective, well-intentioned, and in some sense cognitively stable. Compassion is not an easy emotion: it requires a valuation of the object of compassion and a reflection on the meaning of wellbeing by the observer, and this requires a fairly deep connection between the observer and observed. It is striking that Nussbaum's examples are ensconced within a community or national boundary. Compassion is not, it seems, something for the 'distant other'. Perhaps the 'otherness' is too great to allow the complex mediations of value and emotion to work.

Interestingly, in passing, Nussbaum defines a set of 'impediments to compassion's ethical work': shame, resentment, envy, and disgust: altogether more troublesome emotions and ones that Nussbaum's discussion leaves at the margins. But perhaps these emotions are important to an understanding of the way Africa is seen in Britain. If the kinds of (virtuous) compassion that Nussbaum sets out are – to borrow from Walzer's (1996) language – thin, then whatever compassion might reside in the spectacle of images of distant disaster will be at best unstable, provisional, or poorly defined. And the kinds of 'enemies of compassion' that Nussbaum lists might also reside in the emotional repertoire – generated from a failure to understand the victim's situation, an uncertainty about the viewer's relations to the victim, too overpowering a sense of the uncontrollable and terrible nature of the external world. Who does not feel a hard spark of shame when viewing an image of a famine victim which is, simply and viscerally, a sense that to witness this (mediated) death is to question one's own right to be alive?

If we take Nussbaum's consideration of compassion seriously, then perhaps we should not worry about compassion fatigue but the near-absence of compassion *tout court*? Perhaps the emotions that are more germane for our purposes are shame, disgust, shock, and pity – emotions that do not try to reconcile the complexity and distance between observer and observed but to express it.

Unstable witness

This chapter started with a personal reflection that was less than honest. Although it was true when I started writing this chapter that I couldn't find the Sudan photos, I retrieved a single photo after another internet search about six months after the first draft of the chapter. The image was taken by Tom Stoddart in 1998 at a feeding centre in Ajiep, Sudan. The image was published in newspapers and raised considerable amounts of money as well as gaining general public attention. Finding the photo was obviously upsetting. This was partly because the image had remained in my memory during the writing of this book as a poorly defined phantasm, an image that I started the chapter with because it had a strong impact on me personally. Viewing the photo in its definitive form made the image real again: less ambiguous, fresher in its significations.

Finding the image makes me think about the motility of images. I had clearly lost much of the detail over the ten years or so between viewings. There is only one image, not three as I had thought, tracing the stages of theft that I had imagined in the description that starts the chapter. The 'boy' is also certainly a minor, but more grown than I remembered.[21] Stoddart himself narrates the theft in a way that is pretty true to the way I narrate the imagined three pictures. The boy's face does indeed communicate a complex array of emotions. The key for Stoddart is the disdain of the boy; I can still see a resignation and a pleading.

Speaking and writing about images like this is to generate values, and to communicate difficult ethical issues. In this sense – and minimally – an engagement with images of suffering is part of Nussbaum's eloquent humanism, perhaps even part of a deliberative process (cf. Wenar, 2006). Part of the 'upheaval' (to use Nussbaum's phrase) that I experienced in seeing the Sudan photo I had searched for and written about from memory was, I have come to realise, a result of my realisation of how unstable a witness I am.

We can open this personal and emotional reflection out. There is no definitive reason to suppose that people's emotional reactions to images are stable and coherent. Emotions, subsequent sense-making, and reaction will all be complex – especially for imagery of suffering which makes for difficult viewing. Consider the almost schizophrenic emotional veering expected of viewers of Comic Relief Red Nose Day television: from celebrity comedy events directly into reportage of extreme poverty and disease, the shortest of pauses, and back to a compère who introduces another celebrity short. Advertisements which appeal for donations to provide water to emaciated children can run immediately before luxury cat food ads. These loose phenomenological observations surely attest to the instability in subject positions involved in viewing images of suffering.

In light of this instability, making perfect sense of representation is a fallible project, but nonetheless a valuable one. The following chapters will move away from direct emotional reflection but will nevertheless be aware of the ways in which sympathy, humanitarianism, eudaimonism, pity, shame, anger, and disgust all feed into broader political processes. Without emotions – complex, incoherent, powerful – it is difficult to see whence the generative force for the politics of representation derives.

Notes

1 We use the term sympathy largely in the same way that Adam Smith did in *The Theory of Moral Sentiments* (2009), although his understanding is strongly couched within a methodological nationalism and a certain concern with the way a good society functions. For an interesting contemporary reflection on Smith's notion of sympathy, see Boltanski (1993). The cognate term 'empathy' is less appropriate because it implies a common/shared feeling rather than a 'fellow' feeling.

2 A thought-provoking and image-rich analysis of whiteness is Dyer (1997).

3 This racist story probably draws on the Old Testament's story of Ham, the sinful son of Noah. The trope of black people having dirty skin has various manifestations in

British culture: from the sixteenth century (Sherwood, 2001: 2) to the advertising campaigns of soap brands in the early twentieth century (Ramamurthy, 2003).

4   Emotional relays of guilt are enhanced by statements made by the media and campaign NGOs to the effect that children are dying 'one a minute' (Brookes, 1995) or the finger-click ads that Make Poverty History used.

5   This kind of view is aptly summarised by Giblin and Maddox as 'Merrie Africa' (1996). Their work relates the romantic view to Western idealisations of a pre-industrial past and a certain colonially generated view of environmental management. See also Brockington (2009).

6   A kiSwahili neologism meaning literally 'the Benz people'. It alludes to Kenya's nouveau riche and particularly those who import luxury cars.

7   We will return to this in subsequent chapters because the Biafra appeal/campaign is a major marker in British campaign history.

8   More broadly on the deadness of images, see Barthes (2000).

9   Adam Smith's description of lament as sympathy for the dead ends with a rather metaphysical belief that fear of death acts as a constraint on social injustice.

10   In other contexts, lamentation can become part of a political militancy – for example in the public lamenting of those who have died in combat.

11   Chouliaraki (2006) uses the term 'pity' as the cornerstone of her analysis of suffering imagery, but her understating of this term includes a range of emotions and identities. In the main, she associates pity with Smith's notion of fellow-feeling just discussed and which perhaps is more easily mapped as compassion or sympathy rather than pity. Pity, it seems to me, is coded more strictly with a hierarchy between observer and sufferer.

12   See www.imaging-famine.org for examples of this, or the front cover of Benthall (2010).

13   De Waal's argument is that famine is a denial of a right and therefore centrally a political question.

14   Foucault will be returned to later in the chapter, trying to bring in a focus on the emotional self to his concepts.

15   This seems to be changing with the growth of the electronic media and the ability of protagonists and witnesses to record and take photographs and video footage with mobile phones.

16   A phenomenon coined as the 'Biafra syndrome' by Mai Palmberg (2001: 205)

17   The 'composite homogenised picture of Africans' (Sherwood, 2001: 16) is a common metonymy in which Africa becomes a single body or personality.

18   Internal in the standard sense used in International Relations theory: rule over citizens/subjects within, not external sovereignty which relates to the ability to defend spaces. A detailed theoretical treatment of this distinction is Walker (1992).

19   This more expansive notion of biopolitics is outlined in Rose (2001).

20   The *locus classicus* here is Marcuse (2002).

21   The young who are subjected to hunger and starvation have stunted growth, making them seem possibly younger than they are.

3

Africa–Britain: a short history

Introduction

This chapter makes a review of British-African interactions through history. It does not make a claim to anything but the most general review, and this is because the purpose here is simply to provide the general coordinates for the more detailed considerations of the historical changes in Africa's representation in Britain in subsequent chapters. The focus is on the nature of the political relations between Africa and Britain and the main ways in which Africa has been 'domesticated' into the British polity.

The story is one of relatively unstructured representations of Africa giving way to more robust and persistent frames. This is part of the rise of British national identity and specifically a national identity based in maritime ascendance. This chapter will show how representations of Africa interpolate themselves into the imperial commerce of slavery and the 'civilising' mission of colonialism. The struggle for independence in Africa generates subsequent layers of representation based in the notion of development, a concept which both affirms a certain kind of African sovereignty and also legitimates persisting British involvement in Africa. This chapter demonstrates how the collapse of nationalist projects ushers in a bolder interventionist framing in response to famines and humanitarian disaster. The section ends with an exploration of more diverse post-colonial currents of Britain–Africa relations.

Pre-modern encounters

Britain's interactions with Africa began well before the period under scrutiny within these pages. There is an argument that Africans were present in Britain before the Roman empire, although the historical evidence is far from straightforward (Luke, 2007).[1] Certainly from AD 200, Africans – including a Roman Emperor – were present in Britain, leading Fryer to make the striking observation that 'There were Africans in Britain before the English came' (2010: 1).

Before Britain's emerging modern nationalism in the mid-seventeenth century, British sailors, travellers, and itinerants visited Africa in a relatively patchy and *ad hoc* fashion, bringing back to small and selected British audiences a diverse set of narratives. From the 1500s onwards, British traders involved themselves in commerce with the West African coast. But there were two patterns to this trade that significantly influenced British involvement and the prospects for the representation of Africa within Britain. Firstly, British (and European) trade with Africa was relatively equitable; in some cases it seems that African traders pushed terms of trade in their favour and were fairly indifferent to the kinds of goods that Europeans offered (Thornton, 1998: Chapter 2). Secondly, British traders and the British state were only minor players in a European mercantile system dominated by the Iberian peninsula. Throughout the sixteenth century, Britons played a small role in the thriving Mediterranean economy (Braudel, 1993). Some Britons were captured and enslaved by wealthy North African households (Colley, 2005). For some Britons (and Europeans more generally), becoming enslaved meant losing freedom and being forced into an alien society; but it also led some to convert to Islam or even to gain a certain amount of social status. The reportage from these sources tends to express admiration for host societies – or at least facets of them. The enslavement of Britons by North Africans again reveals the rough parity of interaction during the period before Atlantic slavery.

Representations of Africa were in keeping with the broader nature of the sixteenth and seventeenth centuries. In the first place, there was no systemic Africa imagery of the kind detailed throughout this book: no familiar tropes, no persistent codes of power and powerlessness, no attempts to use African imagery for the broader purposes of public mobilisation or state legitimisation. Rather, imagery was more idiomatic, more likely to be the result of specific acts of collection[2] for private purposes.

Secondly, images of Africa were largely positive: either as '"noble" beings living in harmony with nature, or as political allies whose vast kingdoms and empires were believed to be commensurate with the most powerful of royal monarchies which reigned in Europe' (Grinker and Steiner, 1997: 682). Before the 1600s, Mudimbe identifies more sameness than difference in Africa's representation in European cultures (1988 :8)

In sum, British encounters with Africa before the mid-1700s were not systematised into a political economy of imperial exploitation and rising British pre-eminence. As a result, the kinds of imagery brought back to Britain were both more diverse, less infused with racism and imperial arrogance, and generally less prominent. It is only with Britain's rising imperial nationalism that African imagery becomes a key component in the way that this national thinks about – and represents – itself.

Britain and slavery

Britain's maritime ascendance was enshrined most clearly in the Utrecht Treaty (1713) in which Spain gave Britain the *Asiento* to trade slaves in the Spanish colonial realm. From the mid-seventeenth century until the end of the eighteenth century, Britain was *primus inter pares* in the Atlantic system (Curtin, 1964: 6). This system was built on the integration of an early industrialising Europe, the colonisation of the Americas, and the evacuation of slaves from West Africa. Britain's heavy involvement in the Atlantic slave trade generated more systemic representations of Africa and Africans than had previously been the case, and it erased both the indeterminate hierarchy between Britain and Africa and the variegated nature of the encounters between Britons and Africans.

It is striking that during the period when Britain aggressively pursued a dominant role in the slave-plantation system – embedding it into the wealth of its political class, generating flourishing port cities in London, Bristol, Liverpool, and others – there was little in the way of a 'humane' representation of African people. By and large, the leitmotifs were the hazards of the 'slave coast' for British mariners and the exoticism of the environs.[3]

When Africans figured, it was mainly as a cargo, not as humans. Until slavery as a system was challenged in the late 1700s, the debate about slavery was largely one concerning its economy: the numbers transported, the efficiency of slaves' work, concerns with the reproduction of the labour force, attrition rates,[4] and so on (Drescher, 1987). Pro-slavery groups and individuals referred to slavery as the means to 'save' Africans from idleness. Slavery was based on a dehumanisation and racialisation of Africans, their rendering into units of labour, or as a feral half-people: 'they were sub-human savages, not civilised human beings like us' is how Fryer encapsulates prevailing attitudes during the height of the slave trade (2010: 7).

Even conversion to Christianity did not necessarily upset this hierarchy: slavery could be articulated as the ordination of God. Slavery as a condition was associated with a natural order or servitude, often expressed through references to Christianity or specific Bible text. If God loves all persons, and ordained orders of slavery in the New World, then one could even be a Christian slave (Rozbicki, 2001: 33–35).

This was a period in which 'blackness' became powerful political and moral coding. In the context of the Enlightenment and emerging empire, blackness became increasingly strongly associated with the devil and sin, and whiteness became associated with God and virtue (Baaz, 2001: 7; Dyer, 1997; Nederveen Pieterse, 1992). This basic dyad has persisted in various formulations into the present day, and was prominent throughout the Victorian period, even being projected onto the English poor and the Irish (Rozbicki, 2001).

But one can discern also an early humanitarianism in the British polity in the mid-1700s (C. Brown, 2006). Interestingly for this book, this protean fellow feeling was articulated as a meditation on Britain as a moral space. The best example here is the small number of cases in which enslaved Africans were, it was argued, free once they were on British soil. The basis of this argument – sometimes referring back to Elizabethan law or the Magna Carta – was that the British constitution (scattered as it was and is in laws of varying provenance) enshrined the freedom from enslavement for all.

The best-known case here is that of James Somerset, defended by Granville Sharp against the claims of his 'owner' who considered Sharp's case as theft of his property.[5] But, in Somerset's case – as with that of the slave Jonathan Strong previously – the nub of the controversy seems to have been the nature of Christian morality[6] and the constitutional status of freedom within Britain rather than the claims, thoughts, or identities of the enslaved. It is as if these two were custodies of a broader argument between slave owners, judges, and intellectuals in London concerning the nation's moral boundaries.

The first African voice within the abolitionist movement was that of Ottobah Cugoano which emerged later in the century. Cugoano's *Thoughts and sentiments on the evil and wicked traffic of the slavery and commerce of the human species* (1787) offers a powerful moral case against the Atlantic slave trade, one framed within a challenge to British moral integrity.[7] Cugoano was, in effect, succeeded by the better-known Olaudah Equiano, whose *Interesting Narrative* (2003 [1814]) was framed less as a challenge to British moral hypocrisy (self-declared Christian civility and brutal slavery) and more as an appeal to British moral virtue – a tenor that set him as a key advocate within the abolitionist movement.[8]

Abolitionism and beyond

In essence, the period from the mid-1600s to the late 1700s was one in which Britain rose to become the major maritime power. Britain's capitalist political economy at this time was based in workshop industry, freehold agriculture, and the benefits of the plantation-slave system in the New World. Although historians describe the Industrial Revolution and British ascendance from the late 1700s, this process was not one that many were aware of at the time. British society was still what one might now describe as 'undeveloped': literacy was low, national identity was weak, levels of poverty and disease were high. The British state was besieged by wars with France, American Independence, and a constant fear of social movements within its own territories – not least those in Ireland, Wales, and Scotland.

In retrospect, it seems a fair judgement to say that the abolitionist movement around the turn of the century provided the only publicly recognised representation of Africans. But the discourse of abolition also fed into Britain's own political turbulence and uncertainties about the nature and future of the British state. Abolitionism produced the first stable representation of Africa and Africans in Britain; this also helped to 'settle' or consolidate a sense of Britishness at a time of exceptional change and uncertainty. At the heart of abolitionism was a desire to construct a stable sense of British virtue and also British global predominance, and it attempted to do this through a strong and exoteric dissemination of British national identity. Later chapters will look at abolition in more detail. The historical marker set here is simply that from the late 1700s there emerged a widespread appeal to abolish the slave trade which evoked the humanitarian sentiments on Britons in order to recognise the suffering caused by slavery.

Abolitionists campaigned as Britain found a fairly solid – and globally contextualised – footing for its national development. Representations of Africa were now engraved with the underlying inequality that has, *mutatis mutandis*, remained throughout the period under consideration in this book. The primary feature of this inequality was (and is) the representation of Africa as subordinate to Britain. There are two facets to this inequality in regard to the question of Africa's representation. One is in a sense more straightforward. It is the denigration of Africa: the derogatory racial epithets, the assertion of British agency over passive Africans or Africa, the location of Africa behind, below, or beneath Britain. The second facet is more agonistic: it remains steeped in the constitutive inequalities constructed and maintained during and since the slave trade, but it represents Africa as a place that might be saved, as an evocation of Britain's special (moral) place in the world as leader of civilisation. Empire, or Britain's actions in Africa specifically, can be criticised, but *immanently*: as part of a project to make Britain's involvement in Africa 'better' or perhaps more faithfully representative of what Britain is. Criticism was not aimed at empire or colonialism *tout court*.

It is the interaction of these two facets that serves as the ideational underpinning for a great deal of Africa campaigning, as shown throughout this book.

Abolitionism was, then, situated within this historical context: it expressed both a concern with the inhumanity of Britain's involvement in the slave trade, and a sense of Britain's pre-eminence. Indeed, often abolitionist entreaties were for a more morally upstanding British empire, rather than a radical rethinking of British global expansion. After all, the legacy of abolitionism and anti-slavery was a drive to colonise Africa and make it 'civilised'.

One can see a connection between empire and virtue growing on the heels of an increasingly successful abolitionist movement in the early 1800s.[9] After this, British missionaries travelled to Africa (especially southern Africa) with a remit of saving souls. This was directly connected to abolitionism: salvation from the chains was morally associated with the salvation of the soul. Price identifies how the creation and values of the London Missionary Society generated a protean humanitarianism out of the comingling of the task of evangelising and the values of abolition (Price, 2008: 5). This humanitarianism was constructed for a British audience, a 'domestic culture of empire' (*ibid.*: 10).

There is a fascinating historiography of the fortunes of British missions: the complexity of their encounters with African societies, their relationship to state-driven processes of colonisation, the rivalries between different missions in different parts of Africa, their often patronising attitude towards African subjects, and so on. What is worth emphasising here is the fact that returning missionaries and missionary correspondence disseminated narratives about Africa to the growing congregations of Britain's churches: relaying progress in the Sisyphean and global task of making the world in God's (or the British) image. Herein, the connection between British involvement with Africa and Africans, already established by abolitionism, was reinforced: the white man's burden was to wrest Africans from ignorance through the word of God, but also through the habits and customs of 'civilisation'. Thus, missionaries would provide education on how to cook, dress, sew, and so on. Basic literacy (in English) was a prerequisite for Bible study and progress towards virtuous personhood. Correspondingly, missionary images and discourse depicted Africans as child-analogies: as delinquent or obedient to the requisites of Christian mission.

Missionaries were not the only group pushing into Africa in the wake of abolitionism. The Africa Association was created in 1788 to promote scientific knowledge of Africa's terrain, flora, and fauna. The Royal Geographical Society (founded in 1830) also promoted scientific exploration as a progressive post-abolition project, sponsoring David Livingstone and Henry Morton

Stanley. After 1808, it also saw its work as part of a broader post-slavery dissemination of enlightenment in Africa. Indeed, the exploration project was seen as part of an ongoing imperial virtue which expunged Britain of its leading role in slavery (Koivunen, 2009: 24).

Perhaps the best-known early explorer was Mungo Park, who carried out two excursions up the Niger River. His *Travels in the Interior Districts of Africa* (2002) was an early example of a genre that grew throughout the nineteenth century, of personal accounts of exploration.[10] Each of these volumes tended to relay two core images: one was of the morally steadfast and intrepid explorer (even if expressed in characteristically British understatement) and the second was the nature of the African (or perhaps the tribally defined African). The 'savagery' of Africans was certainly constructed through explorer accounts, delivered to academic and scientific communities as well as published in books, even if a closer reading of explorer accounts also reveals an awareness of existing African cultural and scientific technologies and in places expresses a respect for African individuals and societies.

Preparing for colonialism

Britain's colonial endeavours in Africa commenced in the early nineteenth century in southern Africa, but colonisation outside of South Africa (the Cape in 1795 and in 1843 Natal) was generally feeble.[11] In West Africa, British settlement was restrained by disease and a lack of interest. Scientists, travellers, and missionaries relayed imagery of Africa to a broadening British readership.

David Livingstone embodied – or was represented – as everything that Britain wished to be in Africa. His modest origins, his missionary zeal, and his conviction that Africans could be saved through commerce and Christianity was avidly broadcast into British public culture. His book, *Missionary Travels*, sold 70,000 copies (Jeal, 2001: 163). The London Missionary Society made great efforts to promote Livingstone's image as a way to increase donations and subscriptions for the great cause of conversion. In effect, Livingstone attained what would now be called celebrity status – having to move about London quietly to avoid admiring crowds and being invited to many high-profile speeches and dinners. Over the thirty years of his travelling through Africa, Livingstone moved from national hero to national saint (Sebe, 2009: 43), and was finally buried in Westminster Abbey.

Henry Morton Stanley's books were also broadly read by the standards of the times, endowing upon him fame and notoriety in Britain. The explorer and missionary narratives during the early and mid-nineteenth century epitomised the 'darkest Africa' imagery, and Stanley's books propounded the trope of 'darkest Africa'[12] to a greater extent than any other single text or image. His account of his travels – to follow the Congo River upstream, to find David Livingstone, and to 'rescue'[13] Emin Pasha – relayed a narrative of the determined white explorer overcoming the physical adversity of the environment and the endless problems caused by Africans – either those in his employ or those encountered during his traverses. Stanley became something of a 'celebrity' in his day: he was playfully described as such by a friend when returning to Britain and a mix of fame and infamy (Jeal, 2008: 136).

Stanley's reception in Britain encapsulated the agonistic public reflections on Britishness noted in regard to abolitionism. Although born in Wales, Stanley claimed American citizenship and toured Africa with patronage from an American newspaper and then, notoriously, the King of Belgium. However, he also displayed a strong sense of Britishness, stating for example that it should be the British flag that flew over the territories that he traversed (Hochschild, 1998: 59), and of course, having the iconic meeting with Livingstone. As such, his popularity in Britain was attenuated by his unclear national identity. The salacious interest in his accounts of exploration was tempered by a moral anxiety about the brutality he relays. The accounts of whipping and killing were related to questions about the veracity of his achievement and often associated with his Americanness. His naturalisation as a Briton – even to the extent of gaining a seat in Parliament – accompanied the resolution of this tension into a standard narrative of his intrepid civilising mission. In other words, his repatriation was accompanied by a moral 'cleansing' of his travels in Africa.

Livingstone and Stanley's books and speeches, and the embracing of their explorer images by the media presents a specific example of a broader cultural familiarity with explorer narratives which might properly be said to have commenced with Mungo Park, but was very prominent by the late 1800s as a result of various explorer books, presentations, and interviews in the press (McLynn, 1992). The explorer generated a powerful pre-colonial contrast between a 'savage' Africa and a virtuous British expansion.

Moving further into the nineteenth century, images of Africa within fiction played strongly upon the theme of exoticism: of bizarre and arcane cultural practices (a theme supported by the emerging discipline of anthropology) and of primitivism. These tropes were affirmed through fiction and poetry (Boehmer, 2009): the works of Kipling, Haggard, and a raft of lesser-known writers confirmed Africa as a space very much below Britain and often as a place within which the redoubtable essence of Britishness was tested and offered for the avid consumption of generations of (male) adolescents and provided ideas for the film industry in the early twentieth century (Mayer,

2002: 30).[14] The fictional narratives were expressed through British protagonists who were logically the focus of the books. Figuratively, Africa ran as a series of scenarios presented to the protagonist, serving as foils and challenges to define the nature of the British exploratory/imperial male self. In the process, Africa's darkness was also feminised as an abstracted body to be explored.

In 1851, the Great Exhibition at Crystal Palace curated Africa as a reality possessed by Britain – artefacts brought to Britain were displayed with authoritative scientific, ethnographic and exploratory knowledge. Subsequently, throughout the late Victorian period, British museums generated various displays of exoticised African culture for British audiences. Museums – in the late 1800s and into the 1900s well-attended – relayed many of the values associated with this period in which African imagery became richer and more diverse, even if almost entirely assembled within the growing sense of British colonial pre-eminence. Thus, as Coombes (1994) shows in detail, museums could curate to express scientific knowledge over Africa, to evoke humanitarian sympathies, or to provide frisson to those in search of the exotic and erotic within ostensibly 'respectable' circumstances.

In sum, the period between abolition and full-blooded colonialism (which was the bulk of the nineteenth century) generated a raft of representations of Africa largely through the framing of exploration. This was the period in which, as Philip Curtin argues, images of Africa 'hardened' into a set of references familiar in British culture (1964: xii), a period in which exploration fixed Africa as a subordinate place vis-à-vis Britain. Exploring Africa was, in essence, exposing Africa to a range of British spectators: intellectuals, politicians, churchgoers, readers of newspaper serials and books, and so on. By the end of the nineteenth century, all of these 'domestications' of Africa's image were extant within British public culture.

And it was at this time that Africa began to be photographed by the portable Kodak camera. The taking of photographs ushered into British public discourse a key new reference point: authenticity. The claim made by photographs (and photographers) was that these photos depicted the real Africa. The general culture of the Enlightenment produced the appropriate cognitive category: that the photographer was an external agent to an existing scene or depiction of reality. In fact, photos of Africa were highly staged and contrived, often taken after receiving instructions from those at home who wished to make Africa bend to their own purposes (Koivunen, 2009: 38). Africa was generally photographed as a hostile terrain and a place full of wild beasts. Africans themselves were photographed as exemplars of tribes, often with an explicit (and to the present-day eye, extremely ugly) referencing to eugenics: profiles with dimensions, head sizes, and a focus on supposed physical distinctions[15] (Landau, 2002; Ryan, 1997). Photographs of Africa were (and are) 'introverted': as Landau observes in regard to imperial imagery of Africa generally: 'the history of the European view of non-European peoples has always reflected Europeans' history of imagining themselves' (2002: 2).

Colonialism and Britain's imperial flush

It was only in the late 1800s – and marked by the Treaty of Berlin in 1884/5 – that Britain endeavoured to define the spatial limits and the nature of the colonial project in Africa to move from a cognitive geography of the expanding frontier to the territorially fixed colonial state. This final stage in Britain's long imperial history might be seen in retrospective as a 'last hurrah', a brief period in which Britain saw itself as the centre of the world, the now infamous late Victorian map of pink focused around the (disproportionately large) British Isles. Another key image of this ascendance was the 'Cape to Cairo' assertion which was portrayed graphically by an imperious Cecil Rhodes striding across the continent in Atlasian form.[16] Some parts of Britain's colonies were settled – notably the 'white highlands' of Kenya and southern Africa. British companies invested in plantations and mines.

During this period, the geographers' and ethnographers' gaze intensified: British Africa was zoned by environmental and 'tribal' categories. An equivalent of the French colonial distinction between *l'Afrique utile* and *l'Afrique inutile* created images of mines and plantations contra scrub or 'bush'; (relatively) 'civilised', 'martial' or 'savage' 'tribes';[17] lines of rail and empty spaces. Much of this geography entered school curriculums – a new source of representation and one that was significant for its spread and impact on young minds.

By the late Victorian period, as a result of the colonial expansion and the relaying of colonial imagery into Britain, it was possible to speak of an 'imperial citizen' (Price, 2006: 617): socialised as such through narratives of heroic battles, colonial projects, humanitarian missions, and British pre-eminence. The British – like all European powers who were signatories to the Berlin Treaty – had to demonstrate some exertions to 'effectively occupy' the territories they claimed. This led to the violent imposition of colonial state rule over diverse and often rebellious populations. It also led to the development of a class of British politicians, bureaucrats, and expatriates who identified their Britishness with the colonies (Ranger, 1995). Indeed, the conspicuous display of Britishness (it is worth noting here that the Scots were enthusiastic participants in the British colonial project in Africa) in the colonies provides another aspect of how the colonial project contributed to the evocation of upstanding Britishness.

During the colonial period, direct involvement in Africa became a key reference point in Britain's sense of its place in the world: contrasted with supposedly more brutal colonialisms (especially those of King Leopold), and associated with enlightened Christian mission. It was only in the late nineteenth century that British culture began to replace an explicitly Christian sentiment for overseas intervention with one based in a 'compassion for humanity' (Himmelfarb, 1991: 4) – not that this meant the removal of Christian values. Rather the Christian and evangelical sentiments of saving others and acting virtuously were often the implicit motivations for humanitarian action, something that made humanitarian appeals something of a 'surrogate religion' (*ibid.*).

Towards the end of the colonial period and into the twentieth century, questions emerged concerning the financing of the colonies and their ability to generate revenues for the British state and economy. This led to a protean 'development' narrative in which the British government began to spend in its African colonies to develop infrastructure and some aspects of the economy.[18] Relatedly, in the 1930s, the notion that African colonies would be good for Britain was disseminated widely through the Empire Marketing Board (EMB). The EMB produced advertisements portraying the plantations of southern and west Africa as the source of tropical commodities such as tea and cocoa, but it also framed these in strongly patriotic ways, as embodiments of imperial vigour. (Chapter 7 will return to this theme.)

In regard to colonialism more broadly, 'effective occupation' was constructed around two broad strategies: one based in white settler communities and the other 'indirect rule' in which African communities were 'tribalised' into low-level colonial state structures of power. This was encapsulated in Frederick Lugard's *Dual Mandate in Africa* (1923). The 1930s and 1940s saw the British political establishment – and associated groups of scholars in Oxford and London – become increasingly concerned with the 'native problem', which effectively boiled down to the issue of how to control the social changes taking place in African societies as a result of colonial capitalism. Hailey's *African Survey* (1938),[19] the largest and most prominent of a set of synoptic overviews provided the raw material for a political debate about Britain's role in Africa (both as a state and as the sovereign authority over colonial states) and what constituted prudent 'custodianship' (Cowen and Shenton, 1998). The Colonial Development Act (1929) set out a moderate agenda of controlled modernisation and development investment. The Fabian Colonial Bureau (1940–) generated ideas about moderate progressive modernisation in British African colonies.

Even though we can identify an elite British engagement with Africa around colonial strategy, it is important to consider this in context. True, the late 1800s and early 1900s provided a last great flourish of British co-lonialism, and this colonialism was centrally focused around Africa and it seems reasonable in hindsight to see this period as especially formative. But, in the sense of having 'won' the nineteenth century (histories of global politi-cal economy speak of a *pax Britannica* and a global British 'informal empire' during this period), Britain's colonial occupation of Africa was in retrospect the last playing out of British power projection in an increasingly competitive system of nation-states.

The first half of the twentieth century witnessed the decline of empire and a palpable loss of imperial self-regard in Britain. From the 1920s, nationalist resistance to British colonial rule emerged in Africa (Davidson, 1978) on the heels of a brutal and nationally divisive European War. The global recession of the 1930s buried the vestiges of the (supposedly) liberal international order under British hegemony. The Second World War had multiplex repercussions: the vulnerability of Britain in Europe, the mass participation of African men in the Allied forces and their subsequent changing political identities, and the difficult social and economic legacy of the war all played into a sense that Britain's imperial age was coming to a close.

Decolonisation

In the 1960s, decolonisation worked its way through most British colonial possessions. There is a substantial history here of struggle, reform, and politi-cal manoeuvring which underpins decolonisation, but what is most germane to this account is the impact of decolonisation on British representations of Africa.

As ever, the ways in which Africa was represented was the outcome of both changing forms of involvement in a changing continent and also the patterns of change within Britain's political culture itself. The 1960s saw the strength-ening of the politics of the Left, and political cultures of radicalism that interacted with the margins of the Parliamentary and party system (especially in regard to the Labour Party).[20] In this context, there emerged a campaign movement concerned to advocate self-determination in parts of the British empire – a movement that focused mainly on Africa throughout the 1960s. The Movement for Colonial Freedom was created in 1954; Fenner Brockway was a Chair leading advocate of self-determination. Interestingly, as seems so often to be the case in leading Africa campaigns (see other personal examples later in the book) Brockway was the child of a Reverend and member of the London Missionary Society.[21]

The 1950s and 1960s also witnessed a moment in which Africa campaigns for Independence merged with the political activism of African intellectuals in Britain, who had been galvanised by the Pan African Congress meeting in Manchester (1945), an event that was remarkable in its assembling so many of Africa's most powerful political thinkers and future politicians. This connection between British Africans, Africans in Britain, and a broader 'solidarity' movement within Africa campaigning can also be seen throughout the anti-apartheid Movement's campaigning, even if this connection has generally been far less discernible in the more 'developmental' campaigns of large NGOs.

Decolonisation introduced what Paul Gilroy has called post-imperial melancholia (2004). Within public culture generally, decolonisation profoundly questioned the notion of Britain as a global power. Coming after the Suez crisis,[22] decolonisation signalled not only the assertion of sovereignty throughout Africa against British colonialism; it also added a final clinching piece of evidence that the Western world was now under the hegemony of the United States. As a result, British political culture had to reconcile itself to a significantly different world-view: rather than considering Africa in the context of an expanding British power – even an ideology of global hegemony – Britain faced a world in which African states were asserting their sovereignty, and Britain's place in the world (cognitively and in terms of military and economic power) was now 'second tier': one of a number of large European states, a close member of the American-led 'free world'. For Gilroy, this created a racialisation of British political culture, strongly articulated to xenophobic concerns with African and Caribbean immigration. Within Britain's racisms, Africa was simply 'back home': a place where (in the crudest and most generic sense) black people should return to.[23]

In terms of government, in most cases, Britain maintained close relationships with its ex-colonies and, because decolonisation took place largely in the absence of armed liberation struggle,[24] British companies and expatriates remained. Indeed, it was the continuity in British–Africa relations that led Africa's new generation of radical and nationalist politicians and intellectuals to speak of neo-colonialism and 'flag independence' (e.g. Nkrumah, 1965).

In Britain, decolonisation served to decrease the prominence of Africa within the media and public culture. Occasionally, wars, coups, and humanitarian emergencies brought African countries into the purview of the public, and the ongoing liberation struggle in South Africa remained an active issue in British politics, as Chapter 4, the exploration of the anti-apartheid campaign will show. The post-independence period witnessed the emergence of the electronic and print media as mainstays of Africa's representation in Britain. Specific high-profile events in Africa would be transmitted to a British audience, often articulated as stories of disaster or chaos: the Congo wars of secession, the Biafra secession, Idi Amin's coup, the Sahel famine of

1973/4, the Ethiopian famine of 1974, and of course Band Aid in the early 1980s.

The post-Independence period also witnessed an increase in the immigration of Africans into Britain, something that – in addition to the larger immigration of African-Caribbeans into Britain – led to changes in Britain's national culture and, lamentably, a rise in racist politics and violence. African diasporas and Britons of African origin and heritage have generated a diversity of organisations that 'look south' to Africa. But, generally, these organisations have not achieved a broader public presence or been effective in addressing issues to the British government which has, by and large, been indifferent to these groups. The signal exception is the Anti-Apartheid Movement which brought together various African and African-Caribbean groups and people within a very broad and nationally recognised campaign.

One final theme of British–African relations after independence is that of development. Arturo Escobar (1994) has argued that the concept and practice of development has served as a way for Western states to exert power over formally independent states. It generates a relationship between Western states and 'Third World' states in which the former are advanced and the latter undeveloped, in which the former exert agency over the latter, and in which the West contains the properties of development and the latter betrays an absence in these properties. Clearly, this general understanding of development chimes with the way this book understands British–African relations in that development (as a discourse) generated a politics of opposition and hierarchy within which countries like Britain legitimately intervene in countries like those in Africa. And concerning the post-independence period, Britain's aid programme was focused on African countries which were largely ex-colonies. In 1965, the Overseas Development Ministry was created with a remit (set out in a White Paper) to pursue Britain's moral duty to promote development in the post-colonial regions.

The construction of a national 'duty' to provide aid offered a palliative to the sense of national loss ushered in by decolonisation. It generated public norms of 'generosity' and virtue and maintained a certain kind of national esteem (Kapoor, 2008: 76*ff*.). Anglophone Africa – by virtue of its recent decolonisation, close relations with Britain, and strong impetus to promote economic development – served centre-stage in this construction. The narcissistic aspect of aid giving to Africa has also been embraced by British governments – no more so than New Labour which represented its involvement in Africa through what Julia Gallagher evocatively calls a 'resplendent image' of Britain: associating Britishness with goodness through Africa (Gallagher, 2011: 22*ff*.; see also Chandler, 2007).

Beyond post-colonialism?

As the title of this section suggests, there is some difficulty and controversy in making a reasonably robust historical categorisation that might succeed that of decolonisation and post-colonialism more generally. The previous section sets out the main facets of how Africa mattered for Britain in the 1960s and 1970s[25] and how this period was constructed on an interplay of post-imperial melancholia and a sense of colonial continuity embodied in discourses of development. But, of course, things have changed.

Crawford Young (2004) wrote a thought-provoking essay, asking if it would be a better judgement to move beyond the concept-periodisation of post-colonialism in which Africa's politics has changed to an extent that the colonial–post-colonial continuity is now less significant. Young's interest is in the ways that we might theorise African politics and the state, but much of what he says has relevance here. The stable sovereignties that were either extant or assumed in the 1960s and 1970s (Jackson, 1990) no longer exist in much of Africa; relations with other countries and regions have become more diverse than simply the legacy of colonialism with a superpower patron added in; and of course, Western countries have themselves changed a great deal.

We can note some significant changes in Britain's relations with African countries. Structural adjustment from the 1980s onwards multilateralised global development politics, centred on the World Bank and IMF (Callaghy, 2001). As a result, donors such as Britain have increasingly practised development both in consortium with other donors (through institutions such as the OECD or the more informal 'Paris Clubs' of bilateral donors) and legitimised their development credentials through their influence on – and attitude towards – the World Bank and IMF. Certainly, the former Chancellor Gordon Brown involved himself heavily in the policy directions of the IMF through his heading of the Policy Committee and ideas about development finance. In a sense, the British government's assertions of 'developmental legitimacy' relate as much to its role in multilateral institutions as they do its involvement in specific countries.

Secondly, and also in the 1980s, development NGOs took up activities of campaigning and appeal-making with great energy. The key point here was the Live Aid/Band Aid events and the subsequent professionalisation and increased revenues of large NGOs. This tended to lend development activities a more populist edge: less concerned with government-to-government aid and more about the 'grassroots' or the 'human face' of development.[26]

Outside of discourses of development, the excrescence of civil wars and complex emergencies has lent a more 'securitised' aspect to British considerations of African countries (Abrahamsen, 2005). During the 'war on terror', a period in which 'good news' concerning Britain's role in global politics was extremely sparse, perhaps the most prominent – even for some celebrated – event was the British intervention in Sierra Leone. From 2000, after a military coup ousted Sierra Leone's elected President, the British government deployed troops to secure the main airport, subsequently pushing RUF rebels out of the capital city and ensuring the return of President Ahmed Tejan Kabbah. In 2002, the British media reported how Sierra Leoneans in Freetown publicly celebrated the British presence and especially the British Sierra Leone Ambassador Peter Penfold.[27] It was Sierra Leone that served as the best case of New Labour's proactive and interventionist liberalism rather than the chronically awful interventions in Iraq and Afghanistan.

And, in regard to security and conflict as points of departure for Africa's representation, it needs to be noted (Duffield, 2007) that any representation of Britain as altruistic intervener is juxtaposed against more or less subtle racialisations of Africa as a place of disorder and violence – a place where 'people find liberation in violence' in one writer's words (Kaplan, 1994: 6).[28]

One underlying theme of this book is the interplay between the aesthetics of consumption and representations of Africa. In relation to this overview, it is worth noting that some parts of Africa (notably Egypt, the Indian Ocean coast, east and southern African game reserves, and South Africa) have become increasingly popular destinations for progressively inexpensive and often 'package' holidays. This has enhanced a 'commoditised' imagery of Africa that relies on 'tribalised' Africans, wildlife, and ersatz adventure narratives. For some time, television has enhanced this framing of Africa as exotic and adventurous wilderness. Contrastingly, the rise in ethical consumption has provided an image of Africans as small-scale family or cooperative farmers who require a better price for their crops.

If the ever-changing aesthetics of consumption have generated changes in Africa's representation, it remains the case that prevailing public attitudes towards Africa are defined by two tropes: poverty and corruption. This is borne out by the annual public attitudes surveys commissioned by the Department for International Development (DFID) since 2006. The 2007 report exemplifies this most clearly in the key findings which include that the survey revealed that 'the UK public believe poverty in Africa is still an important issue' and that a majority felt that aid was wasted as a result of corruption (2007: 9).

It would appear that the post-colonial representation of Africa is – in keeping with post-structural aesthetics more generally – more pluriform than during previous periodisations. This seems to ring true when looking at campaign representations, as seen in Chapter 8. One way to understand this shift is to consider the ways in which British national identity is changing.

The ongoing broadening of consumer-related identities and the increasingly 'cosmopolitan' outlook that is disseminated through new media and global tourism have 'layered' relatively new images upon older but enduring ones.

Context and campaign

This chapter has provided the key coordinates for the layering of the Africa campaigns that are the focus of the rest of the book. This is not simply a case of providing the general line of events within which campaigns fit; there is also a more political consideration here. Campaigning necessarily has to gather together familiar imagery, prevailing public attitudes, and popular discourses in order to be recognised and supported by a public. As such, campaigns are not a separate part of the African presence but very much a constituent part of it, relying on and enhancing some representations that derive from other agencies, and challenging or rejecting others. For example, abolition rejected the dehumanised imagery of Africans as cargo, but also affirmed an evangelical humanitarianism that led Britons into Africa and created the powerful trope of the civilising mission. British NGOs have shared ideals about development intervention in Africa with governments, even if at particular instances they are also critical of British government (in)action. As noted in Chapter 1, there is within the Africa campaign tradition a sense of 'cordial adversarialism' in regard to campaign–government relations, one that tries to rescue Britain's (post)imperial identity rather than challenge it. In more recent times, campaigns have innovated very effectively to internalise the public messaging of the private sector through use of polished advertisements and public relations consultancies.

Table 3.1 offers a schematic but representative accounting of the general African presence in Britain. This allows one to consider the work done by campaign organisations – both in terms of constrains and opportunities – more fairly in subsequent chapters.

In light of our historical methodology one can treat each representational form as a 'layer' which might be substantially erased but also persist – albeit in modified forms – in subsequent layerings. For example, the 'development' representation remains powerful into the present day. The next chapter will show how more specific campaign organisations fit in with this general schema.

Table 3.1 The African presence: an overview

Period	Institutions/agencies	Prevailing forms of representation
c. 1500–c.1700	Pirates, traders	Piecemeal, equitable
1700s	Slave traders, plantation owners	Sub-human, unit of labour, non-Christian
mid-1700s–1808	Abolitionism, some exploration	Enslaved victims, human, (potentially) Christian
1800s	Missionaries, explorers, anti-slavery campaigners	Savage, (indigenously) enslaved, redeemable
late 1800s–1930s	Colonial states, colonial office and academics	Wards of British colonial project, tribes, Africa as a resource
1930s–1960s	Colonial states, British government, mass media	Imperial decline, self-determination
1960–1980s	Government, development NGOs, media	Africa as developing countries, aid recipient
1980s–	Government, development NGOs, media	Africa as aid recipient, space of humanitarian disaster
2000s–	Government, development NGOs, media, celebrities, campaign businesses	Africa as space for self-realisation, insecure place

Notes

1 Luke and other contributors to this book see traces of Africans in difficult and slender evidence, taking very grey written evidence and assigning Africanness to it, often in a way that relies on racial typology.

2 Although it is worth noting that the act of collection and curation was intrinsic to Britain's colonial project proper (Cannadine, 2002).

3 The West coast of Africa (the Guinea coast) was known as the 'white man's grave', and death rates for Britons in Africa remained high until the use of quinine as an anti-malarial (Curtin, 1964).

4 Either as a result of death during transportation or death from overwork.

5 For accounts of the 'Somerset case', see Fryer, 2010: 120–126; Hochschild, 2005.

6 Sharp provides an early and definitive exemplar of the close association of Africa campaigning with religious morality: he was the son of an archdeacon, grandson of an archbishop, had two brothers as Anglican clergymen, and interacted with Quakers and evangelicals throughout his life. We will return to this theme throughout the book.

7   By the mid-1700s, there were an estimated 10–15,000 former African slaves in London (Rozbicki, 2001: 46).

8   Olaudah's dedication notes Britain's 'liberal sentiments, its humanity, the glorious freedom of government …'. One should see this Dedication in the context of the book's appeal towards abolition, but it remains a striking affirmation of the British political elite's self-perception of a country blessed with God's providence and liberty. The rest of this remarkable book maintains a careful balance between the inhumanity of various Britons and an appeal to humanitarian sentiment.

9   The London Missionary Society was formed in 1795.

10 Although it is worth noting that Park's narrative is distinct in both its relatively modest and favourable judgement of many of the peoples that he encountered through and also the (in light of his successors) remarkable lack of public profile in Britain (Park, 2002: Chapter 26).

11 The British presence was restricted to specific entrepôts such as Lagos.

12 Two of his books contained the Africa-dark association.

13 The claim that Emin Pasha needed rescuing is more ideological than factual, fitting in with the prevailing sense of explorer and missionary heroic narrative.

14 Most obvious here is the *Tarzan* series, based on books by Edgar Rice Burroughs.

15 This obsession was literally brought to Britain in the person of Sara Baartman and the 'scientific' masculine interest in her genitals (Crais and Scully, 2009). Interestingly, in light of the 'agonistic' character of Africa's representation, it is worth noting that Zachary Macauly (abolitionist and member of the Africa Institute) sued the 'manager' of Sara Baartman.

16 Rhodes was referred to heroically in the press as the Colossus.

17 With apologies for so many quotation marks, but all of these categories – including the very notion of tribe – were created by Europeans and were far from self-evident and pre-existing.

18 The term international/overseas development is now centrally embedded in the parlance of international politics, but it is worth noting that the term only became generally recognised in British political circles after the First World War as Britain and other European powers came to reflect on the prospects for their African colonies. The first Colonial Development Act was passed in 1929. On this, see Kelemen, 2007.

19 For a favourable review of the making of the African Survey (Cell, 1989).

20 The uniquely intense interactions of the UK Labour Party with left-wing and Christian-socialist intellectual and movement currents is detailed clearly and intricately in Vickers (2011).

21 The historical 'sinew' seems to be from evangelical abolitionism through missionary humanitarianism into the more (but not entirely) secular developmental campaigns of organisations like Oxfam and the Jubilee debt campaign.

22 It is worth recalling that the Suez Canal was substantially owned by the British state after the purchasing of shares by Disraeli, an act seen as evidence of Britain's dominance of Egypt/Sudan and enhanced maritime mobility. The nationalisation of the canal and the opprobrium visited upon Britain and France for their attempts to

undermine that nationalisation perhaps symbolised Britain's slipping grip in Africa more than any specific act of decolonisation.

23 The rising racism of British and American societies in the 1950s and 1960s indeed led to an intellectual movement to go back to Africa, generating politicised and romanticised images of Africa as a place of spiritual rootedness or a place where more positive identities of 'blackness' might be created (Howe, 1998).

24 The key exception here is Kenya where the 'Mau Mau' insurgency provoked a brutal counterinsurgency by the British. The peaceable transition to independence rather obscures the concentration camps and summary executions perpetrated by the colonial state (Anderson, 2006).

25 One might add issues relating to the Cold War to that account, but in fact this aspect of Africa's international politics was felt much more keenly in the United States. For an excellent case study see Wright, 1997.

26 Chapter 5 will return to these concepts.

27 Both Penfold's name and appearance resembled the kind of quintessentially English government representative that one might recall from a Graham Greene novel.

28 Kaplan's views provoked a good deal of controversy – largely because they were facile and poorly thought through. An insightful engagement is Englund, 1998.

4

Africa campaigning in the framing: from abolition to Make Poverty History

This chapter reviews the Africa campaign tradition. It does so in a purposefully selective manner in order to bring the framing analysis set out in Chapter 1 to bear on campaigning, and shows how the African campaign tradition has come to rely upon a set of diagnostic, prognostic, and motivational framings that have mainly focused on a norm of good Britishness generated through the 'introverted' nature of campaign representation. Chapters 5 and 6 develop how these representations have been devised in more detail.

The abolition of the slave trade

A great deal has been written about abolitionism in Britain. The aim here is to discern the three frames and consider the ways in which the African presence within them serves to promote a notion of virtuous Britishness. It should be recognised, however, that abolitionism is exceptionally complex to map: it endured for twenty years (1787–1807)[1] and involved a diversity of social groups and ideas. What follows is selective, but not unrepresentative.

Diagnostically, abolitionism was based in the cruelty of the slave trade. The economic arguments concerning abolition and especially emancipation[2] were less foregrounded and were indeed very complex and less amenable to the popular politics of campaigning (Brion Davis, 1999; Drescher, 2002). If there are two icons of mass abolitionism – icons that were at the heart of abolitionist politics – it was the ship *Brookes* diagram of a slave ship deck, and the Wedgwood cameo 'Am I not a man and a brother?' The first image chimed with a more 'scientific' sense of inhumanity and the second a more obviously emotive request for help. Recall that the question is being asked by a kneeling

– almost beseeching – African man, looking upwards and addressing what must surely be a British Christian.

Abolitionism's framing of a humanitarian appeal was very much one that focused on a powerful emotional relay of sympathy in its most tragic realisation: of African victims who were filled with sorrow and wished to be saved from slavery by abolitionists. The history of rebellion, maroons, and piracy that was also a central part of slave historiography was absent (Linebaugh and Redicker, 2002).

The diagnostic frame of abolitionism was infused with Christian appeals against cruelty to other humans. The 'Clapham Sect' of politicians (who were defined by their religious beliefs and went with the epithet 'the Saints') and Thomas Clarkson both based their discourses on the violation that slavery did not only to enslaved Africans but also to proper Christian practice.[3] More broadly, abolitionism and its growing success was inextricably interlinked with the growth of non-conformist Protestantism in Britain, especially those of a more evangelical stripe. Churches organised petitions, spoke of the evil of slavery, and conjoined ideas of liberation from godlessness to liberation from slavery (Drescher, 1987: Chapter 6).

Prognostically, abolitionism was in the main – for all of its ambition, endurance, and historical significance – a moderate political movement in terms of its strategising. The main actions proposed by abolitionists were petitions, political lobby and argument centred around Westminster, and boycotts. In regard to petitions and political lobbying, it is clear that these forms of action were minimally adversarial; rather, they *appealed* to an ideal of proper British governance. Much lobbying involved presenting the facts to British parliamentarians in the expectation that full knowledge of the privations of slavery would change minds (Hochschild, 2005).[4] The prospective of abolitionists' engagement with the British polity was that the movement could bring about the best in British governance which was based in national propriety as a liberal Christian nation (Austen and Smith, 1969).

Concerning boycotting, abolitionists framed this political action in striking terms: sugar produced in slave-worked plantations was referred to as 'slave sugar' in order to associate the cruelty of the plantation system with the refined cane sugar imports from the Americas. The moral impetus behind the notion of slave sugar was that to consume it was to benefit from the extreme suffering of distant others. The suffering of slaves generated its own genre of emotive stories, paintings and poems (Fulford and Kitson, 1998), but this was coupled by a prognostic appeal to Britons that was often expressed through alimentary imagery. Boycotts were framed as both an appeal to religious and humanitarian sensibilities and also to a sense of abstemiousness in which the consumption of slave sugar was portrayed as a kind of pollution in which British consumers would ingest the fluids of slaves as well as sugar.

The motivational dynamic behind abolition was based in an appeal to Britain's and Britons' global reach. The British parliament's attempts to pass bills to abolish the slave trade and then slavery itself were seen as of global import and indeed anti-slavery reforms were sometimes compared favourably with other European nations' laggardliness (Drescher, 1987).[5] The same sense of British global leadership was also extant in boycott campaigns. Consider this passage from an anti-slavery pamphlet:

> It is the duty of the people of England to put an end to... slavery... They can, to a certainty, put an end to it, by the rejection of that produce, which forms the chief support and encouragement of slavery, and to abstain from using such produce is therefore their bounden duty. But that, which is the duty of the people of England *collectively*, must, of necessity, be the duty of everyone amongst them *individually* ... I am resolved, for one, to maintain on this point, a conscience void of offence towards God and towards men. (In Sussman, 2000: 37)

This tract presents opposition to slavery as a question of British propriety and religious rectitude. It conflates the good Briton with the great nation – all under the eyes of a Christian god. Motivationally, there is within this passage and other campaign literature a powerful aspirational/inspirational quality. Abolition was framed as an exercise in global power; a political and moral endeavour which was in part an assertion of British global leadership and virtue. Relying on the universalisms of liberalism and the empathy of Christianity, British citizens and parliamentarians were entreated to make the world a better place.

Abolition campaigns provide something of a datum for the Africa campaign tradition. Although one can identify earlier forms of anti-slavery in England and Britain (C. Brown, 2006), the modern abolition movement put in place a protean frame which has consolidated itself in subsequent decades and centuries. One can see a diagnostic frame based in Christian and liberal norms and a concern about their violation in distant places, a prognostic frame that identifies Britain's greatness with prospects for the spread of rights and religious proselytisation, and a motivational frame in which Britons and their government are encouraged to feel like the virtuous lords of humankind.

Interlude

Having set out the originating Africa campaign and delineated its framing as an appeal to British national virtue, it is worth recalling the historical approach set out in Chapter 1. The rest of the chapter will not proceed to demonstrate how each subsequent campaign 'fits' into the template set by abolitionism. Although at a push one might be able to use the evidence to do this, it would require considerable sleight of hand and a misrepresentation of the general features of Africa campaigning.

The frames set out in Chapter 1 change: this is what makes historical 'layering' relevant. Furthermore, one aspect of the argument regarding the African presence is that the dynamics of Africa's representation and British national identity are from our perspective coeval. That is to say, we are not studying the changing representation of Africa against a stable British national culture; rather, we are exploring how changing representations of Africa are an integral part of a changing British public culture of national identity. In a sense, the African presence and especially its articulation through campaigns produces a liminal space, a 'co-production of Africa and Europe over centuries of economic and political engagement' (Guyer, 2004: 14), even if this co-production is realised on the highly uneven terrain of (post)imperialism.

This point is most apposite in regard to the impact of decolonisation on Africa campaigning:[6] this is the moment in which British nationalism has to resign itself to a world of sovereign states rather than Victorian pink imperial swathes on the atlas. Profound geopolitical changes such as this both reveal how changeable the Africa campaign tradition is – but also, in other respects, its resilience.

Table 4.1 offers a synopsis of the ways that the most prominent Africa campaigns have been framed. There is clearly considerable variation, but also some connections. Diagnostically, there is a sense of Africa as a place of suffering and in need of help; the prognosis is that the British government should act and will do so in response to campaigning; the motivation is based in appeals to good (Christian/liberal/humanitarian) citizenship based in national self-esteem. Around these threads, one can discern the articulation of various motivational norms: liberal concerns with rights violations, Christian concerns with the same, charitable appeals, solidarity with struggles for self-determination, and so on.

There is a lot to deal with here. The next sections will proceed by taking each frame in turn and discerning how major campaigns worked within these frames. This will give a sense of how the campaign tradition has been layered and how each campaign has to some degree affected its successors. We will then be in a position to reflect on how the representation of Africa in campaigns has served to affirm and construct a sense of British national identity.

Table 4.1 Summary of major campaign framing

Campaign	Diagnostic	Motivation	Prognostic	Similar campaigns
Abolition of slavery	Unchristian cruelty, rights violation	Good citizenship, national propriety	Boycott, petition, lobby of government to illegalise slave trade/slavery	Congo Reform Movement, British Missionary Society, Anti-Slavery Committee
Biafra campaign	Violation of self-determination, famine	Saving innocent victims, national propriety	Emergency relief, lobby of government to recognise/assist Biafra	Sanctions against Rhodesia, support for POLISARIO, EPLF. Band Aid, NGO famine appeals
Anti-apartheid	Rights violation, racism	Supporting struggle for rights, anti-racism, solidarity	Boycott, lobby government to ostracise the South African government	Mozambique Angola Committee
Band Aid/Live Aid	Famine	Saving innocent victims, charity	Emergency relief to Ethiopia	NGO famine appeals
Make Poverty History	Unjust and extreme poverty	Good citizenship	Lobby of government/ G8 on aid, trade, and debt	Trade Justice Movement, Jubilee Debt Coalition, UKAN

Campaign framing

Diagnostic framing

There is a basic but profound point to start with here. This is that Africa campaigns all rely on a simple juxtaposition: of Africa as lacking something that Britain can provide through intervention. The foundational diagnostic in regard to Africa campaigning is British action to help Africa. This is an imperial legacy. A remarkable ideational turn was performed during abolition in which Britain (often embodied as Britannia) was portrayed as friend and liberator of the slave (Colley, 2005), setting a precedent for the basic dyad of mendicant and patron. This interaction is specifically between Britain and Africa: British relations with other world regions are different or more complex. British popular culture generally sees Africa as a place in which discussions about aid and charity take place in a way that is unique (Cohen, 2001; Moeller, 1999).

The lack/intervention dyad has been articulated in different ways to provide a diagnostic frame. After abolition, campaigns formed within (not against) the colonial project which appealed to the British government to intervene as a responsible custodian of African societies as they underwent the tutelary transformations of colonial state formation (Cheesman, 2009; Grant, 2005). Here, the lack was 'civilisation' and later 'development', and British colonialism was the advocate and/or midwife of these phenomena.

Independence profoundly shifted the intellectual terrain for campaigns. It defined a space of self-determination and autonomy which problematised what had previously been assumed: that Britain had a 'natural' right to intervene in Africa as it saw fit. In the 1960s, Africa campaigns articulated a diagnostic frame that has come to be the most powerful and persistent of all frames: famine. The diagnostic of famine intervention enabled a weakened or conditional African sovereignty to persist.

Initially in the Congo (1960–1961) and subsequently in Biafra (1967–1970), famine images were presented through campaigns[7] for emergency relief. The diagnostic here is a powerful and simple one: innocent people are dying from lack of food and we should therefore provide the food as quickly as possible. This framing has an awkward relationship with the more political aspects of campaigning – especially those concerned with rights and self-determination (de Waal, 1997). The Congo appeals were presented as simple issues of malnutrition; the Biafra campaigns were more politicised.

The Biafra campaign was partially constructed by a group of humanitarian relief organisations that were largely based in a Christian ethic: Nordic Church Aid was one of the most dynamic relief agencies in Biafra.[8] The British humanitarian reaction to the starvation caused by war was strengthened by a longer tradition of sympathy for famine victims (Heerten, 2009). The malnutrition caused as the Nigerian army moved into Biafra created widespread kwashiorkor in children. The image of the swollen-bellied but emaciated child was disseminated widely in Britain, through the mass media and also through emergency appeals on TV programmes such as *Blue Peter*.

Additionally, the Biafra campaign was propounded through a more political movement: the British Biafra Association (BBA). The BBA emphasised the legitimacy of Biafra's claim for self-determination, questioned the colonial borders of Nigeria, advocated on behalf of the Biafran government, and condemned the actions of the Nigerian military even to the extent of using the label 'genocide'.[9]

Thus, the Biafra campaign not only generated a definitive image of Africa – the famine victim – it also conjoined humanitarian appeals and a set of less publicly prominent but more politically sophisticated arguments about self-determination and rights. In this sense, the diagnostic framing was not entirely coherent: mixing charitable and solidarity norms.

The next 'layer' in the Africa campaign tradition – anti-apartheid – recapitulated the comingling of appeals/fundraising and rights/solidarity diagnostics. Fundraising was a major part of anti-apartheid campaigning in the 1960s, focused on providing legal support for detained political activists (Klein, 2009; Skinner, 2009). Subsequently, the anti-apartheid movement – which sustained a single-issue campaign from the mid-1950s until 1994 – developed a complex politics which was increasingly focused around solidarity with the African National Congress (ANC), but also included strong socialist currents, and of course a focus on Nelson Mandela as the avatar of the struggle. Underlying the multiplex political currents was a simple diagnostic: that apartheid was illegitimate and that Britain should cut relations with the apartheid state and support struggles against apartheid.

It is the anti-apartheid movement that fits least well into the Africa tradition because of its extended political engagement in African rights and struggle. Indeed, the coalition anti-apartheid Movement[10] came to act in close consultation with the ANC in London and to generate lobbies and MP coalitions within the British polity. Most obviously during the Thatcher years, the British government was represented largely as part of the problem, not the solution (Fieldhouse, 2005: 180ff.).

If the diagnostic framing of the Africa campaign tradition was partially 'destabilised' during the anti-apartheid campaign, subsequent campaigns have powerfully calibrated that instability and overlain the tradition with the more familiar 'lack-intervention' diagnostic.

Band Aid/Live Aid was not a campaign but a charitable appeal, but it is difficult to exclude from the topic at hand here for a number of reasons.[11] Firstly – it worked within the Africa campaign tradition, generating imagery reminiscent of the Biafran campaign (the starving child) and presenting Africa as in need of external assistance.[12] Secondly, Live/Band Aid was supported by the major British NGOs through the Disasters Emergency Committee, and each of the large NGOs contained/contains within them varying admixtures of campaign and fundraising activity, each of which tends to blur into the other. Thirdly (and rather teleologically), Live/Band Aid fed into subsequent campaigning activities because of its massive public prominence: Live/Band Aid did not invent the celebrity endorsement but it used it to such an extent that any subsequent campaigning would have to work against the grain in not engaging celebrities. Live/Band Aid engaged with the media (especially the BBC) so effectively that subsequent campaigns have become a lot more effective in working through the media – presenting campaign ideas/ideals in mass media-friendly ways. We shall see how the Live/Band aid legacy became a salient issue for the Make Poverty History campaign later on.

Live/Band Aid's diagnostic was very similar to the main facet of the Biafra campaign: the issue was famine and a desperate need to move relief supplies into famine-affected areas.[13] Live/Band Aid's success in raising money was also a success in strongly consolidating public views of Africa in the mould of famine and aid.

Make Poverty History (MPH) consciously aimed to distinguish itself from the Live/Band Aid legacy. Although it was, *ab initio*, a coalition of the major British charities, the campaign platform was based in three issues – debt, aid, and trade – and it did not appeal for money. The diagnostic frame was that mass poverty was intolerable and required bold action by the world's most powerful states in these three key areas. This diagnostic frame represented a concerted effort to shift the representation of the problem away from 'lack'/charity and towards something more akin to injustice.[14] As with all the other campaigns, MPH was significantly driven by church groups, especially on the 'high street' (Martin *et al.*, 2005: 21, 29).[15]

Prognostic framing

We now have some sense of the framing generated by each campaign. Diagnosis and prognosis are closely interlinked. The interest here is in how campaign organisations, having set out a representation of a problem, articulated a solution – one which located the campaign organisation itself at centre stage.

With reference to Biafra, we have seen how the campaign included both a humanitarian and a rights framing. The humanitarian framing tied into a donation/appeal prognostic framing. This was effected through appeals in the electronic and print media bolstered by the powerful emotional impetus of the *kwashiorkor* child image. The Biafra appeal was effected through development NGOs and humanitarian organisations such as the Red Cross, and it also involved the involvement of a clutch of celebrities who endorsed the appeal.

The rights aspect of the campaign (which was also embodied in some of the relief organisations who saw Biafra's secessionary struggle as legitimate) was less publicly prominent because it was based in a prognostic framing of advocacy and appeal to the British government. The British Biafra Association did include prominent public personalities but its prognostic framing was highly political and therefore more complex, engaging with public policy, party political, and diplomatic circles. Thus, the prognostic frame for the Biafra campaign was characterised by a tension between charitable appeal and advocacy/lobby – and internal tension that has been carried through other campaigns' prognostic framing.

As with the diagnostic framing, the anti-apartheid campaign's prognostic framing was rendered complex as a result of the endurance of the struggle against apartheid. Key facets of the prognostic frame can be discerned as follows (from Fieldhouse, 2005; Gilbert, 2007; John, 2000; Thorn, 2006).

- Consumer boycotts. Initially boycotts of South African products, but subsequently boycotts of banks (John, 2000) and companies that had subsidiaries in South Africa and cultural boycotts against certain musical and sporting events.
- Protests and vigils. Public manifestations of opposition to apartheid, focused on the South African embassy in Trafalgar Square. The vigil at the embassy came to be a daily event in the 1980s.
- Petitions. These were addressed to the government – part of the work to compel governments to reduce links with the apartheid state.
- Membership of the Anti-Apartheid Movement. This movement grew into an activist network in which campaigning became part of the prognostic frame itself. Attending meetings, debating, reading anti-apartheid news, and encouraging others to join the campaign became part of the prognostic frame in a way that was unique to the Africa campaign tradition.

Collectively, these prognostic actions draw on a variety of norms. The boycotting refers to the ethics of consumption, the vigils to Christian notions of observance,[16] petitions to the accountability of government to citizens, and membership to the aspiration to build a social movement. In its initial phase the anti-apartheid campaign was led by churches and especially Father Trevor Huddleston and Canon John Collins. Throughout the anti-apartheid struggle, there was a strong current of liberal Christian support which drew upon the emergence of unorthodox and radical Christian ideas which had gained prominence during abolitionism and were also present within some NGOs involved in Biafra. But we should not overplay this point; anti-apartheid's prognostic framing was diverse. From any kind of liberal perspective, apartheid was sufficiently heinous to endorse a wide range of actions to undermine it – a fact revealed in the general support for the armed struggle of Umkhonto we Sizwe, the ANC's armed wing.

Moving on to Live/Band Aid, we can see a clear and ostensibly simple prognostic framing that was delivered infamously by Geldof on the night of Live Aid: 'Give us the money now. Give me the money now.'[17] The prognostic frame was very direct, apolitical, and time-limited. In these senses, it was very different to the campaigns on abolition and apartheid. This campaign accrued no complexity but succeeded in gaining widespread cultural impact. It affirmed the charitable prognostic framing in such a way that it would be no exaggeration to say that subsequently, the charitable appeal for Africa (or more correctly specific regions at specific times) has become ingrained in British public culture.

The framing of Live/Band Aid left a difficult legacy for MPH prognostic framing. MPH was devised with a non-charitable prognostic; the campaign wished to present an series of unique opportunities for British citizens to influence important international meetings – most prominently the G8 meeting taking place at Gleneagles in July 2005. The prognostic revolved around the mass lobby. The campaign encouraged people to write postcards, text, email, and demonstrate. The demonstrations around Gleneagles were organised not as protests but as an assembly, an appeal to governments: 'to welcome the G8 leaders to Scotland and to ask them to deliver trade justice, debt cancellation and increased aid' in the words of one organiser.[18] The event was described by Rootes and Saunders as 'more a procession of witness than a protest' (no date: 2), a contrast which evokes a certain Christian imagery of public gathering.

MPH did not involve a charitable appeal: the campaign was financed by contributions from the larger NGOs and private donors. The white wristbands became an extremely prominent part of the campaign: 8 million were sold and 'brand recognition' of the wristband was widespread. This, in fact, blurred the lines between a lobby campaign and the post-Live/Band Aid prognostic connection between Africa and charity.[19] This connection was only further blurred by the Live 8 concert (which was not part of MPH), which was curated by Bob Geldof and which graphically evoked a direct connection with Live/Band Aid by bringing onto stage Birhan Woldu, a survivor of the Ethiopian famine who was filmed in 1984.[20] In summary, the prognostic framing of MPH struggled against the well-established charitable prognostic framing that had been established by the Biafra appeals and significantly consolidated by Live/Band Aid.

More generally, a range of solutions to the diagnostic framing in the previous section have been formulated by Africa campaigns, but out of these, two key forms of action can be discerned: giving money and petitioning government. The next section will look at the ways in which campaigns have propounded messages to encourage people to pursue campaign actions.

Motivational framing

The Biafra and Live/Band Aid campaigns evoked norms of sympathy and humanitarianism in their motivational framing. This was done principally through the famine image which, in its ideal type, is a photograph of an emaciated child, focused on an upward-turned face (VSO, 2002). The countenance of the famine child is pleading and it directly addresses the viewer in order to appeal to their desire to help. This kind of framing has been reproduced in many other famine appeals for southern Africa, the Sahel, Sudan, Somalia, Niger, Ethiopia, and east Africa. It is the main motivational frame of the Africa campaign tradition.

The second motivational frame appeals to people's sense of citizenship. It is centrally based on appeal to people's sense of power: that people can (through a campaign) change the British government's policy or change the way that certain commodity producers behave. Make Poverty History was steeped in a very positive aspirational sense of citizenship: the logo for MPH put 'make' and 'history' in bold type, suggesting subliminally that engaging in the campaign would mean making history. Other aspects of the campaign's messaging strongly affirmed this idea.

A third and related motivational framing is derived from a sense of propriety concerning to British government action. Much of the diagnostic and prognostic framing of the Africa campaign tradition is based in a concern with existing government policy and a sense that policies will change for the better through public action. Motivationally, this requires a positive situating of the British government: as 'leader' (as it was framed in regard to abolition and MPH), or as a particularly powerful/influential agency in rotation to African issues (as it was with campaigns on Biafra and anti-apartheid).

Other motivational framings are extant but more diffuse. They tend to revolve around political norms of the British Left[21] and Anglican/protestant Christianity (Howe, 1993). Distilling the motivational framings into these three major norms – charity, citizenship, and Britain's place in the world – usefully brings together a broader sense of the campaign tradition's characterising features as outlined in the previous section. Christianity bequeaths a charitable/sympathetic motivation, empire bequeaths a sense of national self-esteem, and liberalism bequeaths a sense of connection between distant others, civic action, and British government response. This section has shown how these key features weave through each organisation and its framing activities. The concluding section will consider the ways in which this campaign tradition and its framing can be understood as an 'introverted' conversation about British national identity.

Summary and a look forward

This chapter has set out some analytical coordinates oriented around the African presence: Africa campaign organisations and the ways in which they have framed Africa for their purposes. In doing so, these campaign organisations have reflected and contributed to a broader sense of British national identity and have largely done so in a specific way: to present Britishness as virtuous and hegemonic. Within these political currents, Africa's imagery has changed throughout the last 250 years but not in ways that are entirely unmoored: the powerful sense of domination and intervention remains throughout. The sketch of the major Africa campaigns presented here will be looked at in more detail subsequently, not only to provide an introduction but also to associate these campaigns with their main framings.

Notes

1   Or more correctly, it has carried on to the present day in different institutional guises. The Anti Slavery Society was created in 1839; in 2007, Anti Slavery International used the bicentenary of British abolition to remind us that slavery is far from abolished.

2   This chapter focuses mainly on abolition of the slave trade rather than emancipation because this was a period in which 'the Africa' was the focus of campaigning. After 1807 when the slave trade was abolished by Britain, abolition campaigns became significantly more focused on the plantation economy and the new cultures of slave communities in the New World rather than the appropriation of people on the West African coast and the privations of the Middle Passage.

3   Perhaps the strongest argument regarding the Christian morality behind abolitionism is Anstey, 1981.

4   This kind of representation was affirmed in the 2006 film *Amazing Grace*. It is worth noting that Britain aggressively pursued dominance of the slave trade in the 1700s and was in fact the world's main slave trader in the mid-1700s. Also, a great swathe of the British ruling elite had investments in the plantation system – even some churches. It is difficult to square this with the notion that better knowledge of slavery in itself would lead to a straightforward moral rethinking by the British establishment. The numerous rejections of slavery reform Bills by the House of Lords demonstrates this.

5   Something of an echo of this nationalist celebratory tone was clear during the bicentenary of the abolition of the slave trade. This is one aspect of the tensions dealt with by Tibbles, 2008. Waterton and Wilson show how public commemoration of the abolition of the slave trade produced an 'ontological gerrymandering', creating a 'positive us' and 'negative them' (2009: 382–384).

6   A fascinating study of the Church of England's shift from 'civilising' missionary campaigning and representation to something more akin to support for African nationalisms can be found in Stockwell, 2008.

7   At this time especially by Oxfam (Black, 1992).

8   The Red Cross was also important, but provided medical assistance and relief to both Biafra and the Nigerian government.

9   A strong example of this explicitly political approach to Biafra is Forsyth, 1977.

10 The capitalised Anti-Apartheid Movement (AAM) here signifies the official coalition of anti-apartheid activities which was hegemonic from the mid-1960s onwards.

11 Retrospectively, Bob Geldof claims that Band/Live Aid was political. Interview, episode 5 of the Sky Arts documentary *Get up Stand up: The Story of Pop and Politics*.

12 The association of the African child with the need for external assistance is analysed by Manzo as a 'colonial metaphor' (Manzo, 2008: 635–636).

13 It is important to note that the nature of the famine in Ethiopia was not simply about drought. The famine hit specific parts of Ethiopia and the famine that took place was a result of the dynamics of conflict and migration as well.

14 On the tensions between charity and injustice, see Papaioannou, Yanakopoulos and Aksoy, 2009.

15 Something of a division emerged between the large NGOs in London and the local church groups in other towns and cities. This came to the foreground when MPH was ended at the end of 2005.

16 Although by the 1980s when the vigils became continuous, they were sponsored by the 'far left' City of London Anti-Apartheid Group (Fieldhouse, 2005: 218–227). I am grateful to an anonymous reviewer for bringing this to my attention.

17 Although a more profane version of this quotation has seeped into modern folklore.

18 Quoted by John Pilger at www.johnpilger.com/articles/the-ghost-at-gleneagles, accessed 22 April 2011.

19 A survey commissioned by MPH suggested that people's views of MPH, Live 8, charity, and Geldof were indistinct (Fenyoe, 2005: 7). Another rough post-MPH survey found that 42 per cent of respondents thought MPH was 'founded by Bob Geldof, Bono and other celebrities' (World Emergency Relief, 2005).

20 *The Sun* reports: 'Birhan Woldu hugs Sir Bob Geldof at the Live8 supershow and beams "Thank you world"' (4 July 2005). There is an elision in this text in which Geldof might be seen as representing humankind. Geldof's ability to generate affective impetus in campaigns and appeals is dealt with in detail in Westley, 1991.

21 Associations here can be made with the Campaign for Nuclear Disarmament, and Jubilee 2000, the latter of which might well be fitted within the Africa campaign tradition because of its focus on Africa – rather like MPH.

5

Africa and the search
for Britishness

Introduction

The previous chapter explored issues of representation in terms of Africa's general association with mass suffering. This association is itself an outcome of a series of representational acts within British public spaces, and especially by campaign organisations. The next two chapters review the British campaign tradition, that is, the historic development of Africa campaigns from abolition to contemporary NGO campaigns. These chapters do not tell a linear story of the evolution of the Africa campaign tradition; rather, the chapters focus more closely on the argument of the book which is set out in Chapter 1: that representations of Africa within British campaign materials (and more broadly British popular culture) are principally focused on constructions of virtuous national identity. Africa's representation might be more or less detailed, complex, and multiplex, but it seems that representations of Africa are best understood as narratives about Britishness first and about Africa second.

Consequently, the following two chapters work as a pair, exploring the ways in which Africa campaigns have developed a sense of Britishness both by looking inwards (this chapter) and outwards to Africa (Chapter 6). This chapter focuses mainly on campaign organisations; the next chapter analyses forms of representation.

A very British tradition

The African presence as a campaign tradition

Make Poverty History consciously associated itself with the campaign to abolish slavery, the Anti-Apartheid Movement, and Jubilee 2000. In launching

MPH, Nelson Mandela referenced abolitionism and apartheid.

> The Global Campaign for Action Against Poverty can take its place as a public move-
> ment alongside the movement to abolish slavery and the international solidarity
> against apartheid. And I can never thank the people of Britain enough for their sup-
> port through those days of the struggle against apartheid. Many stood in solidarity
> with us, just a few yards from this spot. Through your will and passion, you assisted
> in consigning that evil system forever to history. But in this new century, millions of
> people in the world's poorest countries remain imprisoned, enslaved, and in chains.
> They are trapped in the prison of poverty. It is time to set them free. Like slavery and
> apartheid, poverty is not natural. It is man-made and it can be overcome and eradicated
> by the actions of human beings.[1]

In a short book written to engage people in MPH, the section 'Become
Part of History' provides a potted history of abolitionism, anti-apartheid and
drop the debt in order to define a tradition which also embraces MPH, and to
demonstrate the power of campaigning and the role of campaigns in making
history (Bedell, 2005). The reason for this historical placing was to shape a
(potential) campaign constituency: that the British public had a tradition
of progressive political activism that had as its focus a humanitarian regard
for Africa and Africans. As a campaign strategy, the value of this historical
placing is readily apparent: MPH is portrayed as one recent expression of
Britons' concern for the well-being of Africa. MPH's awareness of its placing in a campaign tradition is not unique; indeed, it builds upon a raft of
campaigns that have made associations with those they consider to be their
predecessors. Campaign organisations generally have a Janus-like quality:
looking forward to their successes and backwards to their antecedents. One
might imagine that MPH's historical narrative will be subsumed into future
campaigns which will refer to MPH as part of a tradition that they are now
carrying forward.

These self-identifications, then, provide a *prima facie* argument that one
can speak about a tradition of Africa campaigning. This is a tradition that
has been 'self-aware', not a tradition that is implicit and immutable but rather
one that has been constructed through references to a certain kind of notion
of Britishness. To take Hobsbawm and Ranger's (1992) insightful aphorism,
it is an invented tradition, or perhaps better, a constantly *re*invented tradition. In other words, tradition is understood here as a mixture of both real
common features through time and the political construction of an awareness of those features (whose presence or force might vary considerably) as
parts of a single political and historical narrative. The dynamics and global
linkages of the Africa campaign tradition are outlined in Table 5.1.

Table 5.1 A bicentenary of Africa campaigning

Campaign	Moral continuity	Cross-references
Abolition	Nonconformist Christian ethics Empathy Humanity	Scattered references to ancient English rights and law. Some philosophical and religious axioms.
Anti-apartheid	Anglican Christian ethics Humanity Solidarity	Abolition
Jubilee 2000	Christian ethics Humanity Poverty alleviation	Abolition, anti-apartheid
Make Poverty History	Christian-Fabian ethics Humanity Poverty alleviation Justice	Abolition, anti-apartheid, Jubilee 2000

Christian sympathy and the benighted African

Throughout our period of study, British moral virtue is and was strongly underpinned by a confluence of liberal and Christian values, what Stephen Howe calls a 'Nonconformist and Radical-Liberal tradition' (1993: 169). The emergence of this tradition was very much part of the late eighteenth-century campaign for abolition but it also endured throughout the nineteenth century initially through campaigns against 'indigenous' slavery and then through the colonial 'civilising mission'. The strong Christian ethos was articulated through a sense of universalism and humanitarianism – what Drescher calls a 'religious liberalism' (1987: 125). This tradition was very much a part of the emergence of a Protestant liberal ideology that worked closely with Britain's emerging sense of imperial grandeur. Both abolitionism and the nationalist self-esteem generated after the complete abolition of slavery favoured the ideology of 'social reforms of evangelical Christianity' (Blackburn, 1988: 137) which would, through campaigns and the scriptures, generate the 'freedom and dignity... of African peoples' (Brown, 2008: 42). The premise of this bundling of ideas was that all people were similar and united under God and that it was the moral duty of a good (British) Christian to remake the world in His image: a global community of the faithful; 'global assimilation into a Christian brotherhood' (Lester, 2010: 142).

This notion of providence, mission, and Britain's ordained global role therein underpinned abolitionism, subsequent anti-slavery campaigns, and it fed into all of the other campaigns analysed here, even if the explicit religious references have tended to dampen as time has gone by. Campaigns will be covered in more detail in later chapters, but perhaps a taster of the interconnections between Africa campaigns and Christian liberalism can be offered here. In regards to the anti-apartheid Movement, one of the key pillars of the coalition was the Church of England: Fr. Trevor Huddlestone was perhaps the best-known and respected moral authority in the UK on the abhorrence of apartheid. Jubilee 2000 was strongly based in local churches, and the notion of a jubilee derived from the Old Testament: Martin Dent (one of the founders of Jubilee 2000) coined the campaign name in reference to the Biblical notion of a writing-off of debts (Dent and Peters, 1999).[2] The practices of representing Africa, especially reporting its tragedies and sufferings, which were central to Africa campaigns, carries on a tradition of missionaries as interlocutors of Africa campaigns that was especially important in modern British history (Maxwell, 2011; Stuart, 2008: 103). Relatedly, the churches that had previously provided the bulk of the campaign energy for Jubilee 2000 also served as the 'grassroots' for much of the MPH coalition.[3] MPH encompassed a large number of Christian organisations, both development NGOs such as Christian Aid and CAFOD and church-based associations. Thus, it was not difficult for one coalition member, the Brompton Holy Trinity, to write a pamphlet titled 'Make Poverty History' in which the three policy 'asks' of the coalition were entirely expressed through Christian idioms and references to the New Testament (Gumbel, 2005).

The Christian ethos behind so much Africa campaigning is also extant in the large campaign NGOs, more or less explicitly. Oxfam owes a lot of its origins to churches that saw charity and relief as core parts of Christian virtue.[4] More obviously, the emergence of Catholic Aid for Overseas Development (CAFOD) and Christian Aid established a strong association between both Catholic and Protestant Christianity and Africa campaigning. Indeed, the notion of charity as a public sentiment has a lineage back to the profusion of mission societies in Africa from the mid-nineteenth century: returning missionaries would show drawings and photos of their mission stations and appeal for donations (Curtin, 1964: 324–327; Maxwell, 2011: 45).[5]

The liberalism contained within Anglican and Dissenting British culture from the late eighteenth century was certainly more complex than a simple conviction in universal freedoms. Liberalism contained within it both a racist, nationalist, imperial, and anti-imperial strain, and it is not uncommon to find facets of two or more of these in liberal texts. It is now well-known that key liberal thinkers such as J. S. Mill argued both for universal freedoms but also made distinctions between some states or communities and others (Jahn, 2005a). Jennifer Pitts shows how liberalism offered a set of ideas to promote Britain's 'Turn to Empire' (2005); Sankar Muthu (2003) reveals the ways in which liberalism's cynicism of nation-states and cultural difference undermined imperial notions of racial or national superiority; Wright Mills (1997) shows how liberalism's notion of rights has often been formulated as a racially exclusive contract between states and citizens.[6]

Finally, it is important to note that liberalism's ascendance throughout the nineteenth century was a result of its ability to produce the orthodoxies of political economy: the comity of individual freedoms and laissez-faire. This binding together was also strongly associated with the self-perception of Britain as a 'free trade empire', liberating peoples through the vigorous incentives of competition and trade (Gallagher and Robinson, 1953).

Thus, we are not looking at Protestant Christianity or liberalism *tout court*; the diversity of interpretations covered in the previous paragraphs strongly suggests that a single liberal or protestant tradition of political thought is unlikely to be anything more than the most general principles and convictions. Rather we are interested in the liberal humanitarianism that became (as noted in Chapter 4) a surrogate religion – mixing Christian universalism and 'fellow feeling' in ways that provided powerful emotional drives for campaign framing. The repercussions of this conscious tradition-building go beyond questions of the efficacy of any specific campaign movement. The tradition that these campaigns have built is itself a component in the construction of British cultural nationalism. Modern nationalism is, as all agree, in pivotal senses invented but, *pace* Anderson (1991), the means and forms of invention are manifold: Africa campaigns constitute one facet of Britain's 'imagining'. Furthermore, they rely on a morality which is a mixture of sentiments of national grandeur and empathy for Africans. In this sense, these campaigns compose an imperial[7] tradition that has as its dual premises a narcissistic view of Britishness and a projection of British moral virtue onto Africa. A self-perception of a nationality uniquely shaped as 'possessors and patrons of liberty' (Colley, 2005: 360) with an 'unexampled portion of civil liberty' (abolitionist text, cited in Temperly, 1977: 109) is at the heart of the emergence of Britishness.

It would seem, then, that a brief reading of the tradition of Africa campaigning in Britain reveals a 'thread' connecting each campaign 'moment', however different each campaign might be in terms of political posture, organisation, and success. The connection here is the way that campaigns are premised on a notion of a particularly or uniquely morally virtuous British public which will – with the requisite efforts made by the campaign – support a cause which appeals to their sense of propriety. But, this campaign virtue and purpose can only be articulated *through* representations of Africa.

The Africa campaign tradition

The Africa campaign tradition is constituted by numerous organisations, each in some ways relying on and innovating on its antecedents. The list would include: the Society of the Abolition of the Slave Trade, The Congo Reform Association, Aboriginal Protection Society, Anti Slavery Society, Africa Bureau, Movement for Colonial Freedom, anti-apartheid Movement, and Make Poverty History. These campaigns are not only diverse in important respects but also span two centuries – from slavery through colonialism, from independence to economic crisis and indebtedness.

Table 5.2 Britain's modern history of Africa campaigning

Global context	African context	Policy	Examples
First stage imperialism	Slavery 1700–1833	Abolition emancipation	Society for the Abolition of the Slave Trade, churches, unions, women's groups
Second stage imperialism	Colonialism 1884–1960s	Transformation	Aboriginal Protection Society, Anti Slavery Society, Congo Reform Association
Decolonisation, Cold War	Sovereignty 1960s–1994	Self-determination	Africa Bureau, Movement for Colonial Freedom, AAM, Mozambique Action Campaign
Globalisation	Indebtedness 1990s–present	Poverty reduction	J2000, Oxfam *et al.*, MPH

Table 5.2 provides a sense of historic change and global context within which campaigns emerge. Each campaign will be affected by its international context (Busby, 2007; Thörn, 2006). This is not just to say that campaign

issues change during colonialism and again after independence (Bush, 1999; Howe, 1993). It is also to recognise that the agency of Africans also 'feed back' into British campaign politics and more broadly (McCaskie, 1999; Thompson, 2005).

These historical and global dynamics that have affected campaigning in Britain might be understood to undermine the extent to which we can identify a *British* tradition. That is, the global historical context poses the possibility that the Africa campaign tradition is primarily an instantiation of a global politics. However, there are limits to how far one can push this argument.

Firstly, Africa campaigns are thoroughly 'introverted' in the sense that they rely on British public values and political practices and focus mainly on the British government. The fact the campaigns might reflect 'thinner' international norms is certainly relevant, but not necessarily 'dominant' in that all domestic campaigns are likely to chime with some aspects of transnational moral discourse. It is a question of balance rather than either/or: the strong nationalism that we will see in each campaign analysed here tends to suggest that references to Britishness prevail even if campaigns key into international norms and organisations.

Secondly, it is precisely the *persistence* of a British tradition in relation to global normative change that is of interest. An endeavour to maintain continuity is intrinsic to the notion of tradition, understood politically: not so much a primordial essence, and more a evocation – creative and imagined – that might either oppose change or integrate it into its own notions of continuity. In sum, it will be argued that the British Africa campaigning tradition has focused principally on notions of national virtue, but has interacted with broader international political flows, drawing upon these flows in order to reaffirm the tradition's relevance and importance.

The next section will look at the lineage of Africa campaigning in order to define the continuities in campaign morality and strategy and thereby illustrate the ways in which this tradition has created for itself a repertoire of moral and political arguments that are now understood to be intrinsic to British public sensibilities. Four major campaigns will be looked at with a view to discerning their core political demands and their place within a broader campaign tradition. This is not to argue that each campaign is *entirely* integrated into some kind of template; indeed, some campaigns have contained within them tensions and attempts or move away from the tradition set out here. Nevertheless, what these different campaigns have done is generate a historically embedded public sensibility about Africa within British national identity.

Abolition

Britain and slavery

By the mid-1700s, Britain was a key exporter and trader in enslaved Africans (Pettigrew, 2007): annual shipments of slaves by Britain roughly tripled over the eighteenth century (Sussman, 2000: 4) so that between 1791 and 1805, British ships carried 52 per cent of all slaves carried across the Atlantic (Kaufmann and Pape, 1999: 634). It was clear from the beginning of the Atlantic slave trade that this was a brutal enterprise. A scattering of political, philosophical, and religious voices condemned the trade throughout its practice, but the slave trade was not significantly challenged until the late 1700s.[8]

What the Society for the Abolition of the Slave Trade did was create the basis for a campaign infrastructure that would draw on and build a basic moral argument: any Christian that believed in the notion of an empathy with other human beings as fellow children of God had a religious duty to support abolitionism. This might seem commonsensical now, but it was a considerable ideational turn when 'between the 1780s and the 1820s the heathen African became a fellow Christian' (Drescher, 1987: 121). This is a key facet of Christianity's comingling with protean liberal ideas in early modern Britain.

The origins of abolitionism are diverse, and the growth of the campaign only serves to make analysis of the movement potentially extremely complex. Histories of abolitionism each make their own arguments as to how one might account for abolitionism's popularity and social base. But it is certainly the case that in terms of ideologies of abolitionism, Christian morality – or actually the humanitarian Christianity emerging at the time – was vital to abolition campaigning. The three personalities most associated with the emergence of abolitionism – Granville Sharp, Thomas Clarkson, and William Wilberforce – were all Church of England Christians.[9] In regard to the constitution of the Society, nine of the original 12 members were Quakers (Brown, 2008: 39). Much of the energy that allowed the campaign to grow was derived from a Protestant Dissenting tradition in which struggling against adversity was seen as especially virtuous, analogous with the quashed hierarchies and modest prayer of the Quakers and Methodists. In day-to-day parlance, abolitionists called their cause the 'holy cause' (Dent and Peters, 1999: 31).

Abolitionism's Christian morality integrated well with an emerging popular imperial nationalism. Abolitionism became Britain's first fully mass national political mobilisation, an 'emblem of national virtue' (Colley, 2005: 354) or even national 'redemption' (Kaufmann and Pape, 1999: 645). From 1787 an abolitionist movement emerged which encompassed the entire British polity

(Coupland, 1933; Hochschild, 2005; Oldfield, 1998). It engaged workers' associations, businesspeople, the clergy, women's associations, industrial towns, provincial towns, and villages (Austen and Smith, 1969; Drescher, 1994; Hall, 2002). It emerged in London but also in Sheffield, Manchester, Birmingham, York, Edinburgh, Leeds, and a number of other provincial cities and towns. It created an influential body of support in Parliament.[10] In 1791, William Fox's abolitionist pamphlet, *An Address to the People of Great Britain on the Utility of Refraining from the use of West India Sugar and Rum* was as popular as Thomas Paine's *Rights of Man* (Sussman, 2000: 114).

Abolitionism was sufficiently popular that its relationship to British nationalism was symbiotic rather than parasitic. In other words, it did not just flourish within a context of emerging nationalism[11] but it was itself a dynamo of that nationalism. Britain's role in the world was *thought through* abolitionist debates – both in the defence and the criticism of the slave trade or slave plantation system. Abolitionism was driven by a 'parochial religious and a political imperative to reform their domestic society' (Kaufmann and Pape, 1999: 632). Abolitionism's popularity – however widespread historians consider it to be – was also in a sense constructing the notion of popularity itself. The prognostic frame of Britons engaging a well-meaning British government was articulated within the *Anti Slavery Reporter* as a distinct political relationship: of popular opinion as the 'steam which will enable Parliament to extinguish slavery with one majestic stroke' (in Dent and Peters, 1999: 119). Here, then, is an early iteration of the campaign tradition's reliance on a mass British political sentiment speaking to a responsive and upstanding government.

Abolitionism produced a repertoire of campaign tactics which remain as the template for all of the subsequent movements in this tradition and beyond: the petition, the lobby, the pamphlet, the creation of iconic public speakers, and the boycott.[12] Petitioning was perhaps the mainstay of popular abolitionism because of its ability to connect as large a constituency as possible to the demands to abolish the slave trade.[13] Indeed, Hilton calls the Manchester abolition petition of 1788 the first mass petition in British political history (2006: 184). In that same year, a total of 102 petitions were delivered to Parliament (Blackburn, 1988: 141). In 1792, the Society sent 519 petitions to the House of Commons, the largest number ever sent in a single parliamentary session (Kohn and O'Neill, 2006: 204). If we recall Anderson's histories of nation-creation through the census, map, and museum, we might consider the mass petition as analogous to the census: an aggregate register of citizens, not to categorise and delimit a population as Anderson argues, but to mobilise them for a national cause.

The broad reach of the abolition campaign and the development of a broad range of political actions served not only to bind abolitionism into a successful movement. Also, abolition contributed to the construction of British national identity – an identity based in its Christian and humanitarian credentials. This is not to say that abolitionism was straightforwardly 'good'[14] – although one can hardly carp at the successful outcome of the campaign – but rather to emphasise how abolitionism *portrayed* a changing Britishness. Here was a notion of British self-esteem that became the datum for subsequent campaign organisations.

Of course, during the campaign itself, the emotional impetus of abolitionism was conflicted. Appeals to the Christian and humanitarian essence of the British served as aspirational – or inspirational – appeals. But the contemporary barbarism of the slave trade – encapsulated in the accounts and paintings of the slave ship *Zong* from which ill slaves were thrown into the Atlantic to cut losses and recoup insurance – meant that abolition discourse also evoked a kind of national shame, a 'great national crime' in the words of one abolitionist missionary (in Brown, 2008: 78). The evocative language of sin was juxtaposed with a purported otherwise virtuous nationalism throughout abolition debates: a 'foul blot' on British national character, a form of 'pollution' and so on.[15] This tension was resolved with the final acts of abolition which were represented as much as a national victory as a liberation of enslaved Africans.[16]

Britannia: friend of the slave

In 1807 the British government made trading in slaves illegal. In 1833, slave labour was made illegal in British possessions. Britain was the first slaving nation permanently to ban its merchant ships from carrying slaves.[17] In no small measure did abolition in 1807 contribute to the narcissism of British nationalism after abolition, animated also (as in most matters at that time) through comparisons with France.

The prominence of Britain as a slaving nation was enthusiastically elided under a wash of self-congratulation: pictures in the newspapers and paintings in galleries represented ex-slaves throwing off chains under the beneficent gaze of Britannia. In the words of a contemporary poem: 'Hail to Britannia, fair liberty's isle; her frown quailed the tyrant, the slave caught her smile; ... and slaves sprang to men at the sound of her voice' (in Colley, 2005: 356). The ideology of Britain as a beacon of freedom, protestant Christian idealism, and as a global leader of civilisation were all articulated through abolition (Anstey, 1975, Chapter 4). The enslaved African iconography was replaced by imagery of a liberating and caring Britannia (Katz-Hyman, 2008: 225).[18]

The abolition of the slave trade and slavery enabled a nationalist resurgence that involved a historical sleight of hand. The major involvement of the British in slavery[19] was de-emphasised and Britain's love of freedom and global progressiveness was affirmed (Gott, 2010: 109), a 'new national ideology of beneficent imperialism, of English[20] superiority and of national unity' (Sherwood, 2001: 10). Successful abolition gave fillip to launch a nationalist imperial mission based in a sense of British providence sanctioned by God (Brown, 2008: 79) which supposedly involved 'Africa redeemed through peaceful commerce' (Blackburn, 1988: 146).[21]

Representing Africans and Africa

Remarkably, throughout the campaign, very little attention was paid to Africa or Africans. The African presence within the abolitionist campaign was largely a means to the narcissistic nationalistic gaze (Kowaleski-Wallace, 1997: 38). The iconic image of the African – diffused throughout the country as pamphlet cover and 'logo' for the middle classes' emerging consumerism – was that designed by Josiah Wedgwood: the prostrate and beseeching chained African man, asking: 'am I not a man and a brother?' One might think of this image as one of Britain's first generally recognised brand images (Koehn, 2005). It came to be deployed by Wedgwood in a range of different products: snuff boxes, pendants, bracelets, and brooches. Furthermore, other manufacturers of personal items made cruder copies and adaptations of the prostrate slave design (Oldfield, 1998: 157). As the 'brand' became more popular, its commodity status became more apparent, as Thomas Clarkson noted: 'At length the taste for wearing them [the cameos] became general; and thus fashion, which usually confines itself to worthless things, was seen for once in the honourable office of promoting the cause of justice, humanity and freedom' (in Katz-Hyman, 2008: 220).[22]

Beyond this symbol, there was scant information or imagery of Africans within the campaign. As noted in Chapter 1, the framing of campaigns relied on a principle 'other' of the British government; Africans were the figurative 'other' on whose behalf campaigns worked. Occasionally paintings of suffering Africans in various images of the 'middle passage' and brief narratives of slaving on the West African coast were employed, but generally very little was known of Africa because there was *no need* to know anything else. The abolition campaign – for all its humanitarianism – did not concern itself with an understanding of Africa or Africans beyond that required to evoke a morality of empathy to drive a campaign focused on the British state. In the words of one prominent abolitionist, Alexander Falconbridge, 'I cannot say what the practice in Africa is, not having lived there, but when my opinion is asked, I give it freely' (in Austen and Smith, 1969: 76).

The pleading (praying?) African man served to construct the Christian empathy that served as the moral basis for the campaign. The campaign's success depended on its mobilising a national sentimental abhorrence of slavery which in turn relied on an image of Africans infused in tragedy and sympathy. Recalling Chapter 2, one can see in the Wedgwood cameo a protean emotional appeal to Britons' pity and humanitarianism. This mixture of sympathy and tragedy also infused anti-slavery fiction (Carey, Ellis and Salih, 2004; Carey, 2005). In a sense, the event of abolition then became a moment of powerful national self-affirmation, or perhaps a validation of a national biopolitics of moral virtue. Abolition produced a profusion of self-congratulatory imagery in which the prostrate slave of Wedgwood was replaced by the celebrating and grateful African and the canonisation of individuals such as Thomas Clarkson and William Wilberforce. For example, a range of commemorative medals were produced, including one that updated the Wedgwood image thus: 'we are all brethren' (note the more explicit Protestant notion of community), set into an image of an 'Englishman proffering a hand to a native African, while in the background five (black) figures dance jubilantly around a tree. Underneath is the legend "Slave trade abolished by Great Britain 1807"' (in Oldfield, 1998: 162).

Just as abolitionism was based in a faith in public morality, so it was also based in a faith in Parliamentary politics and lawfulness. The intense petitioning of Parliament and the reformist politics of the 'Clapham sect' MPs who wished to promote the abolition of slavery generated a political campaign that was based in the due procedure of legislative change (Brown, 2008: 31). The complete abolition of slavery took sixty years, was based on incremental Acts of Parliament, long and torturous debates in the House, and corridor lobbying (Hochschild, 2005) . More generally, the major advocates of abolition not only conformed to lawful means of campaigning, they evoked British Law and Right as campaign resources. This was the case for Thomas Clarkson and even more so for Granville Sharp who referred to Acts from Elizabethan times to advocate for the freedom of African slaves when in Britain.[23] As the franchise expanded, abolitionist propaganda focused on the ways in which candidates had voted or spoken in regard to slavery (Austen and Smith, 1969). Abolition made Britain – great slaving nation that it had been – believe it was 'un-British' to involve oneself in the slave trade. A revealing example of this is the literal and metaphorical national boundary marking embedded in abolitionism – the proposition that footfalls within British national space must be from free men and women.[24] British self-perception as the special land of liberty was given an immense boost after abolition.

In sum, abolitionism created a campaign strategy based in the mobilisation of British public sentiment of empathy for enslaved Africans through protestant humanitarianism. Although abolitionism was by no means a 'London-centric' affair (Hall, 2002; Hall and Rose, 2006), it focused its campaign activity on parliamentary reform through lawful popular support and extensive reasoned argument. Throughout the campaign, the African presence was entirely rendered through tragic and sentimental imagery that both portrayed the predations of enslavement and the supine pleas for respite from romanticised African individuals.[25] These key facets might be condensed summarily into three key terms which work historically as 'threads', weaving subsequent campaign movements into a single tradition: tragic Africa, British moral virtue, and British state agency.

Anti-apartheid

Britain and apartheid

Anti-apartheid activism began in Britain in the early 1950s, provoked by the detention of black South Africans who were challenging aspects of apartheid law, especially the Pass Laws. Anti-apartheid activism began as part of the campaign politics of pro-sovereignty organisations such as the Movement for Colonial Freedom and was then institutionalised into the International Defence and Aid Fund (IDAF) and the Anti-Apartheid Movement (AAM). The initiation of an anti-apartheid campaign with the prospect of a broader mobilisation began with the creation of the AAM in 1960 after the Sharpeville massacre (Fieldhouse, 2005: 20), which generated some powerful imagery of unarmed and wounded black South Africans, including children.

As with abolitionism, we are studying a successful movement, and it is difficult in this light not to endow the movement with a certain kind of immanent progressiveness. But, like abolition, the anti-apartheid campaign experienced highs and lows, shifts in politics. In broad brush, one can discern a period from the 1960s to the 1980s in which AAM was strongly based in a liberal Christianity not dissimilar to that of abolitionism. From the 1980s onwards, AAM became broader and influenced by student groups and unions. Throughout the entire 45 years of struggle, AAM was also strongly influenced by the ANC.

It is also important to note in this introductory historical contextualisation that there is an immediate 'Britishness' to AAM that derives from Britain's own colonial legacy *vis-à-vis* South Africa. Britain pushed into South Africa during the 1800s, challenging and displacing African and Boer populations. The South African war at the turn of the twentieth century generated a palpable 'jingoism' within the British public – a legacy one can see today in constructions such as the South African war memorial in Hull, built through public subscription. South Africa was the starting point for Cecil Rhodes' Cape to Cairo imperial claim. From 1948, the National Party in South Africa consolidated and imposed a fully racialised polity on South Africans and in 1961 it left the Commonwealth and became a republic.

Apartheid was, then, connected to Britain's own colonial racism, and also its own politics of anti-colonialism. Thörn notes how anti-apartheid campaigning emerged from the Christian Fabian liberalism which characterised the Movement for Colonial Freedom and Congo Reform Society (2009: 76; see also Thörn, 2006). Britain's relations with South Africa were, then, analogous to Britain's relationship to the slave trade: Britain benefited from a colonial legacy with South Africa in terms of investment and trade, but the Africa campaign tradition posed the morally troubling and insurgent notion that Britain's 'greatness' was betrayed by its indifference to – or connivance with – the mass brutality and explicit racism that was apartheid – something that, in a post-holocaust world, was generally seen as morally beyond the pale.

Anti-apartheid: Christian liberal origins

This section should start by acknowledging that the religious framing of anti-apartheid was not of a magnitude comparable to abolitionism. Indeed, it is the case that the Christian morality of abolitionism becomes progressively more *sotto voce* as the campaign tradition develops. It is not the purpose of the argument in this chapter strictly to attach Africa campaigns to a Christian template. Rather, it is that the secular and liberal discourses are layered upon a Christian liberal Protestant discourse in ways that produce synergies in the way justice, empathy, and charity are expressed. Nevertheless, the Christian facets of Africa campaigns remain salient.

In regard to the anti-apartheid movement, we can certainly identify secular and radical liberal points of origin. These derived from Britain's emerging New Left in the 1950s, as well as the politicised African diasporas that emerged in post-war Britain. However, it is worth bearing in mind that two of the main pro-sovereignty campaign organisations were driven by men who had found their moral compass through Protestant Christianity. The Africa Bureau was headed by Revd Michael Scott,[26] and Fenner Brockway of the Movement for Colonial Freedom (and a doyen of British independent socialism) was schooled at Sons of Missionaries and cut his teeth as a writer in the *Christian Commonwealth*.

In 1956 Canon John Collins[27] formed the Treason Trial Defence Fund out of a previous organisation, Christian Action. Christian Action (1946) itself had roots in the Anti Slavery Society, the organisation taken on by Thomas Buxton after Wilberforce's death with a remit to see an end to slavery in the New World and Africa. The Treason Trial Defence fund became the International Defence and Aid Fund which supported black African detainees on treason charges. In this empirical sense, one can identify a connection between abolitionism and anti-apartheid, but the sense of connection was deeper still.

Anti-apartheid emerged in Britain very much from an Anglican Protestant milieu, a network of 'prominent churchmen' working individually (Gurney, 2000: 129; Thörn, 2006: 288). If there were three key people behind the emergence of anti-apartheid, it would be Father Trevor Huddlestone,[28] Canon John Collins,[29] and Anglican Priest Michael Scott. Huddlestone – who was president of the AAM between 1981 and 1995 – was perhaps the most important public moral spokesperson for AAM, representing a religious humanitarianism and anti-racism that gave AAM a strong support base in the Anglican and other protestant churches. Collins worked to create the IDAF in 1952, inaugurated at St Paul's Cathedral in London. Perhaps the most visually striking and impressive form of protest was the vigil, held outside the South African Embassy in Trafalgar Square throughout the AAM's existence. The vigil attracted a diversity of people – the broad church that AAM came to represent. But the notion of the vigil is certainly infused with Christian references – wakeful observation of injustice – and it was supported and to some extent hosted by the St Martin in the Fields church which also faces into Trafalgar Square (the 'few yards from this spot' that Mandela mentions in the opening quotation for this chapter).

Organisationally, the AAM had many church members within its coalition and also collaborated with faith-based NGO campaign groups. During the Rivonia trial (1963–64),[30] AAM worked with Christian Action for example (Klein, 2009: 459). Subsequently, the AAM continued to be strongly based in the churches, although through the 1970s and 1980s, the 'Britishness' of its (especially Anglican) base was replaced by a stronger influence from South African churches themselves (Gurney, 2009: 477). During the 1970s and 1980s, English churches were prominent in the End Loans to South Africa campaign (John, 2000: 421–423).

AAM prognostic framing

The AAM in Britain was created in 1959, becoming active in 1960. During its 34 years, it campaigned virulently for the ostracisation of South Africa from the community of states. At its height, it had widespread public prominence, especially during the 1980s when there were a series of disruptions and protests at sporting events, a 'Free Nelson Mandela' vinyl single released by Special AKA, and Free Nelson Mandela concerts at Wembley in 1988 and 1990. By 1990, 184 local activist groups had affiliated with AAM (Thörn, 2009: 5), and in 1998 AAM had a total membership of 18,000 (*ibid.*: 85). Membership hardly exhausted the level of support for the anti-apartheid cause though: in 1985 an anti-apartheid demonstration in London attracted about 100,000 people.

What were the AAM's main campaign activities? It campaigned through petitions, lobbying for sanctions, demonstrations, boycotts, theatre and other cultural performances, and inviting South Africans to speak. It developed local groups in cities and towns, and it produced propaganda to encourage the participation of others. More than any other campaign action, it was the boycott that came to define the AAM. Indeed the AAM emerged out of the Boycott Movement *via* the Anti-Apartheid Committee (Fieldhouse, 1995: 21, Klein, 2009: 455).[31] This involved not only a boycott of South African produce (especially fruit), but also a boycott of South African cultural events in the UK and of British firms that were heavily involved in South Africa. The boycotting of South African goods was seen as a mass action, a 'people's sanctions' (Thörn, 2009: 89). Boycotting also expanded away from a simple decision not to consume certain products. The Musician's Union boycotted South Africa as a venue for performances and also protested when South African artists performed in the UK.[32] There was also an emerging 'buycott' in which positive consumption was encouraged: the best example of this was the 'Free Nelson Mandela' T-shirt, which was for a time a rival to Che Guevara's image.

Finally, we should note that AAM was heavily involved in parliamentary politics. AAM always contained within it prominent politicians, notably Barbara Castle, and David Steele. AAM was generally supported by the Labour Party, although not always very strongly when Labour was in power. Such was the obvious racism and brutality of apartheid that open support for the South African government was difficult to articulate.[33] As with abolition, conservative arguments tended to refer to consequentialist arguments, focusing especially on Cold War concerns and the prominence of the South African Communist Party within the ANC. Both the Labour and Conservative parties, under pressure from AAM, groups within the parties, international anti-apartheid actions through the UN and governments, introduced sanctions.

'There are strong parallels between the ... anti-slavery movements and the anti-apartheid Movement. Not least the repertoires of both movements

included consumer boycotts' (Skinner, 2009: 4000). The abolitionist boycott icon was 'slave sugar'; the anti-apartheid boycott icon was the Outspan
orange. Thus, in a sense, the AAM relied upon a campaign politics that was
defined by and derived from abolitionism. One might imagine that boycotting is such a widespread form of activism that this connection is not especially
important. However, it is interesting to see a 'deeper' overlap than a simple
urge for preferential purchasing. As Chapter 7 will show in more detail, the
slave sugar boycott was infused with a morality of pollution, one which relied
on the image of slave sugar being metaphorically soaked in blood, sweat and
tears. The idea here was simply to bring the suffering undergone in producing
plantation commodities as close to the consumer as possible. The Outspan
orange was sometimes covered with stage blood by campaigners in order to
produce the same effect as abolitionists had done with sugar – metaphorically and literally inscribing Outspan oranges as 'blood oranges'. One might
also consider the campaign against blood diamonds from West and Central
Africa in the same light.

Representing Africa

If we can identify a moral lineage between AAM and abolitionism based in
their strategies and their liberal Christianity, it is important also to note that
the AAM became a far more diverse movement (in a sense a 'movement of
movements' before the term was coined) than this. The AAM also encapsulated various Marxist and socialist groups, was partly run by a South African
ANC diaspora, received support from party politicians, most notably and
consistently Barbara Castle, and received strong support from labour and students' unions. The complexity of the movement's politics is documented in
immense detail by Fieldhouse's remarkable account (2005) which gives the
impression of a campaign whose unity of purpose was matched by its diversity of constituency. Nevertheless, it is worth pointing out that the campaign's
unity was increasingly focused around Nelson Mandela's imprisonment and
that this was framed in a way that was both politically moderate (necessarily so in order to hold a broad coalition together) and appealed to a mass
British public (Klein, 2009: 467). This aspect of the AAM campaign came to
a peak with the two Free Nelson Mandela concerts held at Wembley in 1998
and 1990. The complexity of the ANC's struggle – let alone the rebellion in
the townships and the other organisations fighting against apartheid – was
condensed into the iconography of Mandela as representative of the ANC
and progressive forces in South Africa more generally. Representationally,
Mandela's image has become the most powerful positive image of Africa in
British history.

Drop the debt

One of the closest parallels to the debt crisis is the Atlantic slave trade. It, too, was a system of international oppression accepted for generations as a normal and necessary part of trade and life. And it, too, resulted in the West benefiting from the resources of the southern hemisphere while southern countries, and particularly sub-Saharan Africa, were devastated.

But in 1833 the slave trade was abolished in all British possessions. It was not because of one powerful individual or institution, but because of the concerted effort of thousands of people. People resisting slavery on plantations were backed by ordinary people in Britain. They were convinced by the uprisings and leadership of slaves and by the passion of individuals like William Wilberforce that the status quo was wrong and could be changed. Powerful people in Parliament, like Wilberforce, took up the cause, but it needed the agreement and support of thousands of ordinary people to ensure the destruction of the slave trade.[34]

Jubilee 2000 was created in 1997 (in response to the Highly Indebted Poor Country (HIPC) initiative) but had close antecedents in various groupings throughout the 1980s, especially the Debt Crisis Network. The extended quotation from the Jubilee 2000 campaign derives from a document titled 'Who We Are'. In this passage, very succinctly, the campaign self-consciously sits itself within the Africa campaign tradition. Martin Dent, one of the founders of Jubilee 2000, was the great-great-great-grandson of the prominent abolitionist Thomas Foxwell Buxton, a genealogy that Dent affirms as part of an explicitly Christian humanitarian tradition (Dent and Peters, 1999: 15). As Mayo argues, Jubilee 2000 'participants consciously drew upon the experiences of international campaigning in the past, especially abolition' (Mayo, 2005: 181–182).

Throughout the 1980s, indebtedness was rhetorically associated with slavery: thus terms such as 'debt peonage', 'modern slavery' and 'enslaved to debt' became common campaign currency. Jubilee 2000 chose as its icon the breaking of chains: a direct reference back to abolitionist imagery.[35] The frequent metonym of the chain and international debt encapsulated both a reference back to abolitionism's Christian humanitarianism and a more explicit advocacy of liberation which for many campaign members chimed with a more secular politics of liberalism and also social justice. As with the AAM, Jubilee 2000 encompassed these various political currents within the unifying theme of dropping the debt. Like anti-apartheid, the moral case to drop the debt was sufficiently powerful to hold the coalition together.

Jubilee 2000 was very centrally created by Christian groups (church and lay) in Britain. The notion of a Jubilee derives from Leviticus and Deuteronomy in the Old Testament. Just as in abolitionism and anti-apartheid, 'its key principles are that each person is endowed with essential human dignity as a child of God, and individuals and institutions are obliged to protect and promote the dignity of persons' (Donelly, 2007: 100). This succinctly condenses the liberal Christian and empathetic codes that define Africa campaigning. Mayo notes that the campaign's effective networking began when it moved into the offices of Christian Aid (Mayo, 2005: 179).

Jubilee 2000 generated a build-up of letter writing to the Prime Minister, the Chancellor,[36] and MPs, focused on the millennium. Letters to the PM and Chancellor were phrased in ways that would appeal to their declared Christian progressiveness (Mayo, 2005: 178). The campaign's normative focus was the 'forgiveness' of debt and a 'wiping the slate clean' to allow Africa (and a smaller number of highly indebted countries in Latin America) a fresh start. To this end, the campaign created a 'human chain' around the G8 in Birmingham 1998, a visually striking gesture that the British government in conjunction with other powerful heads of state could make a historic decision to relieve the burdens of millions.

The imagery of this rally recalled a norm developed from abolitionism: the signification of enslavement, and the appeal to release nations, corporately enslaved, from the burden of indebtedness. Also, the surrounding of the venue provided a physically-arresting appeal to the G8, placing the meeting 'within' a popular movement. About 70,000 people attended the rally at Birmingham, again revealing a broad constituency for Jubilee 2000, beyond its 110 member organisations (Mayo, 2005: 174). This event was striking in its cordiality and in its motivational framing – especially in contradistinction to demonstrations against the WTO. The premise of this demonstration was a faith in the G8 premiers and in a 'moment' when a problem might be addressed. This focus on the heads of state and their ability to deliberate morally in order to take a profound decision fits well within the Africa campaign tradition's appeal to the better nature of political leaders. Jubilee 2000 achieved great success in attaining general national recognition through celebrity support at the Brit music awards and through the public support that the coalition received from major politicians (Josselin, 2007: 25).

Nevertheless, it is clear that Jubilee 2000 did not attain the kind of broad support of abolitionism or anti-apartheid in the late 1980s. One might speculate on the reasons for this. It seems likely that the relatively policy focused aspects of the Jubilee cause made it more difficult to propound to a mass audience quickly. The representation of Africa within the campaign was also rather unorthodox if we take the abolitionist tragic victim as the datum. By and large Jubilee 2000 avoided representations of Africans as tragic victims (Mayo, 2005: 175), in keeping with the shift towards 'positive images' which will be analysed in the next chapter. Indeed, Jubilee 2000's campaign materials were as much political economy as they were evocations of sympathy.

Major campaign messaging focused on unfavourable comparisons between debt and interest repayments by poor countries and levels of expenditure on primary health and education for example.

This section ends with a consideration of the innovations of Jubilee 2000: the ways in which the campaign tradition was modified as a result of its campaigning. Jubilee 2000 certainly contained its own diversities and tensions. Perhaps the major tension emerged precisely as a result of the campaign's Britishness. Its connections to other national movements (notably the US and Sweden),[37] the UN (Klein, 2009: 457; Reddy, 1999), and of course the ANC were generally handled harmoniously. However, in regard to Jubilee 2000, concerns with representation from the Global South and issues regarding the extent to which political strategy should be more radical and globalised emerged within the campaign, eventually leading to the creation of Jubilee South and the Jubilee Debt Coalition in the UK.

Make Poverty History

Dear Friends.

How wonderfully you have supported us in our struggle against apartheid. You did make Apartheid history! Thank you, thank you, thank you. Thank you for wanting to make poverty history. Well done. Go on to the Jubilee, on to Trade Justice and on to Make Poverty History![38]

The passage above, like Mandela's at the start of this chapter, asserts a historical precedent for MPH which is very similar to what is portrayed as the major campaigns in the Africa campaign tradition. Similar historical placings were pronounced throughout 2005. In an *Observer* article (15 May 2005), campaigners placed MPH 'in history along with the abolition of slavery and the extinction of apartheid'. Clearly, the core aim of this trope was to generate a sense of historical import, to frame MPH as of epochal importance. This basic sensibility was reinforced through a general narrative of 'now or never' as the G8 meeting approached. But it is also noticeable that the retrospective discourse also *constructs* the tradition it claims to be part of: the anti-apartheid struggle is retrospectively fitted into the contemporary campaign as 'make apartheid history'. In terms of how campaigns are framed, history matters a great deal. Without a strong adversarial framing, a sense of provenance provides a key way to endow a campaign with a clear identity. In the Africa campaign tradition, looking backwards is also looking inwards: statements like the one above affirm a historical story about the British public: its humanitarianism, its sense of justice, its concerns for Africa. The sense that this campaign tradition is to some degree infused with a Christian public morality is suggested by the personality of the speaker: Archbishop Desmond Tutu, former Primate of the Anglican Church of Southern Africa.

More broadly, MPH did not develop a discourse that keyed into notions of Christian humanitarianism to the extent that previous campaigns did. As Chapter 8 shows, this was mainly a result of the ways in which MPH managed its public relations. Thus, one might note the incremental secularisation of the Africa campaign tradition, embodied in MPH. However, we should not overstate this: in interviews with MPH campaign managers, it became clear that the 'grassroots' of the campaign was to be found in local church groups, often linked to Christian Aid and CAFOD. During 2005, churches posted MPH banners on their facades, distributed pamphlets, and interacted with other local groups based in campaign NGOs and other faith groups.[39] While the success of MPH as a 'logo' was a result of very effective public marketing, the emergence of local campaign groups under the MPH banner were commonly based around churches. MPH chimed very well with the social justice narrative of Christian Aid and CAFOD, articulated through campaigns such as 'We Believe in Life before Death' which plays with a statement of faith to express a statement of justice.

What MPH shows more than other campaigns is the incremental self-awareness of this campaign tradition. In this sense, we need to bear in mind that this tradition is not simply a result of shared moral codes and forms of political activism; it is also a result of a 'layered' discourse in which campaigners see their organisation (partially) through the characteristics of campaigns of the past.

Campaign nation

In late 2003, individuals within some of the major campaign NGOs started to consider the development of a campaign coalition based on the major themes that they shared: aid, debt, trade, and the environment. At the same time, the British government (and especially Gordon Brown) was working to shape an international development agenda, especially around aid and debt: recall Brown's articulation of an International Finance Facility and his his launching of the Commonwealth Debt Initiative in 1997 (Josselin, 2007: 31).

The campaign was launched in the first week of January 2005 and immediately had to deal with the impact of the humanitarian emergency caused by the tsunami in the Indian Ocean which affected the South Asian seaboard and especially Indonesia. In the aftermath of the tsunami, MPH's priority was to grow and attain widespread public awareness of the campaign.[40] The coalition's launch in earnest took place when Nelson Mandela spoke in Trafalgar Square to 20,000 people in February. In the main, the demands of the coalition remained general desiderata that all coalition members could agree on. It is fair to say that MPH's progress in early 2005 was moderate. It was only when Comic Relief became centrally involved with the publicity effort that MPH became the high-profile campaign that it did.

Make Poverty History was the most broad-reaching public mobilisation campaign in British history. Although estimates vary, about eight million people purchased the MPH white wristbands.[41] Some 300,000 text messages were sent to the Prime Minister, and *The Observer* stated that MPH had the active support of 2.7 million Britons. MPH attained 87 per cent 'brand awareness',[42] especially via the white wristband. It grew to incorporate over 540 member organisations. A quarter of a million people assembled in Edinburgh for the G8 summit. The campaign's success was most visible in June/July 2005, when a series of high-profile events and publicity actions focused on the G8 summit in the Gleneagles Hotel, Edinburgh. More than 200,000 people marched through Edinburgh during the G8 summit. It was during this period that celebrity endorsement became especially prominent, especially through the Live 8 event in Hyde Park which drew more public attention than the Edinburgh rally; and although not strictly speaking part of MPH, was largely perceived to be.[43]

As with other iterations of the Africa campaign tradition, MPH both established a place for itself within the tradition, and also expressed a certain kind of novelty. Most striking (and problematic, as we shall see in Chapter 8), MPH decided to work within a very constrained schedule. It took 2005 as its 'campaign year', and the coordinating team of MPH decided during MPH's constitution that it would be disbanded at the end of the year: something that produced some acrimony as the year wound up, not least from local church groups. This meant that throughout 2005 MPH had a kind of impatience that the more 'long haul' campaigns reviewed above did not. MPH became, in fact, a mass lobby of a single international meeting: the G8 summit at Gleneagles. In order to achieve maximum public support for this rally MPH also worked hard to employ marketing techniques in its campaigning, to an extent that some of those involved in its management were uncertain about the balance between the dissemination of the campaign and the 'depth' of people's commitment.

MPH closely adhered to the campaign lineage in many ways. Not only did MPH make references to other campaigns within the tradition, it also aimed to engage the British public in its entirety. That is, like the other campaigns in this tradition, MPH's motivational frame was to mobilise a *nation*, not a class, sect, or interest.[44] This might seem commonsensical, but there are in fact some striking conclusions that derive from the paramountcy of engaging Britons as a whole. MPH maintained a faith that everyone was a potential participant in the campaign.[45] It relied on the premise that British citizens had at their heart a sense of empathy with distant others and a faith in civic and governmental politics within Britain that would allow a substantial wrong to be righted. This is, of course, the same premise that drove abolitionism, and it was the most prominent premise in the other campaigns as well. This shared premise meant that both campaigns not only maximised their scope of engagement – mainly through mass petitions and their present-day counterparts the text and email – but also that they served to construct and reinforce a certain kind of public national politics.

The breadth of the campaign, covering both the 'active engaged' and 'nuns and mums'[46] meant that the messaging of MPH had to be as broad and accessible as possible. As a result, the relatively sophisticated politics that was evident in the internal planning of MPH fell away to simple headline messaging which was essentially 'aspirational'. Aspirational campaigning meant emphasising the greatness of the British public and is encapsulated in one of the contenders as a main campaign slogan: 'Be Gr8', and as mentioned in Chapter 4 the MPH logo has 'make history' in bold text, with poverty sandwiched between in ordinary text, suggesting that the main message is to entreat people to make history through poverty campaigning.

In interviews, many of the members of the Make Poverty History Coordination Team[47] recognised that the campaign messaging was very simple and that engagement was by and large very 'shallow' (for example sending an automated email or buying a white wristband). There was a strategy to ensure 'migration' with the newly engaged so that they might become more deeply involved in specific NGO-based campaigns, but this did not achieve as much as was desired.[48] Thus, evaluations of MPH argue that the very high 'brand recognition' of MPH and the massive numbers of texts, wristbands, etc. did not evidently represent a process of politicisation or campaign participation, but was rather a moment in which some simple messages chimed with a broader public, especially as they were articulated through celebrities.

The focus on the G8 was articulated largely through pressure on the British government, as the 'host'. This served to reinforce both the Britishness of the campaign, and a sense of British global leadership. Bono (who spoke as part of the coalition through the NGO he is involved with, DATA) articulated this sensibility very well at his speech to the New Labour party conference: 'If Britain can't turn its values into action against extreme stupid poverty ... if this country, with the reigns in its hands, can't lead other countries along this path to equality ...'.

MPH also served to frame a certain approach to the British government which is very familiar to the Africa campaign tradition: that proper and effective campaigning should be cordial towards the government, making requests rather than demands and accompanying civic actions with intensive and close engagement with politicians. This was something that created some internal criticism of MPH which leaked out to the media (Hodkinson, 2005; Quarmby, 2005). It was also expressed by MPH spokespeople, who encouraged Blair and Brown to act 'historically', 'show global leadership' or to be 'heroes' at the G8. At the Edinburgh rally, a spokesperson explained MPH's purpose: 'The intention is to welcome the G8 leaders to Scotland and to ask them to deliver trade justice, debt cancellation and increased aid' (in Bond, Brutus and Setshedi, 2005).

What matters for our purposes here is that the campaign was largely focussed on a celebration of British civic politics, the potential of the British government to lead the world in making poverty history, and only very brief and cursory representations of the distant poor themselves. The energetic participation of perhaps one of the most prominent contemporary cultural producers of Britishness, Richard Curtis, contributed significantly to the 'introversion' of the campaign: both the special episode of the *Vicar of Dibley* and the drama *The Girl in the Café* resonate with cultural references to Britishness. Indeed, as if to reinforce that persistent notion of progressive Protestantism and reformist British politics, after the showing of the *Vicar of Dibley* Dawn French led a contingent of 600 vicars to Downing Street to submit a petition.[49] Relatedly, quite early in the campaign year, MPH ceded to Comic Relief its campaign publicity. This was done because Comic Relief's institutional history has been one of very effective public messaging and the production of striking campaign imagery, often through the deployment of celebrities. As one of the co-founders of MPH, Richard Curtis and Comic Relief's approach to messaging became the imprimatur of MPH. MPH's messaging was very media-savvy, high-impact, and celebrity-endorsed.

Moralising poverty

The purpose of MPH was to push the British government – and indirectly the other G8 governments – to use the Gleneagles summit to focus on global poverty alleviation and the Millennium Development Goals. The campaign did this by devising three lobby issues: debt, aid, and trade. For each issue, MPH propounded a list of commitments which it argued were the minimum required to 'make poverty history'.

One is struck by the scope of ambition of MPH. The campaign prominently declares that its aim is to eradicate severe poverty, although it was never clear how one measures the level of achievement in relation to poverty. Taking the headline figures from UN organisations, one might suppose that making poverty history would involve material improvements to the billion people living on less than a dollar a day. This would be the most modest target that would make poverty history, but it is not at all clear how increases in aid, debt write-off, or trade reform relate to the well-being of this diverse mass of extremely poor people.[50] One might argue that well-devised reforms in these three areas will promote economic growth, and some poverty reduction, although the relationship between growth and poverty reduction is not straightforward either.

The salience of poverty reduction within MPH was, then, based in a direct and simple association between the aims to reduce debt, increase aid, and 'make trade fair' and a desired outcome of substantially reducing poverty. Considering the immensity of the task, it is perhaps remarkable how little public discussion took place concerning the links between the campaign 'asks' and the explicitly epochal aim to eradicate mass poverty. 'Poverty' in the MPH campaign attached itself to a triad of policy demands, had little to do with the modalities of poverty alleviation, and it evoked a public morality that was pivotal to the campaign's mobilisation successes.

The detail of what it might mean to make poverty history is not as relevant as one might suppose when thinking about MPH. What matters for our purpose is the utility of poverty as a resource to mobilise campaign support. This is not to argue that extreme poverty was cynically deployed as a way to maximise the impact of the campaign: it is clear that the vast majority of those who worked for MPH were highly motivated and dedicated people with a genuine commitment to tackle international poverty. Rather the argument here is that the aim of attaining mass public recognition and support rendered the notion of 'poverty' as an increasingly powerful moral reference, one which did not require much reflection on how mass poverty might be reduced significantly but certainly did require the evocation of an epochal opportunity to (in some vague sense) make poverty history.

Much campaign literature would start with stark headline statistics about poverty in order to generate a sensibility of moral outrage or perhaps even just 'shock'. The common procedure from thereon would be to present the G8 as a historic window to deal with mass poverty. Finally, the message was that ordinary people could make history by participating in MPH. The campaign's messaging strategy was based on the same logic: in the planning frameworks, developed by the Coordination Team, campaign actions were divided into know, feel, act: in other words, awareness of poverty, moral indignation, and cognisance of ways in which one could act on this indignation.

Thus, poverty served as a means to generate moral engagement with the campaign. Of course, all campaigns require a framing that contains simplifications, strong moral messaging, and even heroic world-views. 'Poverty' served MPH as a way to make the campaign effective in becoming well-known within British public culture even if 'poverty' as a phenomenon to be combated remained largely unspecified. The ways in which MPH connected the G8, poverty and its combating, with a certain sense of agency brings us back to the theme of introversion.

Consider the following passage: 'The G8 leaders have it within their power to alter history' (Bob Geldof in Barnett, 2005: 1). Here, we see a clear hierarchy of agency: MPH as the driver of historic change, and the leaders of the G8 as the immensely powerful controllers of the destiny of a benighted mass population to such an extent that one meeting might (in some magical fashion) usher in a new world of mass rapid poverty reduction. There is a sense of historic condensation, of reducing a large, structural, and complex social problem known as mass poverty to the decisions of 'eight men in a room'.

And the poor themselves? Throughout the MPH campaign, very little was heard from them. As set out in Chapter 1, and indeed as a leitmotif throughout the book, the poor (largely Africa, as we shall see in Chapter 8) remained almost phantasmic; a poorly figured distant problem that could be solved by an effective British campaign and a morally guided British leadership of the G8.

Conclusion

This chapter has reviewed Britain's major Africa campaigns. It has shown how there is a discernible thread that carries through each campaign, based in a liberal Christian concern for Africa/Africans and that this discourse has been deployed by campaigns to evoke a sense of national virtue. The discourse of national grandeur, expressed within a religious and liberal/humanitarian sensibility is strongly posed within the abolitionist movement, and then is iterated within subsequent campaigns. As argued in Chapter 1, each campaign layers upon is precedents, creating not copies but facsimiles of the Africa campaign discourse. In the round, we can see how the religious language of the nineteenth century has softened considerably into something less prominent or more implicit. The next chapter will show how an important facet of Christian morality that has been transposed between campaigns is that of charity, which in British culture became a generally recognised emotion and practice from the mid-nineteenth century when returning missionaries would appeals for contributions to schools, churches, and other proselytising projects in Africa.

Of course, one can take each or all of the campaigns reviewed here and pull out other aspects of their dynamics to tell different stories about the Africa campaign history. But it is clear that these stories are not primarily about

Africa; their dynamics are most centrally about the ways in which these campaigns are produced within British politics and how they bring African issues into the British polity. It is in this constitutive sense that Africa campaigns speak about Britishness through African issues.

Each campaign case study is in an important sense idiographic: each has its own history, issues, and institutions. But, as a campaign – with an imperative to generate frames – each has consciously worked within – and affirmed – an African campaign tradition. We have seen how each campaign has generated admixtures of humanitarian and Christian motivational frames, diagnostic and prognostic frames in which problems in a distant and sketchily figured Africa can be addressed by the British government, pressured by the British people. This chapter has, in a sense, looked at campaigns 'outside-in': it has enquired as to how a vaguely articulated Africa has generated imagery of British agency and morality. The next chapter will look 'inside-out' at the ways in which campaigns have generated more detailed representations of Africa for British public consumption.

Notes

1   Nelson Mandela, speaking in February 2005, www.makepovertyhistory.org/docs/mandelaspeech.doc, accessed June 2009.
2   It was, Donnelly (2007) argues, Catholic Missions which, in the late 1970s, first alerted Western polities to the predations of high levels of indebtedness.
3   This point was stressed in a number of interviews with MPH campaign organisers.
4   The Famine Relief Committee based in Oxford which became Oxfam was galvanised by Edith Pye, a Quaker. The Committee was formed after an invitation from Revd T. R. Milford to a small number of people including Pye to form a relief committee (Black, 1992: 13–14).
5   As the colonial project weakened, mission societies found their role in British public affairs less certain. (Stuart, 2008).
6   For a detailed historical account that relates to Wright Mills, see Prashad, 2007.
7   The term 'imperial' is meant not temporally but politically, that is, as a characterisation of the politics between Britain and Africa which, although substantially changed since Independence, still displays various prejudices and iniquities created during the colonial era.
8   For an analysis of anti-slavery ideas before the late 1700s, see the first chapter in Blackburn, 1988. One striking feature in this chapter is the intellectual ability of writers to claim an anti-slavery sensibility while advocating the Atlantic slave trade by racialising the possession of humanity as European (C. Brown, 2006; Keene, 2007).
9   Wilberforce underwent a conversion to evangelism, a conversion that served to add vitality to his abolitionism.

10   Tellingly dubbed 'the Saints'.

11   The period of abolitionism was also the initial period of the British colonial project, as well as the defeat of Napoleon Bonaparte, and the (limited) expansion of the vote.

12   An estimated 30,000 Britons took part in the boycott of 'slave sugar'. We will return to the boycott as a campaign method in Chapter 7.

13   Abolishing slavery itself did not generate the kind of mass petitioning that abolishing the slave trade did.

14   Abolitionists could maintain all kinds of racialised understandings of Africans – as children, savages, heathens in need of saving.

15   Quotations taken from Gallagher, 2011: 47.

16   And, of course, the idea of reparations was not mooted.

17   For an important caution regarding British disengagement, see Sherwood 2004. British companies continued to benefit from the slave trading of other countries.

18   Relatedly here, see Gratus, 1973.

19   Not only supplying British colonies with slaves but also the plantations of other European nations. A striking investigation into the centrality of slavery for some British cities is Richardson 2005.

20   English superiority was certainly accompanied by Scottish imperial-colonial enthusiasm.

21   The House of Commons also managed to reinvent the British government as virtuous when faced with oncoming nationalist struggles for self-determination. See Cheesman, 2009.

22   Hilder, Caulier-Grice and Lalore also use a marketing analogy to evaluate the abolitionist cameo, describing it as 'viral' (2007: 24).

23   See especially the 'Somerset Case' which judged that James Somerset, a slave entering Britain from Virginia could not be enslaved once in Britain, nor could he be compelled to return to Virginia with his 'master'. For details, see Hochschild, 2005: 48ff.

24   Although of course the notion of 'freedom' was substantially different for men and women. Indeed, there was always concern within the abolitionist activists that women were becoming dangerously politicised by their participation in the campaign, however secluded it was (Jennings, 2005).

25   On the romanticism that infused imperial ideas in Britain more generally, see Fulford and Kitson, 1998.

26   For details, see Yates and Chester, 2006, an appreciative biography.

27   John Collins, who became Cannon of St Paul's Cathedral, also served as a personal focus for anti-apartheid activity in the UK. He was also involved in the founding of War on Want and the CND, making him perhaps the most important 'campaign cleric' in British history.

28   For a biography similar in tone to Yates and Chester, see Denniston, 1999.

29   Huddlestone and Collins cooperated with each other throughout the 1950s and 1960s.

30   This trial saw most of the ANC leadership tried and many imprisoned.

31 The Boycott Movement's creation represented a consolidation of anti-apartheid's British institutional foundations after a period in which there was more involvement of African diasporas. See Fieldhouse, 1995: 11–13.

32 Although this was not a straightforward decision. After all, one could argue that black South Africans could make a legitimate claim that performing in Britain could raise awareness of conditions in South Africa. The ANC advised AAM against allowing this.

33 The creation of Bantustans, claimed by the National Party as autonomous sovereign spaces for different 'tribes' was unsuccessful in deflecting criticisms of apartheid.

34 www.jubileeresearch.org/jubilee2000/about.html#abolition, accessed 3 June 2009.

35 A personal vignette: in Uganda during 2000, I joined a Jubilee demonstration which was led by a woman theatrically decked in chains representing Uganda's indebtedness.

36 Gordon Brown seemed particularly interested in debt restructuring and engaged with campaign NGOs on a number of occasions, including in the run-up to the creation of Make Poverty History. Brown's first speech expressing his sympathy with Jubilee 2000 was made at St Paul's Cathedral, the location for previous anti-apartheid and abolitionist speeches.

37 See Thörn, 2009.

38 www.mph-northeast.org.uk/getinvolved1.pdf, accessed July 2009.

39 Most prominently, St Paul's Cathedral was wrapped in a MPH white wristband.

40 There was a sense within the Coordination Team after the tsunami and the DEC appeal that MPH might flounder.

41 The *New Statesman* has it that ten million were purchased (12 December 2006). It is not clear how the total number sold was calculated, and some interviewees stated that ultimately, the figure of eight million was agreed as a reasonable estimate.

42 According to media analysis firm Metrica. See MPH Press Release 30 January 2006. The advertising value of the white wristband – its publicity value if it was an ordinary commodity – is estimated to be in the hundreds of millions of pounds (Hilder *et al.*, 2007: 44).

43 A perception propounded by journalist Paul Vallely who states that MPH 'culminated in Live 8 – possibly the biggest political lobby the world has ever seen' (Vallely, no date).

44 One gets a sense of this specificity when comparing these campaigns with anti-imperial campaigns left of the Labour Party (Howe, 1993).

45 A very important caveat here is that MPH was criticised for not engaging Afro-Caribbean groups within the UK; indeed for some interviewees, the campaign suffered generally from a 'whiteness' that evoked colonial times. This was not helped by Geldof's selection of musicians for the Live 8 concert.

46 Each of the phrases within quotations here refers to phrases used in interviews by those who steered MPH. The public were commonly divided into 'engaged', 'interested', and 'non-engaged'.

47 The Coordination Team (CT) was a steering group made up of eighteen or so representatives from the larger NGOs and unions. I interviewed eleven members of the CT.

48 The failure to ensure 'migration' was exacerbated by the fact that the coalition de-stroyed the massive email contact list at the end of 2005. The campaign ended by listing all coalition members on its website and encouraging people to follow links to one or more of them.

49 Relating to the theme of liberal Christianity, Dr Mary Bradford of Christian Aid stated that 'the churches have been the backbone of virtually every major campaign against mass poverty over the last eight years or so' (MPH Press Release, 13 January 2005).

50 There is – as ever – a large debate about the relationship between aid, growth, and poverty. Considered overviews of this debate can be found at Glennie, 2008; Lockwood, 2005.

6

Britishness and the search
for Africa

From turbulent waters to consensus building

Representing Africa within British public spaces is an exercise based in aspiration rather than certainty. Over the last 200 years, representations of Africa have emerged within contested terrain. Each claim, presentation, or evocation of Africa has been intrinsically unstable, or at least *in motion*. This is because all representation contains a Janus-like quality. Located above the porticos of British sovereignty, representations of Africa look southwards towards 'the continent' while also looking inwards in order to resonate with some aspect of British national identity. Many discussions about Africa over the years have been in good part discussions about British identity or statehood as much as they have been about 'Africa' in some sense. We have investigated the domestication of Africa in the previous chapter by concentrating on the major Africa campaigns and the ways that they have evoked a virtuous British public morality. This chapter looks at representations of Africa more specifically, and it does so with a more specific historiographical focus – from the early 1980s to the present day.

One can make a useful rough heuristic of the fluidity of the African presence by looking at campaign imagery from the early 1980s and identifying three broad sequences in the framing of African imagery. The first frame is the charitable appeal based in *disaster* imagery. The *locus classicus* here is the Ethiopian famine of 1984 during which International Non Governmental Organisations (INGOs) used images of extreme suffering to appeal for emergency donations (van der Gaag and Nash, 1987: 45*ff.*). The second frame – very much a reaction to the first – is the developmental appeal based in *human face* imagery. The third frame – and the frame most difficult to categorise easily – is associated with consumption and branding and this will be analysed in the next chapter. This chapter will look at each of the first two in some detail.

The context within which Africa campaigns have worked has changed as extensively as the campaign discourses themselves over the last two centuries. Africa has become mainstreamed into British culture via various modes of cultural and political production. This is partly the story of large Africa campaigns such as the ones analysed in the previous chapter. It is also a result of imperial cultural production, the advertising of commodities from Africa,[1] natural history films, media reporting on Africa events such as Biafra, Rhodesia's unilateral declaration of independence, Kenya's state of emergency, the Rwanda genocide, British government involvement in Sierra Leone, South Africa's independence, and so on.

In recent times, the British government – especially under New Labour – has produced bold statements on Africa; mass campaigns such as Jubilee 2000 and Make Poverty History have (in spite of their poverty rather than spatial focus) foregrounded Africa within the polity; the rise of celebrity campaigning (perhaps most prominent in Comic Relief's biannual Red Nose Days and Sports Aid) has enhanced a strongly affective representation of Africa as moral concern; Africa has become gradually more prominent in film and television; and the marketing and public relations industry has become increasingly involved in commercial/developmental appeals such as RED.[2] In general, there has been a 'celebritisation' of Africa (Lonsdale, 2005: 2).

Celebrity support for development campaigns might not be new, but it has taken off since the early 1990s, to an extent that now any development cause, campaign, or appeal is accompanied by the image and/or voice of a celebrity. There are consultancy agencies that advise celebrities on causes that fit with their image production (Samma, Mc Auliffe and MacLachan, 2009: 138).[3] Celebrities do more than dynamise a message by associating it with stardom.[4] They act as 'emotional sovereigns' who amplify the emotional impetus of a campaign or appeal (Richey and Ponte, 2011). Celebrities commonly visit Africa, generating a hybrid reportage in which one receives news, witnesses events, observes projects through the journeys of a celebrity. But also, one is invited into a highly emotional and confessional mode in which the celebrity expresses his/her feelings about poverty, death, and conflict back to a British audience. This can be extremely powerful, but it is striking how in all examples of this (that I have seen)[5] the location of the Africans involved in the shoot is marginal. This is a piece to camera, addressing British viewers, entreating them to empathise with the celebrity's emotional trauma (not the locals' situation). This might be dressed up in light irony, but the positions taken are formulaic.

In 2006, a series of celebrity portrait posters, under the strapline 'I am African'[6] which constitutes perhaps the most high-profile celebrity campaign, linked to a charity that provides medicines for AIDS sufferers. The celebrity roll-call is unequalled: Janet Jackson, Alicia Keys, Tyson Beckford, Iman, David Bowie, Richard Gere, Sarah Jessica Parker, Liv Tyler, Gwyneth Paltrow, and others.[7] Each portrait is a highly polished glamour shot with an 'African' dash of make-up to signify a common genetic inheritance from Africa and therefore a connection with the continent. The text on the website and posters recounts the familiar eschatology of death and redemption through donations elicited by the celebrity endorsements. 'Stop the dying. Pay for lifesaving', a consumerist appeal to be returned to in Chapter 7.

The interface between celebrity and Africa campaigning goes beyond the ability of the famous to lend their images to campaigns and appeals. There is also an increasing prominence given to private philanthropy and famous public intellectuals, each of which intermingle with campaign organisations and other celebrities in ways that seem to suggest the formation of a novel wealth and mobile 'humanitarian class'. DATA – which was founded by Bono and Bobby Shriver – has received funds from the Bill and Melinda Gates Foundation. Bono also toured parts of Africa with Jeffrey Sachs,[8] the latter writing effusively about Bono's humanitarian compassion. Georg Soros also provided DATA with seedcorn funding. Also, infamously, Bono 'made Jesse Helms cry' (Busby, 2007). Warren Buffet and Bill Gates created the 'Giving Pledge' in which the super-wealthy pledge over 50 per cent of their 'wealth' to good causes.[9] Like Soros, these two have developed public personas as humanitarians, making statements about poverty and development and speaking at international summits on these issues.[10]

Bringing this context in is important. Africa's prominence in British public life has grown and become more complex and, as such, each aspect of representation tends to become interpolated by the others. The main agents of Africa's representation in Britain – campaign and charitable organisations – have not only found themselves modifying or even reinventing the frames within which Africa is located; they have also done this against a changing broader context within which other agencies have also put effort into the representation of Africa in Britain. One result of this is that campaign-based, charitable, governmental, commercial, and celebrity representations now mutually interpolate with each other to produce a dense African presence within the British polity that needs some care to unpack. One clear general observation that one can make is that the African presence has become unprecedentedly prominent within the British polity in terms of campaigning.

Another related *prima facie* observation is that the African presence – in spite of its agential complexity – has become highly networked. That is, the different 'nodes' of representation tend mutually to reference and reinforce each other. This might involve either the direct collaboration of, say, campaign groups and government or celebrities and commercial advertising; it might also be the case that different agents 'scope' existing images and campaigns in order to 'place' their own message or image.[11] The outcome of this networking is moderating: the domestication of Africa has become an important part of a consensus about Britishness, a 'median politics' in which Africa is a reference point upon which 'we' can all agree – both about what needs to be done and what 'our' role is.

In search of Real Africa

There is a key point that needs to be drawn out regarding the context within which representation takes place which to some degree explains the unstable nature of Africa's representation. Put simply, it is that a key part of Africa's domestication has been to make truth claims about Africa. One can see this in the travelogues of the eighteenth century (Burroughs, 2009; Coleman, 2004; McLynn, 1992). Proceeding from then, one can identify a more or less explicit set of claims to authenticity or truth in the writings of abolitionists (Clarkson, 1808; Equiano, 2003; Lovejoy, 2006), the *camera veritas* style of disaster journalism in the 1980s, the 'human face' campaigns of charitable organisations in the 1990s, as well as more specific representations such as sponsoring a child or the village story.

Most relevantly for this chapter the concerns of the late 1980s onwards with 'negative' imagery raised the usually rather shadowy figure of a 'proper' representation. Having worked within an Oxfam-funded Development Education Centre in the early 1990s, I participated in the discursive construction of a notion of 'positive' images of Africa in which the concern was to present Africa through personal or 'human' stories in which ordinary Africans had a strong agency. The shared norm that all workers had was that Africa required a more representative set of images that could be rolled out into school curriculums. Looking through Oxfam's picture archives during a trip to the headquarters in Oxford, I was impressed by how strongly the photos in their entirety reflected this ethos, and I think it is possible to see a similar photographic code in all of the campaign organisations.

The ideal of a properly representative imagery is laudable. The kind of ethos described above clearly improves upon the disaster narratives and victimologies presented from the first half of the 1980s onwards. But there are some difficulties here. Firstly, and most obviously, Africans and African societies *are* victimised; some Africans are not just *represented* as victims, they *are* victims – victimised as a result of myriad forces over which they have little control.

Famines are a central part of Africa's modern history (Devereux, 2007; De Waal, 1997), and they are produced by colonial legacies, post-colonial state action (or inaction), market vulnerabilities, and harsh and unstable environmental conditions. Like famines, civil conflict is also a central part of Africa's politics, another horrific manifestation of processes of social turbulence, cominglings of state violence and weakness, warlordism, and the emergence of political economies of pillage (Keen, 2008; Reno, 2011). There are, of course, people, classes, and communities that are victimised by the forces of global capitalism, climate change, and state action throughout the world. Would it be excessive to claim that Africa has housed a disproportionate number of catastrophic and victimising events compared to other parts of the world?

If we can argue that the victimised are a real and true representation of Africa, then we need to reconcile ourselves with the evasiveness of Real Africa as a grand narrative. NGO representations tend to veer between the 'developmental' and 'disaster' tropes, each claiming to draw out something intrinsically African. The notion of a proper representation of Africa suggests a lurking essentialism which needs to be unpacked. Most obviously, the aggregate entity 'Africa' has proven to be something of a chimera: a juxtaposition of odd parts, assembled to produce a single place, the unifying features of which are difficult to discern.

A quick example might clarify: one of the common positive images of Africa is the woman farmer – often represented in order to posit that Africans are hardworking (she might have a hoe in hand) and not simply in need of charity; also the image brings to the foreground the fact that women do the bulk of agrarian labour. The messages embedded in this kind of image are praiseworthy, but they no more capture 'Africa' in the aggregate than an image of an emaciated child. In fact, both 'types' are part of the composite social terrain of the continent – a terrain also occupied by the informal trader, the wage labourer, the musician, the religious leader, or the Pajero-driving politician. The point here is simply that it is unworkable to identify an essential, general, and uncontentious Africanness that can be rendered as a core set of images.

To represent Africa's diversity, one would be left with such a diversity that the *differentia specifica* that defines Africa apart would dissolve; to focus on a narrower African essence would be to open up debates about representation and its purposes once again. This is inescapable. We should simply recognise the dynamic and agonistic nature of representation, and its inescapably political content which is intrinsic to Africa's domestication into the British polity. Making this recognition does not mean that it is necessary to abandon some form of calibration in which imagery is evaluated in terms of an enquiry into the ways that it is related to its signified. Not to do this would be to move into a postmodern resignation that each and every signification has its own value or even 'truth' and that any standard setting is simply an exercise in power.

But, although we might usefully evaluate imagery according to realities in Africa, we should not see these evaluations as progress towards certainty. The representation of distant others will remain unstable and contested. Indeed, the notion that knowledge producers in Britain might be moving towards a perfect mapping of Africa evokes rather worrying normative positions in which the Western episteme desires nothing more than to make the world legible for its own purposes (Scott, 1998; Stoler, 2002).

It is inescapable that Africa's representation is mediated, and mediated in particular ways. Mediation is practised by British agencies; *African agencies very rarely represent themselves to the British public*. One of the best-known and recent ostensible direct representations is in fact one of the most orchestrated representations: that of Birhan Woldu at Live 8, an example considered further later in the book.

The argument so far moves us towards a sense that a singular and stable 'Africa' is unrepresentable. But, in another way Africa is extremely representable. There is a proliferation of representations of Africa, and there is no a priori reason to suppose that any representation is entirely fictional or entirely empirical and unmediated. What matters, then, is not just some evaluation of how representations compare with aspects of social life in Africa or a particular part of it, but also the practices of representation: the agencies, acts of curation, messaging and so on. The example of Birhan Woldu is a good example: no one can deny her authenticity as an African who can directly address an assembled audience of British citizens. But her appearance and words are heavily mediated, almost entirely integrated into a spectacle managed by various others – Geldof, Madonna, the BBC, and so on.[12] If this is the case, we should not strive for a full and proper representation of Africa but rather keep asking questions about the nature of mediation.

Ben Okri makes an important point:

> It is easy to dismiss Africa. It is easy to patronise Africa. It is easy to exploit Africa. And it is easy to insult Africa. But it is difficult to see Africa truly. It is difficult to see its variety, its complexity, its simplicity, its individuals. It is difficult to see its ideas, its contributions, its literature. It is difficult to hear its laughter, understand its cruelties, witness its spirituality, withstand its suffering, and grasp its ancient philosophies. (Okri, 2009: 8)

This point brings us to the third point for discussion. If representation is rendered intrinsically unstable by practices of mediation, this instability is also rendered complex by the fact that, as mentioned above, campaign organisations are not alone in their representing work: government, media, and private companies have all represented Africa and have done so in ways that conform to or even borrow from the techniques of campaign messaging. This is part of the story of constructing an orthodoxy or consensual imagery of Africa. Thus, campaign organisations might be seen as lead authors of a broader public effort at representation, alongside the references to Africa occasionally made by politicians or DFID, the ersatz campaign narratives of companies that have bought into the RED franchise, the celebrity endorsements of campaign headlines that employ both theatre and politics, and dramatic cultural output via television and film which almost always comes with a political message.

So far, we have set the scene concerning Africa's representation through development campaigning and noted how networked representation has become; how – in the absence of 'genuine' representation – there are various claims to authentic representation; and how practices of mediation in Africa imagery are key. This chapter will substantiate and investigate these three introductory points. It begins by looking at the history of representation from the late 1960s, and the movement between two sensibilities – negative and positive. Secondly, it will consider the repercussions of mediation, focused around themes of Africa's irreducible plurality/complexity and the mediating endeavours of British 'domesticating' agencies. Finally, having recognised the dynamic and mediated nature of Africa's representation, it will consider the ways in which contemporary Africa representation has become unprecedentedly dense and networked, leading not only to mediation but also *moderation*.

Disaster Africa

This section will review the construction of the disaster Africa frame. It does so following the broad historical sequences set out above, and concentrates on the ways in which this framing (as with the others) relies upon a mediation that aims to domesticate aspects of Africa's politics in order to pursue agendas in British politics. The disaster Africa framing is centrally oriented around imagery of mass suffering and especially the representation of human suffering.

The Biafran war of secession

In 1967, the Biafran war commenced after the political tensions and violence of Nigeria's federalism led to the secession of the south-east under Colonel Ojukwu.[13] The federal government's response was severe, strafing the territory with bombs, blockading international trade (including oil exports) and pushing the Nigerian military into Biafra. Furthermore, Biafra's unstable sovereignty was recognised by few countries (Tanzania, Zambia and France being the major ones), making it nearly impossible to establish any commercial relations with other countries. The result of the three-year war was a drastic disruption of agriculture and trade throughout Biafra. The conflict also created displaced populations, made highly vulnerable and reliant on the extremely basic support that the rudimentary Biafran government and a small number of relief organisations could provide.

The Biafra war of secession was, as Alex De Waal argues, the first instance of international humanitarian disaster (1997). Biafra's cause for self-determination was constructed on a failing Nigerian federalism and a pogrom in which those identified as ethic Igbo had been subjected to violence and terror in northern Nigeria, leading to mass population movements (up to a million people) back to the south-west. Biafra's claim to self-determination contained a strong popular and republican theme.[14] The war itself agitated what has proven to be an enduring tension within British (and wider Western) polities: the contesting norms of sovereignty in its statist formulation and the liberal belief in the self-determination of peoples. The British government clearly aligned itself with the Nigerian government and denied Biafra any statehood in international politics. But, for others, Biafra was a cause: a struggle for *popular* self-determination against a post-colonial sovereignty.

The campaign for Biafra in Britain contained two core motivational frames. The first was rights-based and political. The British Biafra Association (BBA) saw the war in Biafra as a political-military campaign forcibly to re-integrate Biafra into Nigeria. The mass suffering that resulted was a political weapon to weaken and discipline the Igbo population. There was an argument made that the Igbo people were being subjected to a genocide (Waugh and Cronje, 1969: Chapter 6) – that is, a systematic liquidation of a people by a state.[15] The language of the BBA is exclusively political: it relied on a historical account of Nigeria's colonially determined boundaries, the legitimacy of secession, and the culpability of Britain in the war against the Biafran people. As a campaign, it was the latter that animated the BBA. The prognostic frame was focused on the British government's military support for Nigeria's war: lobbying and political journalism. This framing did not propound a charitable or humanitarian appeal; it asked people to see their Member of Parliament, lobby parliament, join public demonstrations, attend BBA meetings, and write to the Secretary of the BBA. Pamphlets were designed around short texts explaining the politics of Biafra; there were no images (BBA, no date).

The best-known case of political journalism[16] was Fredrick Forsyth's (1977), based in visits to Biafra during the war. He portrayed Biafra as a progressive nation in search of self-determination under siege from a federal government and its international allies. He employed analogies with other virtuous nations in search of a state. Forsyth's principled defence of Biafra led him to resign from the BBC and to become part of a campaign to recognise Biafra's sovereignty and to condemn the Nigeria government's reoccupation of Biafra.

The second motivational frame was humanitarian. The 'Biafran child' was the first post-colonial exemplar of the generic 'African child' that became the common currency of the disaster Africa imagery. Biafra was not only a cause for those who believed in popular sovereignty; it was also a humanitarian cause provoked by internationalised images of extreme suffering. These two moral frames were not mutually exclusive; it was the mass suffering of Igbo people that provided impetus to the self-determination cause, and the political claims to sovereignty fed back into the humanitarian cause, albeit to a lesser degree. But the politics of the Biafran secession were largely effaced in favour of the appeal for donations to charitable organisations that were – again as De Waal so acutely investigates – engaging in an early example of humanitarian relief in what is now known as a 'complex emergency'.

The organisations that involved themselves in Biafra were both Christian and secular relief organisations – Nordic Church Aid and Red Cross respectively. The Christian organisations perceived of Biafra at least in part as a solidarity cause after Biafrans had been attacked en masse in the Muslim north – one of the sources of support for Biafra within Britain was Catholic (Diamond, 2007: 356).[17] Although the justification for flying food aid into Biafra was the well-known Red Cross neutrality doctrine, it emerged that some relief organisations were also supplying fuel and other non-humanitarian supplies to the Biafran government. Nevertheless, the appeals that they launched followed the apolitical humanitarian focus; any 'political' support to the Biafran government was as covert as the night-time relief flights from Guinea-Bissau. Thus, in a way, Biafra was framed as a *natural disaster* – the cause was to help those who had become victims of forces that were outside the concerns of the relief agencies. As such, the appeals were based on representations of suffering which would provoke a humanitarian response in the viewer; they were not concerned with the process of victimisation themselves. The Biafran child – suffering from *kwashiorkor* and half-naked – would be most effective in raising support for relief operations.

The British newspapers also contributed strongly to this framing. Large-circulation tabloids displayed the most sensationalised front pages concerning the Biafra war. The *Daily Mirror* covered its front page with a naked kwashiorkor-ridden boy, stating 'The boy died only an hour after this picture was taken'. The *Daily Mail* produced a front page on an extremely emaciated baby – again naked – with the simple headline 'Save us'. In 1968, the popular children's television programme *Blue Peter* reported on Biafra using various images of naked emaciated children, and raised ten times the amount that they had appealed for. This *Blue Peter* appeal also served to place Biafra as a starting point for another orthodoxy of Africa representation – the disaster appeal.[18]

It is interesting to note that the disaster journalism that emerged from Biafra in 1968 and 1969 was pivotally a result of the Biafran government organising a public relations operation through a (what is now called) public relations company called Mark Press.[19] Mark Press issued over 250 press releases to Western newspapers advocating the Biafran cause (*Time Magazine*, 1968). In the later stages of the war – after the federal army had reoccupied key cities – mass migrations generated the extreme human suffering captured in the image of the emaciated and dying child. The Biafran government invited journalists in order to present an image of suffering which might have allowed them to win what could be called a war of representation against the Nigerian government which relied on arguments of sovereignty and relatedly a Western/British fear of atavistic 'tribalism'. Nevertheless, after each small team of journalists was returned from Biafra to their capital cities, the imagery was employed by editors, producers, politicians, and campaign groups to make the Biafra war of secession a 'British' affair. The politics of Biafra's secession were rarely narrated; nor were the remarkable attempts by the besieged Biafran state to maintain sovereignty. The politics and discourse of the charismatic Ojukwu were largely absent and the tenacity of many Biafrans rarely made it into British public spaces. The graphic suffering of children portrayed by tabloids and television reports was far more prominent than the more 'campaign' journalism which was restricted – although not exclusively – to the broadsheets, and which expressed dismay at the Wilson government's support for the federal Nigerian government's 'famine crimes' (de Waal, 1997).

Like abolition, the Biafra famine/war serves as an originating representational form. It brought the famine child to public attention through the mass media and especially the tabloids. These images were presented in ways that were increasingly attached to appeals for donations. This representation attained more resonance than the political campaign in support of Biafra's secessionism. Retrospectively, one can see here a tension that persists through other campaigns between the familiar, popular, and powerful appeal and the more complex, elite/lobby-based, and political campaign. This tension is evidently instantiated in a case study of Oxfam Annual reports later in the chapter.

The Ethiopian famine

Ethiopia underwent a 'revolutionary' change in regime in 1974 in which the Haile Selassie government was overthrown by a military and Marxist-Leninist government under Haile Mengistu Mariam. With massive military support from the Soviet Union, the Mengistu government stepped up the war against the secessionist Eritrean movement, the Eritrean People's Liberation Front (EPLF)[20] and the Tigrayan People's Liberation Front (TPLF). The offensives prosecuted by the Ethiopian military – called Red Star offensives – were the largest military operations ever in Africa, involving mass troop movements, regular air strafing, the bombing of towns and cities, the commandeering of food, severe restrictions on food trade, and mass displacements of population. As a result, Eritrea and parts of Ethiopia were subjected to severe disruption in livelihood systems. By 1983, general levels of vulnerability were so extreme that hundreds of thousands of people were forced to move towards feeding camps, many dying during the journey or arriving too sickened from hunger to recover. In 1984, the failure of the secondary rains further exacerbated the prevailing famine vulnerability.[21]

Famines are processes rather than events (Macrae and Zwi et al., 1994; Sen, 1983). The Ethiopian famine of relevance here had begun in 1983 and was – hardly coincidentally – concentrated in Tigray and other northern areas where the Dergue's army offensives were most severe. The Ethiopian government purposefully restricted journalist and relief organisation access to these 'politically sensitive' areas, a result of a concern to minimise the broadcast of famine for fear that it would undermine the government and a desire to use starvation as a weapon to discipline the Tigrayan population that was suspected of supporting the TPLF (and indeed the TPLF did enjoy popular support).

Awareness of the famine was widespread in UN, NGO and some journalistic circles. Indeed, the Ethiopian government appealed for famine relief even as it wished to conceal the nature of the famine in the north which was inextricably linked to the counterinsurgency by the TPLF and the war of secession by the EPLF. But there was little urgency within the international networks that were aware of the emerging famine: newspapers and television broadcasters did not see 'Ethiopia' as a headline story in 1983 and the British government itself was largely indifferent to the famine which was happening in a Marxist-Leninist state and involved a secession movement which enjoyed no support from outside states.

As this complex famine intensified throughout 1983 and into 1984, the 'Ethiopian famine' as a single event was pivotally produced by the now famous 'biblical famine' narrative of Michael Buerk. This seven-minute report, and its subsequent prominence, framed the sensibilities of a young generation and ushered in not only a representation of mass disaster in Ethiopia to almost every Briton, but also the beginning of Africa campaigning and appeals to the mass of the British public.

The first film taken of famine in the north of Ethiopia – focusing on the relief camp in Koren – was made by ITV telejournalist Peter Gill (Philo, no date: 7ff.). His film was delayed by ITV as a result of industrial action. Within a week, the BBC's Michael Buerk and others went to the same location (as well as one other). The impetus to visit northern Ethiopia came from Mohamed Amin,[22] a cameraman employed by Visnews in Kenya. It was Amin who ensured Buerk's access to northern Ethiopia, and who 'framed' the famine images in their full horror. It is important to note how Amin's leading role in the production of these definitive images was downplayed or even omitted subsequently as the BBC edited, produced, and scheduled the famine reportage. Amin was a Kenyan Asian who had a long professional engagement with Ethiopia; Buerk had visited Ethiopia briefly once before. As Buerk has said, he would never have got access to the famine sites without Amin. This led to some accusations of racism or at least post-imperial arrogance by the BBC and perhaps the British public more generally. Part of the reason for Amin's relative obscurity was a result of British media regulations concerning the crewing of foreign reporting (Palmer, 1987: 246). However one balances the ethnocentric biases within the Western media and the particular and rushed circumstances behind the production of the Amin/Buerk report, the programme emphasised the importance of the interlocutor and the process of domestication in representation. Buerk was able to domesticate the famine for British consumption in a number of ways.

Firstly and most evidently, Buerk's accent and demeanour cut a quintessentially British figure which, in a way, was thrown into bold relief by the mass famine that provided the backdrop for his reporting. Secondly – as Buerk recognises – he drew upon familiar tropes in order to narrate the famine. The biblical references he recalled from his own experience at Sunday school. Indeed, the American news network CBS had to be persuaded to run the Amin/Buerk film because it seemed so 'English' and considered using a voiceover and edit to make it less so.

As a piece of journalism, the Amin/Buerk report remains striking and in a sense integral. There is clearly a humanity behind the reportage – something that Burke and other journalists report clearly in their recollections. The encounter between journalists and mass suffering is in itself fraught with the tensions that come from the lack of familiar mediation between the two: there is no implicitly understood relationship of interviewer and interviewee, investigator and investigated, witness and observed. In this specific context, the film's underlying sense of unease is intrinsic to the encounter. Burke's steadfastly 'English' demeanour serves as a conduit to relate the encounter to the British audience that he intended the film for.

But, as seen throughout this book, the production of image and text in Africa (and therefore in some sense 'African') is only a moment in the construction of Africa within the British milieu. The Burke report – and the subsequent Gill report – both became key components in a larger cultural spectacle within Britain. This was a result of both a spike in media interest (Howe, 2009; Philo, no date: 10) – one that had been signally absent during the previous twelve months during which efforts by both the Ethiopian Relief Agency and some NGOs to publicise the emerging complex emergency had largely fallen on deaf ears – and the articulation of this spike with the emergence of a mass appeal for donations. Indeed, Philo argues that it was only after ITV's decision to link the Gill film 'Seeds of Despair' to a public appeal that galvanised the BBC hurriedly to send out Amin and Buerk (Philo, no date: 17; Philo, 1993).

Chapter 1 set out a framing approach to understand Africa campaigning. This approach highlights three aspects of representation: diagnostic, prognostic, and motivational. This chapter has also shown how blurred the distinction is between charitable appeal and political campaign: both practices have been prosecuted by the same (or similar) agencies and they rely on certain basic representations (of poverty) to drive their moral impetus. In light of these observations, we can readily see how the now iconic early reports from the camps of displaced people served as focus for a major campaign which was both charitable but also political and which was based centrally on an appeal to a certain kind of British agency. It is in this sense that we come to reflect on Band Aid and Live Aid.

In 1984, largely under the direction of Bob Geldof, a single 'Do They Know It's Christmas' was released, selling 3.5 million copies in the UK. This was followed in 1985 by a 17-hour Live Aid concert staged in London and Philadelphia. These two events were provoked by Geldof's watching of the Buerk/Amin report on Ethiopia (Geldof, 1986: 271).

The Band Aid/Live Aid phenomenon serves as a definitive example of how a specific aspect of African politics – in this case a complex emergency in Ethiopia in which war, mass displacement, and adverse environmental conditions were reduced into a specific film which expressed the horror at mass human suffering – was domesticated into British public culture as a mass event. Band Aid/Live Aid generated a mass sensibility of charitable empathy within Britain, drawing on the deep cultural taproot of Victorian and Christian identities and rendering these identities both vernacular and contemporary through spectacle. It bequeathed a legacy of 'Aids': Fashion,

Sports, even Food (Allen, 1986: 32). The mobilisation of musicians, the staging of stadium gigs, and the urgency of Geldof's *vox populi* created a cultural phenomenon which was unlike any other mass mobilisation that focused on the suffering of distant others.

The contrast with the Biafra campaign throws this into bold relief. The Biafra campaign remained focused closely on Parliament, government action, and specific church appeals for charity. The campaign was domesticated by a small PR firm, a small number of highly motivated journalists and intellectuals, and church leaders. Band Aid/Live Aid appealed largely to the British public as a whole, generating large amounts of money which flowed through British (and Irish) NGOs with emergency relief operations. The more complex political arguments that were articulated through the Biafran campaign were effaced by a simple core political proposition: that it was morally intolerable to allow mass suffering to continue and that the most effective and immediate action was to raise money for emergency relief.

In the process, Band Aid/Live Aid generated an iconic image in order to maximise its normative impetus: the emaciated child. This image was interjected into pop videos ('Feed the World', 'Who's Gonna Take You Home' by The Cars which was played at Live Aid as a film of a near-dead Ethiopian child trying to walk was shown), vinyl record covers, and the effusion of NGO appeals imagery.

Evaluating disaster framing

Returning to the notion of framing set out in Chapter 1, we saw that framing for Africa campaigning could be usefully broken into three inter-related moments: diagnostic, prognostic, and motivational. Disaster imagery – and the genotype image of the famine child – produces the following framing template. The diagnostic is starvation as a single and self-contained fact. The prognostic is to give resources to the starving to stop them dying. The motivation is the charitable impulses of the viewer. The connections between the three aspects of framing is very close and simple: getting food to those who need it. *The Sun's* first Ethiopia famine headline puts it starkly: 'Race to Save the Babies' (28 October 1984). Each stage of the framing is 'pure' in the sense that each stage seems self-contained and self-evident: the obvious horror of famine, the obvious solution in providing food and water, and the obvious fellow-feeling and charitable actions of viewers. The framing is both simple and strong; it has driven the bulk of charitable appeals in Britain throughout the post-Second World War period (Coulter, 1989). But its effectiveness and its immanent commonsensical appeal does not mean that it is entirely unproblematic.

In retrospect, the emaciated child image has become extremely fraught in British campaigning. It both maintains an enduring familiarity and impact which means that charitable campaigns still resort to it, even if in less extreme formulations. But, a number of criticisms have been made of the emaciated child 'icon', which have driven campaigns to see the Band Aid/Live Aid approach as 'negative' and to move towards the second 'positive' framing.

As argued in Chapter 2, the extreme images of emaciated children are, in a sense, images of death. There is a point of malnutrition and dehydration beyond which fragile bodies will not recover. Photographing these 'living dead' people clearly raises moral issues which always murmur underneath disaster reportage but become most urgent in this specific context. What responsibility does the camera-holder have to the subject-in-death? To what extent is the taking of photos in this situation a final act of extraction from a defenceless subject? The best-known case that speaks to these questions is Kevin Carter's photo of a starving child in Sudan with a vulture in the background. Carter won a Pulitzer Prize for his photo, but was subsequently distressed by the photos and his role as both witness to death and award-winner. His suicide has been linked to his inability to reconcile himself with the extremities of his encounters.

Other photos have focused on the famine child but with a wider frame of reference, revealing other photographers themselves. This produces quite different 'texts' for the images: away from the horror of death throes and towards the moral discomfort of the witnesses. Although the 'object' of the photo is the child, the punctum[23] – the point of interest – shifts towards the photographer or others around the child. One gets a sense of stage-setting, of extraction, of exploitation. Subsequently, these kinds of photographers have been condemned as 'vultures',[24] a powerful analogy in the context of mass famine where literal vultures await the extinction of life as a feeding opportunity.

Moving away from the morally vexed issue of how one thinks ethically about the reporting of extreme vulnerability, there are broader issues about the representation of African selves as children. Here, we encounter one of the most robust legacies of imperial representation: the infantilisation of Africa. Recall from Chapter 2 that infancy served both metaphorically and corporeally to represent Africa. Although much of the (explicit) text of these representations is removed after the attainment of independence throughout Africa, some aspects of infantilisation remain. Most obviously, the heavy bias towards child-images produces a trope in which Africa needs help. It connotes an Africa in which self-management, and even agency *tout court*, are absent. Within this absence, external agencies act to redeem and ameliorate. The *locus classicus* here – again an image made iconic during the domestication of the Ethiopian famine appeal – was the white hand of the nurse/aid worker/ doctor holding the tiny black hand of the child (Manzo, 2008: 637). These images might represent a key aspect of emergency relief, but in the absence of any other images, they serve as a reification: Africa as mendicant, Africa as agentless, Africa as incomplete. More extremely, the repeated imagery of child death dehumanises Africans in the eyes of British witnesses (VSO, 2002: 3). It is this politics that leads Wainiana to write the acerbic passage noted early in Chapter 2.

A lyric from 'Feed the World' runs: 'And there won't be snow in Africa this Christmastime. The greatest gift they'll get this year is life.' Although it might be interesting to deconstruct the lyrics to this song, it is worth bearing in mind both the genre and purpose of the song: pop songs are commonly simple things lyrically and the motivation behind the song was to generate awareness of famine and to infuse listeners with charitable agency. Nevertheless, it is striking how unproblematic it remained to speak about Africa as a place (populated by 'them': the Africans) when, as we have seen, the famine itself scourged through certain regions of Ethiopia and Eritrea.

The point here is that disaster imagery both during Band Aid/Live Aid and subsequently was commonly abstracted within campaign literature and within public sensibilities until distinctions between countries, the origins of humanitarian emergencies, or the kinds of societies into which external agencies might intervene all dissolved under the weight of the representation of a single generic Africa, characterised as a disaster zone. 'Africa' serves as a coding for a racial distinction that is implicit in British culture – especially within the media. In other words, 'Africa' means 'black', and 'black' in this sense means disaster-striken. Thus, dictators become *African* dictators (Idi Amin's expulsion of Ugandan Asians or the coronation of 'Emperor' Jean-Bedel Bokassa attracted British media attention of this kind) with all of the implicit baggage about savagery that this word alludes to. The arms to Sierra Leone scandal becomes an arms to *Africa* scandal with its nod to conflations of politics and violence. Famines that took place after the Ethiopian famine in 1984/5 were represented as *another* African famine: Somalia, the Sahel, northern Kenya, etc. all became part of a single representational narrative in spite of the varied causes of famine in each case.

Finally, the African child image expressed a text of simple charity. The image was constructed as an *appeal* image: to elicit a donation. The motivational frame relies on the innocence of children in the eyes of the viewer. Adults, with their complex life-histories and moral equivocations, do not serve this purpose nearly as well – even if adults suffer and die in greater numbers. The desire to help the child fitted very well with the emergency appeal which worked to provide emergency aid. But, relief NGOs became increasingly aware of the limitations of the sudden influx of food aid, rehydration kits, and shelters to famine zones. Underlying vulnerabilities and more complex issues of rehabilitation remained. These kinds of intervention lent themselves far less well to the child image. Thus, as NGOs moved focus from relief to rehabilitation, there was a sense that more 'developmental' images would be required to engage the British people and also to ensure support and funding.

The racially coded, infantilised, generic, simple image of the African child came to be perceived as increasingly problematic by major NGOs as the 1980s wore on. Within NGOs, a cultural shift towards 'positive' imagery emerged – or re-emerged – as some NGOs grew considerably and represented themselves more boldly as development organisations.

Developmental Africa

Positive images

The late 1980s saw a reaction against the disaster narrative. This was not so much because it had failed – on the contrary it had proven very effective in eliciting attention, emotion, and donations. Rather, the success of disaster imagery had led campaign NGOs to become concerned with the socialisation embedded within it: the popular feeling that Africa was simply a space crammed with famine, war, and pestilence. The problems outlined at the end of the previous section led NGOs and some journalists to perceive of famine appeals based in child imagery as either too 'costly' a way to raise awareness and money, or as a necessary 'first step' to gain public attention after which a more complex and contextualised set of representations should be produced. This basic logic – sometimes called 'migration' – remains: that moments of shock or spikes in awareness of Africa can suddenly boost public engagement if simple messaging is used, but this is only justifiable if there is a strategy to encourage people subsequently to ask questions, explore issues, or look for solutions beyond the immediate charitable impulse – to migrate from 'moved' to 'interested'.

The concern was, as the television journalist Peter Gill declared '[h]aving brought hunger and poverty in Africa ... into many people's living rooms and back into the political agenda, television journalism may now be failing in its duty to educate as well as inform' (in Palmer, 1987: 245). It was Gill's documentary that brought the first images of famine in Koren, and it focused on the nature of the food trade regime and European Community food subsidies (Raikes, 1989), one aspect of a raft of factors which researchers identified that made famine look less like an unexpected tragic drought and more like a complex process of 'entitlement failure' (Sen, 1983) which involved markets, states, and international political economy.

Gill's anxieties about the aptitude of the media to recognise and engage with the 'deeper' narratives of famine or poverty seem in retrospect to have been justified: the general trend has been that Africa is largely absent from the media until a specific disaster wins the attention of enough news producers to generate an item. And, by and large, these items are simple human tragedy stories that – to the itinerant viewer – seem to come from nowhere and simply confirm the disaster Africa representation.

On the other hand, NGOs had to engage with Gill's comment in a far more focused fashion. In 1989 the General Assembly of European NGOs wrote a Code of Conduct on the *Images and Messages Relating to the Third World*. The *Code of Conduct* commences with an affirmation that images should 'promote fairness, solidarity and justice' (Manzo, 2006: 9). The key criteria in order to ensure images cleaved to these norms are to ensure that images: contain the values of solidarity and justice; contain context and complexity and represent the realities of situations; avoid images that stereotype, sensationalise or discriminate; ensure images are taken with full consent; ensure subjects have an opportunity to communicate; record whether subjects wish to be identified; respect people's human rights.

The shift from disaster to developmental representations is also part of the story of how NGOs have changed and grown. Oxfam is a good example here. Having been created as an organisation to provide famine relief, it has become a sizeable development organisation. It now considers itself to be working as a relief organisation, a development organisation, and a campaign organisation, and most of the large NGOs also display this three-fold institutions distinction. The emergence of the academic discipline of development studies has contributed to an intellectual shift within NGOs away from famine relief and towards the modalities of promoting development, which is associated with development projects that promote income generation, education, technology transfer, and more recently empowerment. Oxfam was indeed very proactive in the 1960s in establishing for itself an institutional identity as a developmental organisation that aimed to work with progressive ideal and partner governments, such as Tanzania during its village socialism (*ujamaa vijijini*) period (Jennings, 2002).

The increasing developmental activity of NGOs required a different kind of representation. This was not only in order to portray the kind of work that NGOs were doing (building health posts, buying oxen, introducing new crops, promoting women's cooperatives, etc.), but also to encourage a different sensibility in people regarding NGO work in Africa. This sensibility was not one based in the shock of famine imagery and the 'pulse' of charitable giving, but rather something more complex and engaged. The funding structure associated with this change in representation was away from single large donations towards smaller regular donations, contributions that averred that people were involved for the long term.

There are questions that one might raise as to how these kinds of desiderata are operationalised: how might one ensure that an image contains certain values? How can one represent distant others defined by poverty *without* discrimination? But, for the larger British NGOs – Save the Children, Action Aid, Christian Aid and Oxfam – one can see a palpable shift in representational work throughout the 1980s. These representations were generated as a specific genre which – although not new – was increasingly foregrounded in preference to emergency appeals for disaster relief. Although the archive of campaign materials from the late 1980s onwards is massive, the key characteristics of this genre can be captured in the following points.

1   The active subject. The African subject represented as a worker. This was most obviously achieved by showing people at work. Commonly, this meant photographing people in a rural setting, in fields, holding a farm implement such as a hoe. These images brought African adulthood to the fore, but another key image was of the classroom filled with learning children. These images related a norm that was substantially different from the morality of the disaster representation. The claim was that Africans were not desperate mendicants but were labouring under adverse conditions and that development agencies were working with Africans to overcome those adverse conditions. Thus, the justice framing was more complex than the humanitarian framing of the disaster genre.

2   The representative subject. As mentioned in the introduction and extant in the *Code of Conduct*, NGOs became increasingly concerned with representation. The almost exclusive focus on the child was replaced by a more diverse typology of subjects. Most notably, women became more common subjects of representation – especially in conjunction with the first feature: the woman at work. The norm here was not just to make more 'realistic' images but also to address increasing concerns with empowerment: to show powerless or oppressed groups with their own agency by representing them in activity.

3   The contextualised subject. There was an increasing desire by NGOs to produce representations not of individuals but of communities. This relates to the norms of representation and empowerment noted above but it also answered concerns about producing *realistic* images. The isolated subject was seen as contrived; the embedded subject as real or vernacular. Furthermore, images of collectivities were intrinsically more complex –

less easily accused of facile emotional appeal. Relatedly, there was a trend to photograph people who appeared to be oblivious to the camera rather than staring at the camera is if directly addressing the British spectator. The women's workgroup or the classroom provided a sense that the viewer was seeing ordinary life. Once again, these images required more textual work in order to relate representations to campaigning and appeals.

4 Agonistic narratives. Thus, these images – active, representative, contextualised – required a new kind of text to that which simply and directly appealed for money to save lives. In place of this, more complex texts emerged that relied on deeper references to injustice and also relied on question raising as well as appeals. Christian Aid produced a development campaign 'We believe in life before death' which inverted Christian metaphysics but left a very open text in place of certainty. It connoted an issue about quality of life which was based in issues of hardship and injustice, not death and famine.

Taken together, these codes produce a very different framing to that embedded within the disaster imagery, most notably because of the *complexity* of representation. The diagnostic frame of developmental imagery is based in *poverty* not famine. These are obviously connected but produce quite different representational possibilities. Poverty opens up more fertile ground for the representation of agency; for NGOs concerned to produce positive images, representing poverty required a portrayal of difficult livelihoods, of hard work for little return, of remoteness from opportunity. These issues or problems do not directly author the solutions in the same way that famine framing does. Prognostically, developmental framing connects to a series of project funding activities that NGOs are involved with: irrigation, well digging, health care posts, primary schools, sanitation, new (appropriate) technologies,[25] small-scale credit schemes, and so on. Again, then, the prognostic frame (what should be done?) is more open-ended and complex. Poverty is not solved directly through resource provision (which would be the analogue of the disaster framing); rather it emerges through time and through the success of relatively modest and local projects.

The motivational frame is perhaps the most complex of all. Why should people give money for development? The temporal urgency and simplicity of famine framing is absent. The positive image ethic requires that poverty is not represented in the shocking ways that famine is. The motivation is both charitable (based in donations) but also 'engaged'; that is, connected to a sense of solidarity or political-normative commitment that goes beyond the famine/charity reflex. Development imagery may offer people's names, vignettes of their working day, or their views on their futures. These kind of representational acts aim to produce deeper associations between viewers and those within the campaign imagery. This framing requires more cognitive effort and is likely to motivate fewer people than the famine image will – which is an important reason why famine imagery persists (as well as the fact that famine events persist).

The move from disaster to development: Oxfam's annual reports

This representational shift was enabled by the changes taking place within British NGOs. The late 1980s and 1990s saw the larger NGOs grow and develop more effective campaign departments. This was partly a result of the changes in Charity Commission regulations which allowed NGOs to campaign politically strictly in relation to the charitable objectives of the campaign. This regulatory change – a result of pressure from NGOs – allowed imagery to be employed to promote campaigns on international debt, governmental aid, trade regulation, the arms trade and so on.

One can see the transitions from one frame to another dispersed throughout the materials of campaign organisations from the 1960s to the present day. It is worth pinning down a specific way in which representational practice has changed over this period of time in order to pay more attention to the curation of text and image. This section will review Oxfam's *Annual Reviews* (AR). The AR is produced by Oxfam as a short overview of what Oxfam considers to be its main operations and aspirations. The Reviews are addressed to a general public – not a membership or board of governors and they have always aimed to present key messages in a very clear fashion. As such, the ARs provide a good single 'line' of representation which commences in 1958 and takes us to 2008.

How can we analyse the AR? This section will pull out the key ways in which Africa is represented in the Reviews. This involved reviewing material taken from Oxfam's archives; and then from 2001 downloading the reviews which are now available as PDFs. In keeping with the broader research methodology of this book, the aim is not to make a quantitative analysis but to say something more hermeneutic, based in specific instances of representation which characterise a frame more broadly.

It is striking that Africa's debut in the Reviews offers something of an ideal type for the disaster frame. The front cover shows a woman crying while holding an emaciated child – an extremely distressing image. The accompanying text states 'A mother in the Congo fears help may not have come in time for her surviving child.' The two subjects of the image are cut and pasted onto a blue background, so that there is no context: they are entirely abstracted from the place in which they existed. In the rest of the Review, there are two other images of emaciated children. This was in 1960–61, coinciding with the start of Independence and especially the troubled decolonisation of the Congo.

The rest of the 1960s concertedly sets the disaster frame and Africa as a major aspect of Oxfam's identity and representation. In 1962 on the front cover: 'Africa continued to be Oxfam's major concern'. The image accompanying this text was again one that set a certain template for future disaster imagery: the emaciated black child's hand in a larger white hand, the child looking upwards beseechingly. In this image, the (anonymous) white hand signifies Oxfam as caring and beneficent. The child represents Africa as indigent and subordinate.

There is an implicit association of disaster with Independence. Although the Reviews are entirely apolitical – disasters are effectively presented as acts of nature – the countries focused on are those recently decolonised: Congo, then West Africa (former francophone countries) focusing especially on the protein deficiency kwashiorkor and its stomach-swelling symptoms, starvation in Tanganyika and then Kenya. Contrastingly, Oxfam's operations in British Protectorates and South Rhodesia (Zimbabwe but then under British control until 1965 and the Unilateral Declaration of Independence) were portrayed as more stable, a space within which Oxfam could work towards more development-focused and long-lasting solutions to hunger.

The *leitmotif* throughout the period until 1964 is suffering: 'There seems to be no limit to the suffering human beings are forced to endure.' Africa appears as a single traumatised space within which Oxfam works to feed the hungry. Recalling themes set out earlier concerning biopolitics and Africa's embodiment, one could say that Africa is represented as a single starving body begging for nutrition from the charitable interventions of Oxfam and other agencies – many of which were at this time church-based.

After 1964, one can identify a gradual breaking down of the disaster imagery. As argued in Chapter 1, frames of representation are not best seen as sequences; the disaster frame hardly ends in the mid-1960s (or indeed even in the present day as demonstrated in the next two chapters). But we can identify a sedimentation of other representational frames which move Oxfam towards the 'human face' frame.

The key innovation in representation derives from the development of a clearer narrative on Independence. The implied association of Independence with disaster is replaced by a more positive note – one that also brings a more explicitly political facet to the Reviews. A central issue in the 1964 Review is the matching of post-colonial statehood with the characteristics of African societies and the normative desire for self-determination: 'true political and economic independence'. The posing of these questions is novel. Also, the text has some novelties: African voices are heard for the first time; a Kenyan MP comments on the value of an irrigation project in his constituency which receives Oxfam support.

The photos throughout the Review are a mixture of disaster and positive imagery. From the mid-1960s, key visual reference points are the community, work, and happiness – images that contrapose with the disaster images based in abstracted individuals, indigence, and suffering.

It is interesting to note the beginnings of a developmental and 'human face' content in the mid-1960s because it is strikingly foreclosed in 1968 as a result of the Biafran war of secession. This has already been discussed as a key formative moment in the disaster frame, and it impacts heavily on Oxfam's Review imagery. The 1968/9 Review returns to the template of the 1960/1961 Review: a single emaciated child removed from context and set on a blue background. Biafra stands as the key reference point, representing the continent as a whole, and producing a powerful representation of suffering: Africa's 'year of agony'. In the context of the humanitarian emergency in Biafra, the 'return to type' here is understandable, although there is a sense that those Oxfam workers who wrote the Review are aware that Oxfam has become a pivotal agency in the representation of African disasters. An Oxfam-funded medical doctor working in Biafra is reported as describing the children thus: 'virtually all of them look like Oxfam posters'. This suggests the kind of reflexivity that works within acts of representation: a British citizen in Biafra reporting back to a British audience using an association with a familiar image of Africa generated previously by a British development organisation. The review of 1967/8 speaks of an Oxfam-funded expatriate nutritionist describing one child in her health care centre as follows: 'He ... looked like an Oxfam advertisement!' [*sic.*].

These representations suggest that those working within Oxfam's publicity are aware of the frames of representation within which they work, and indeed Oxfam's role in affirming or modifying those frames. Other parts of the text on Biafra in the 1967/1968 Review try to move beyond the direct and simple emergency appeal narrative, although of course Oxfam is constrained by its charitable status from doing this in any elaborate fashion: Biafra's future is dependent on the outcome of the war.

Throughout the 1970s, the focus on Africa falls away – even if Oxfam's spending remains focused on the continent. There is certainly a shift away from disaster framing towards human face framing and it is extant in various ways, in addition to the inclusion of positive imagery and African voices noted earlier. Most notably, Reviews spend more space giving details of projects. Throughout the Review's history, one of its main aims is to report on the work Oxfam has been doing over the year. This has led to a regular set of 'project features'. Initially, these were reported technically – as questions of resource and expertise, narrated through expatriate voices and largely framed around the provision of nutrition or new agricultural practices. In the 1970s, project narratives were accompanied by more normatively or politically explicit commentary: a need for agricultural projects to recognise the 'inter-related knowledge of each others' cultures and problems' (1970/1) – although there is no detail about the value of 'other' cultures or problems in 'ours'. This kind of narrative – of project detail and a sense of development 'learning' is commonly accompanied by work images or education images. These present African subjects as incipient modernisers.

In the 1980s, the human face frame is fully developed, incorporating not only images of agency, but also 'life story' narratives in which people involved in Oxfam projects (as beneficiaries and/or workers) speak through vignettes. In the 1988/9 Review, a page is dedicated to Norah Mumba's story. She is introduced as a mother and widow and her story is narrated as one of injustice rather than material want. For the first time, there is a quotation from an 'ordinary' African (in this case Zambian) rather than an Oxfam interlocutor (although this does not mean that no mediation is taking place). In the same Review, there is also a report on forced removals in South Africa which again includes a quotation from a black South African farmer.

These life stories emerge as a vehicle for Oxfam to foreground a more explicit justice norm which becomes fully established when Oxfam's logo changes from the abstracted child with outstretched arms to a globe with the tagline 'Working for a Fairer World'. This is presented for the first time on the front cover of the 1990/1 Review. In the 1990s Oxfam's Reviews concertedly abandon the disaster framing. There are reports on Oxfam's emergency relief work, but all of these are accompanied by photos of people coping or rehabilitating their livelihoods.[26] Accompanying text takes care not to attribute disasters simplistically to natural phenomenon. In 1989/90: 'Poverty makes people vulnerable to disasters'; in 1992/3 Africa's problems are accounted for as a result of damaging economic reforms as well as drought.

The 1990s Reviews express very well Oxfam's engagement with the social justice framing. There is a frequent critique of economic liberalisation, an articulation of African issues in terms of rights, and a universal integration of African voices into the reportage. This continues into the 2000s.

The 2000s Reviews represent a dense and complex representation of Africa and Oxfam itself. The human face and social justice frames remain at the core of the Reviews, but one can also discern two other developments. Firstly, the Reviews speak in more detail and more forcibly about campaign work. In the 2000/1 Review a key campaign, mentioned numerous times, is the 'Cut the

Cost' campaign which mobilises against the high costs of AIDS antiretrovirals and focuses on the responsibilities of large pharmaceutical companies. From the mid 1990s onwards the Charity Commission has interpreted charities' involvement in campaigning fairly openly, allowing Oxfam to campaign on HIV/AIDS, arms trade, fair trade, and other issues, even focusing on the culpability of the British government.

Secondly, the Reviews take on a more sophisticated design. Production values have improved throughout the Reviews' history, but in the 2000s this is perhaps more noticeable. The 2003/4 Review has an enclosed DVD with film clips which accompany reports within. Pages are set up with engaging headings, sophisticated page formats, and high-quality photos. There is also a strong tie-in with broader media agendas: newspaper headlines and media events are cross-referenced in regard to refugees, arms, coffee prices and so on. There are also cross-references to Oxfam's webpages. There is also a frequent integration of celebrity involvement in campaigns in the Reviews of the 2000s, especially the more engaged celebrities/artists such as Helen Mirren, Chris Martin, and Annie Lennox. Aesthetically, then, the Annual Reports become more 'corporate' in their presentation (Davidson, 2007: 149)

The 2004/5 Review encapsulates the most recent Reviews especially strongly because it was produced during the 'Year of Africa' (see Chapter 7) and engages with the Make Poverty History campaign. In this Review, a single page presents a single bold word: IMPACT, the 'ACT' section highlighted in red to provide a double message, a technique used in advertising generally and increasingly deployed within campaigns. The use of bold short statements relays a sense of aspiration, identity, and world-view rather than anything specific about Oxfam's activities and it keys in with the increasing attention that Oxfam – along with all of the other campaign organisations – pay to branding identity in the 2000s.

Henrietta Lidchi makes an important point when she argues that development or 'positive' images are not straightforward (1993). The ethic of truer representation that drove the production of these images is fetishised in the image itself; far less is known about the *production* of the images themselves, and whether they are any more representative or accountable than other images. An associated point was made in the introduction: that a perfect, complete, or true representation of Africa is something of a chimera, but that facets of African social life can be captured, curated, mediated and presented through different campaign practices. The specific practice of producing an annual report for the public, investigated in the section above, shows how different representations are also different moral practices: trying to convey different messages about charity, development, and the scope of action of an agency such as Oxfam.

Notes

1 On these, see chapters in MacKenzie, 1986 and more broadly Boehmer, 2009.

2 RED is a commodity brand associated with the development organisation DATA (Debt, AIDS, Trade, Africa) which companies buy as a 'franchise' in return for a commitment of profits on items sold to DATA projects. It is unclear what portion of profits goes to DATA for RED products. An incisive study is Richey and Ponte, 2011.

3 A phenomenon brilliantly satirised by Sacha Baron Cohen in the film *Bruno*.

4 The notion of stardom here refers to a phenomenon associated with celebrity in a lot of the literature: that celebrities are both 'like us' and 'different from us' (Street, 2002).

5 Many can be watched on YouTube by searching Comic Relief and Red Nose Day.

6 This campaign, like (RED) has elicited a raft of concerns from intellectuals (Anderson, 2008; Himmelman and Mupotsa, 2008; Hintzen, 2008; Iweala, 2007; Jungar and Salo, 2008; Magubane, 2008; Sarna-Wojcicki, 2008).

7 A more extensive list of humanitarian celebrities can be found in Samman *et al.* (2009: 140). The list gives a strong sense of how close and publicly powerful the association between celebrity and development/poverty cause making is.

8 Sachs's narrative style – when he is not writing as an economist – is either 'personal' or narcissistic, depending on one's judgement. Either way, it plays well into the in-dividual consumer sensibilities of personal feelings and egocentrism. See Barnett, 2005.

9 The donation amounts and what 'wealth' means (income, assets, including stocks and shares?) are unclear.

10 For details on the involvement of celebrities and the super-rich see the largely supportive chapters in Brainard and Chollet (2008). A revealing example of the dis-cursive elision between politics, celebrity and campaigning was Bono's comments that Brown and Blair were the 'John [Lennon] and Paul [McCartney] of the global development stage'

11 We will return to this issue in Chapter 7.

12 Woldu was brought on stage by Madonna. *The Sun* – which flew Woldu to the UK to appear at Live 8 and covered her visit a lot more than other redtops as a result – characterised Geldof and Madonna as quasi-religious saviours. *The Sun* quotes Woldu (who spoke through an interpreter) as saying of Madonna 'The Madonna took my hand and looked into my eyes ...' and of Geldof 'he is a God-sent person who is trying to help people in Africa'.

13 The origins of the Biafran secession have been traced to different antecedents, from the impact of the slave trade through the federating efforts of the British colonial government. In the post-colonial period the key events were the ethnic cleansing of Igbo people in northern Nigeria which led to a migration of over one million people fleeing the violence, and the instability of Nigeria's federal government.

14 Exemplified in Chimamanda Ngozi Adichie's *Half of a Yellow Sun* (2006).

15 The Biafran cause has generally been analysed sympathetically by researchers,

although questions have been asked about the extent to which the Biafran government's intransigence exacerbated the famine and the extent to which it also presented famine to journalists and aid workers in order to elicit international support.

16 On media responses to secession more broadly, see Akinyemi, 1972.

17 Vatican City recognised Biafra's statehood.

18 The 'Bangladesh concert' organised by George Harrison is commonly seen as the progenitor of the mass celebrity appeal – but it was an awareness-raising concert according to Harrison himself who was interviewed in the TV documentary *Get Up Stand Up*. The first concert focused on Africa – reflecting the differences in representation generated by African nationalisms – was the 'We Speak of Africa' concert organised by the Movement for Colonial Freedom in 1962. With no appeals or campaigns related to war or famine, and curated as a largely small-name and African event (although Fela Kuti was playing in the Koola Lobitos), its national prominence was minimal.

19 Once again, Biafra seems to be setting a precedent. The use of PR companies by African governments is now common – perhaps the best-known or infamous subsequent use of PR was by UNITA (the Angolan insurgency) during the 1980s.

20 As with the Biafran secession, the causes of Eritrea's secession can be understood as historically layered. Eritrea was peripheral to the central Ethiopian kingdom before colonialism; it was fully colonised by the Italians which rendered it separate from Ethiopia 'proper'; and it certainly suffered greatly at the hands of Ethiopian militaries both monarchical and Marxist. See Cliffe and Davidson, 1988.

21 The role of rain failure in famine is debated, owing to the fact that different parts of Ethiopia suffered different kinds and degrees of rain failure or delay, and also that the famine appeal imagery largely relied on a simple 'drought causes famine' account.

22 Amin had already filmed in Korem before the 'Buerk report' but it attracted little interest from the international media (Philo, no date: 6).

23 See Barthes, 2000.

24 The *St Petersburg Times* opined: 'the man adjusting his lens to take the right frame of her suffering might just as well be a predator, another vulture on the scene', www.bbc.co.uk/dna/n292/a22083301, accessed 21 June 2009.

25 Appropriate technology means technologies that are sustainable and useable in specific environments, rather than higher-tech or fossil fuel-hungry technologies. Appropriate and intermediate technologies were developed during the 1960s and 1970s when development NGOs became focused on rural development and 'grassroots' involvement in projects (Chambers, 1983; Korten, 1984).

26 In the 1990s, Oxfam built up a fantastic photo archive in which the work of Geoff Sawyer and Jenny Matthews is particularly noteworthy.

7

Representing Africa through the commodity

Introduction

Throughout, this book has shown how unstable British national identities have been and how changing representations of Africa have acted as part of the ways in which national identity has been modified, how campaigns have drawn on Christian and humanitarian motivations to define a virtuous British public and also how post-colonial development campaigning has represented Africa negatively and positively. Retrospectively, it is easier to discern certain trends and the setting of certain orthodoxies of representation – even if these don't necessarily last. This is why the notion of layering is useful – it suggests a sequencing of representations, each drawing on previous ones and each eventually overlain by others. It is, of course, very risky to be definitive about the present day, taking a snapshot of a series of representations, some of which might prove to be passing, some of which rely heavily on previous canons, and some of which seem to be more enduring. This chapter will therefore look in some detail at current representations of Africa by campaign organisations and do no more than think through how they might fit into the representation tradition. But, in doing so – and building on the work done in previous chapters – we can see the significance in some news trends and the endurance of older ones in a context of change. These points will be bought out as the chapter proceeds, but it is useful to foreground the key patterns in representation that emerge from the chapter.

Firstly, we will explore the ways in which representations of Africa have been integrated into appeals to the British consumer. This is not a historically novel trend, but it is certainly the case that the extent and modalities of the sumptuary framing are historically unique, and potentially very significant. The chapter will suggest a distinction between the use of commodities within a campaign and the commoditisation of campaigns, the latter being more profound in terms of its impact on campaign organisations and the way they represent Africa to a British public.

Secondly, this chapter will note the continuing pervasiveness of 'negative' imagery or famine imagery in contemporary representation, looking at some of the ways in which the tensions between this framing and others persist and indeed appear to be constitutive of many large campaign organisations' activities for as long as they involve themselves in both campaign/lobbying and emergency relief.

Thirdly, it will suggest some ways in which innovations in representation open up new ways for Africans to 'speak to' the British public (or a section of it). In characteristically academic fashion, this point will be made cautiously, but it is important to register both the dynamism and potentially progressive ways in which representations might move. To the extent that we recognise 'globalisation' as something real, the ways Africa is represented in Britain need now to be calibrated against the new ways Africa represents itself and also the ways in which British national identity is changing. Of course, this opens up a great many subsequent questions which are well beyond the talents of this author; the chapter will simply recognise this context and focus on the ways Africa is represented in the present day.

Prologue: consumption and campaigning

This chapter requires some brief assimilative work on aspects of the material in previous chapters. The work of representation builds upon the existing resources at hand: the images, norms, associations, and knowledges that have enabled people to speak about Africa previously. In Chapter 4 we saw how there are key threads that weave their way through a great deal of the African presence: a more or less Christianised philanthropy, a sense of Britain's global power, a liberal humanitarianism and a social identity of national virtue. So, looking at the most contemporary trends in representation requires some sense of connection with this broader tradition – even if the more prospective focus of this chapter brings us to focus on novelty and future developments.

Consumption as a reference point for campaigning is hardly new. The two most salient Africa campaigns were centrally speaking about consumption – and more specifically what it is to be a good consumer. The abolition movement's prognostic framing involved a boycott of 'slave sugar' and a preference for 'free sugar' (Turner, 2005: 120*ff.*). The 'am I not a man and a brother' cameo also served as an identification, built into accessories that remind one of the intensive branding of commodities to be explored later in this chapter. And, of course, the anti-apartheid Movement relied very prominently on boycotts of all goods and services originating in or involved with South Africa, from fruit to banking services. Furthermore – and again in ways that key in with contemporary developments – the boycott strategy served to *expand* consumer identity by encompassing the consumption of culture: sporting events and music became the terrain of politicised purchase decisions. Britain's first music campaign on behalf of distant others was perhaps the 'Free Nelson Mandela' concert at Wembley in 1988.[1]

More recently, the Africa campaign tradition has contributed centrally to the public norms of ethical consumption which are now strongly embedded in British culture through cultural events, ethical and fair trade products and concerns with the environment and animal rights (Brockington, 2009; Richey and Ponte, 2008). The increasingly rich – and heavily marketed – appeal to people as ethical consumers is the key reference point of this chapter because it reveals a shift in the way that British national identity is understood. Ethical consumption connects to a self that is individualised, sumptuary and pleasure-seeking.

This, in turn, has repercussions for other aspects of the African presence. In the first place, it poses a different sense of national identity to the one constructed through appeals to generosity and salvation that we have identified throughout the book. This is not to say necessarily that national identities have been inexorably weakened; it is rather that they have changed and come to resemble something increasingly based in an individualised purchasing point-of-reference. Secondly, the refocusing on individualised consumption marks a key shift away from the norms of social justice, a distinction explored later in the chapter.

The argument here is simply that appeals to people's individual consumptive desires – even if framed within references to poverty alleviation or combating AIDS – propound a deeper normative structure which is conservative. The notion of structured inequalities which are unjust is negated and replaced by notions of individual preference and voluntarism. Furthermore, it places the British consumer – with his or her acquisitive sensibilities (Dauvergne, 2010) – as the central reference point for the solution. This is a tendency, not a *fait accompli*. But it does reflect and reinforce more generalised and powerful social trends in British society and as such one would do well to take them seriously. As with previous chapters, there is a sense of intermingling between campaigns and charitable appeals – and then beyond this towards the representational acts of others, in this case especially celebrities and advertising/public relations companies.

Consumption and identity

Consumption

Consumption here relates centrally to the consumer, or better still, the ways in which consumption contributes to the social construction of consumer identities. As such, the concern here is less in consumption as an economic process and more in the moralities and aesthetics of consumption – although the two are hardly separate as will be shown. Consumption is not just a metabolic necessity; it is also a social act and indeed in countries like Britain, consumption is to all intents and purposes only incidentally focused on the basic requirements for life. This section will present key themes in the literature on consumption that are especially germane to our interests: towards an understanding of consumption that allows us to connect it with the African presence and the general argument of the chapter that the African presence is currently in the throes of significant and novel shifts.

Before we go on to flesh all of this out, it is important to make some comments on the existing literature on consumption. Consumption studies (very distinct from consumer studies, which is largely focused on marketing) is a broad and rich body of research. As a genre, one is struck by the diversity of focuses in the research. This is in large part because, in one sense or another, pretty much all social interaction might be labelled as consumption. The originating canons of the literature – Adam Smith, Thorstein Veblen, and Karl Marx[2] – all conceptualised consumption in ways that were in fact about the broader social relations of class, wealth, and production. The more recent innovations in consumption research are commonly based on postmodern portrayals of social change in which the focus is on post-materialism, identity politics, or globalisation. As a result, we need to be necessarily eclectic in what we take from this literature, and also to be as clear as possible in regard to how we are understanding consumption in this chapter.

Consumer identity

This book is concerned specifically with British identities and their interpolation with aspects of Africa's representation. So, consumption refers us to British social identities – and most centrally the moralities that have been articulated to consumer choices. Throughout the book it has been evident how important representations of Africa have been to ongoing evocations of British virtues. It is especially in this respect that consumer identity is important: discretionary purchases are one aspect of the British citizen's broader philanthropic identity, along with donations and campaign activism.

Although Veblen has come in for a lot of criticism, in some ways his work provides a datum for much research on consumption and identity (Edwards, 2000: 25*ff.*). Writing in 1889, he identifies the emergence not so much of a consumer society – there are debates about when one might date the emergence of fully fledged consumerism – but rather the emergence of a particular kind of consumer identity which he associates with Europe's expanding middle classes. Veblen's work goes under the epithet of a theory of the leisure class, but it is as much about consumption as leisure. What makes Veblen an interesting place to start is his association of certain kinds of spending with social virtue.

Veblen's understanding of conspicuous consumption is particularly germane. The phrase 'conspicuous consumption' has now entered general normative discourse, often to allude to the purchasing of commodities to display wealth. One might associate it with 'yuppies' during the Thatcher years. Veblen also associates conspicuous consumption with the rise of an increasingly wealthy middle class, but he does not only connect conspicuous consumption simply with wealth: he also associates it with public norms. Using phrases such as 'reputability', 'honorific' and 'punctilious', he argues that conspicuous consumption projects wealth *and virtue*. He says that there is a socially constructed discernment in consumption that goes beyond simply having the disposable income to purchase expensive goods and services.

There are two coordinates that emerge from Veblen. Firstly, the association between consumption and virtue which makes consumption a moral act: that consumption is intrinsically a statement of identity. The choice to consume one good over another is made partly in reference to its appearance, its ability to signify a certain social identity, a commitment, a morality. Secondly, and relatedly, there is association between consumption and aesthetics: consumption is deeply ingrained in imagery and representation. The reason that some conspicuous consumption might be generally seen as 'vulgar' (again, one might think of the stereotype of the yuppie with a garish sports car) is a result of the ways in which that consumption is aesthetically valued (after all, the same car driven by Steve McQueen might be admired and lusted after). In essence, consumption is coded with socially valued acts of discernment and identification.

Advertising and marketing

If there is a second broad social transition that has fed profoundly into understandings of consumption, it is the rise of the mass advertising industry. 'Ads' have become a currency of social life. There is a great deal written about ads and their impact on economically developed societies. What matters most here is to register the ways in which advertising and marketing have shaped public identities (what is often coined as a 'consumer republic': Coen, 2003), and how the rise of advertising agencies has led to a broader 're-visioning' of society as a constituency of purchasers.

Mass advertising roughly coincides with the emergence of mass consumer societies in the 1950s and 1960s. The story here is a familiar one: an unprecedented growth in real incomes and employment, another wave of suburban development, and the ongoing industrial shift towards consolidated large companies with large-scale production plant accompanied by technological intensification. This broad social transformation happened most distinctly in the USA, but it also spread through Britain.

Advertising increasingly served as the conduit through which competition between producers took place (rather than claims to value for money or quality). Advertising companies became increasingly complex and ambitious in the ways that they marketed commodities. The public was exposed to an increasingly dense range of adverts within the media and public spaces. Marketing represented the British public in increasingly 'consumerist' terms – initially by income bracket and demographic (the term 'youth' was inaugurated in large part as a consumer identity) and towards the present in ways that are far more infused with emotional and attitudinal markers (adventurous, caring, ambitious, patriotic, and so on).

The forms of advertising have become progressively densely aestheticised. An obvious metric of this is the shift from focusing on the product to image-intense adverts in which the product plays a 'bit part' or might not even figure. Increasingly lucrative advertisement contracts and new technologies – as well as the emergence of an epistemic community of marketers with their own journals, networks, awards, and rivalries – have pushed forwards increasingly ambitious and sophisticated advertisements across an increasingly commoditised media space which encompasses radio, television, the internet, tie-ins between commodities, films, computer games, food, and so on. The 'ad' has become a pivotal mediator of social life (de Zengotita, 2005).

The rise of the ad has shifted the expectations of advertisers and consumers alike. Consumers are expected to be both more sophisticated and more difficult to impress; aware of their libidinal sovereignty and less rational and rather fleeting in the preferences. The ironic trope has suffused all advertising with playful, controversial, and obscure messaging – all of which endeavours to appeal to (and construct) a consumer's instant emotions.

Consuming campaigns

What is the relationship between consumer identities and Africa campaigning? There are two facets that orient the following discussion. In the first place, and most directly, there is the relationship between the prognostic framing of campaigns and the discretion in consumption. In other words, campaigns might represent Africa in order to encourage people to consume in ways that conform to a political message. Some salient cases of this (sugar consumption during the abolition campaign and anti-apartheid boycotts) will be studied later in the chapter. The second facet is less direct and broadens out our focus. Here, the interest is in the ways that campaigns have changed in ways that conform and promote a broader tendency towards consumerism within society as a whole. In other words, campaign organisations have tended incrementally to 'see' societies as constituted by consumer individuals rather than as, say, Christians, people with political convictions (usually on the Left), or humanitarians. One can see this in some aspects of campaign publicity (especially the management of the campaign brand) and also in the mapping out of campaign activity in ways that increasingly resemble the marketing of a product. Understanding consumerism in this sense alludes to a broader commoditisation of campaigns.

The great British consumer

The construction of Britain's modern political culture was based in the spreading and deepening of aesthetic consumption. Walvin identifies this historical development and associates it with the onset of Britain's imperial age:

> [In London] From the late seventeenth century onwards, could be seen the most lavish, obvious material signs of consumption. In and around the Court and among men and women of substance, grown fat on the proceeds of commercial and mercantile expansion, the latest whim, the latest styles ... were to be found. From London, the same people transplanted their social habits across the face of the nation. (Walvin, 1997: 155)

The period from the late 1600s onwards has been defined by a deepening consumer culture, based in an expanding middle class and subsequently broader and deeper mass markets (Kroen, 2004). Walvin goes on to show how the fashions of London served as a generator for the aesthetic standards in British civic conspicuous consumption, from the regional cities to provincial towns and villages. And, at the heart of this construction of Britishness through purchase was the importation of commodities from imperial possessions, especially tea and sugar, which were progressively purchased by people in all classes so that, by the start of the nineteenth century, they became national staples. Indeed, a sugared cup of tea (in contrast to the gourmets of other cultures which drank tea unsweetened) became the quintessence of Britishness by the 1900s.

Anne McClintock (1995) shows how close the connections between an emerging Britishness, civic consumption, and empire were in the nineteenth century. Coining the phrase 'commodity jingosim', McClintock argues that consumption generated a 'cult of domesticity' in which purchasing goods for the household became infused with the values of national unity and imperial grandeur. These values were inscribed into the advertisements for soap, matches, biscuits, whiskey, tea, chocolate; the social activities of sport, toiletry, dress, and travel. 'Commodity jingoism ... helped reinvent and maintain British national unity' (1995: 209).

The mass purchase of tea and sugar was not exceptional to more general trends: like other products, grading, presentation, and branding were central to the circulation of the commodities. Tea blends, 'household names', the association of certain brands with well-known individuals, promotions (new blend recently acquired), and carefully appointed tearoom and grocery shop windows were all part of the imaginary of a nation of imperial consumers during the eighteenth and nineteenth centuries. The British sense of identity as an imperial nation was underpinned by powerful aesthetics of consumption, branding, and retail. The nineteenth century witnessed the emergence of the figures of the Great British Consumer[3] and a Nation of Shopkeepers – even if the latter was coined disparagingly by the French (Walvin, 1997: 164) The former was gendered as a woman and the latter as a man reinforcing the public–private distinctions that underpin modern British national identity.

If the aesthetic nature of imperial commodities is at the heart of British national identity, then it can be seen how consumption served as a powerful political conduit for identity construction. And, inasmuch as commodities were symbolic as well as material – loaded with references, brands, and texts – then they also transmitted values.

The values embedded in imperial commodities worked in tangent with the aesthetics: they were addressed to the British consumer through an evocation of Britishness. They were not commonly articulated in ways that provided purchasers with any knowledge of the social origins of the commodity itself. Images and values were not autobiographies of the commodities (Harvey, 1990): they did not represent the plantations, the slave-based systems of work, or the connections with the violence of the slave trade. It is these connections that destabilised the norms of imperial commodities and led to consumer campaigns in relation especially to sugar.

Consumption and imperial nationalism

Virtuous consumption

Many of the constitutive advertising campaigns of the later 1800s were heavily aesthetic and ideologically rich. Advertisements for tea, soap, tobacco, chocolate, and coffee evoked an association between purchase and imperial grandeur. This was achieved through the use of the Union Jack and Britannia, the deployment of images of upstanding British consumption, and the use of exotic imagery culled from imperial possessions. This coincided with the mass circulation of newspapers carrying advertisements after the deployment of steam printing in the early 1800s.

The commodities that became 'Africanised' throughout the nineteenth century were those that either derived from Africa (tropical goods), or that were sold within British colonies (biscuits, medicinal and sanitary products for example). In all cases, advertisements connected the commodity with a sense of British imperial virtue, commonly expressed through some form of racist imagery. Nederveen Pieterse (1992) presents myriad examples of this, many of which present idealised images of the British male imperial agent: upright countenance, perfectly presented, going about the great work of civilisation. As such, advertising presented a romantic image of colonialism based not only in the grossest caricatures of African people, but also in caricatures of the English masculinity that reflected back from African landscapes into English self-identification. In a sense, these images offered British consumers a stereotype of the virtuous, middle-class, and educated male, an important social base for the British colonial endeavour (Ranger, 1995). This masculinised imagery was to persist through the government-funded 'buy imperial' campaigns of the Empire Marketing Board in the early 1900s (Biccum, 2009; Bush, 1999), in which grisly and stout Rhodesian farmers overlooked their tobacco farms.

Africa served as the backdrop for some of the first mass advertising campaigns that drew heavily on symbolism and emotional appeals. One of the pioneers in this regard was Pears soap. Pears soap advertisements have been studied very effectively by Ramamurthy (2003) and McClintock (1995), both of whom recognise the centrality of the association between whiteness and cleanliness in the blatantly racist imagery of many of the advertisements.

But these images are not simply racist denigrations and celebrations of a certain commodity. And, it should be noted, Pears was hardly exceptional: many commodities performed 'commodity racism' in the 1900s (McClintock, 1995). Once again, these images are also in a sense 'involuted': they evoke sentiments of British virtue. Consider the way that the concept of biopolitics was used in Chapter 2: not simply the way people feel biologically but also the way people feel emotionally. In this sense, the constant juxtaposition or contrast between dirtiness/blackness and cleanliness/whiteness provided Victorian Britons with a fillip to their self-esteem not just as clean/healthy individuals but also as a *healthy nation*. White sugar and (usually) white soap,[4] the medicinal qualities of (again) sugar or tea, or the fineness of certain tobaccos, coffees, and teas are associated with discerning taste, intellect, and health rather than the mass system of surplus extraction that underpinned the evacuation of these commodities to Britain. These adverts also 'white-washed' the dirt, squalor, and poverty of Victorian Britain.[5]

All nationalisms are in a profound sense culturally produced through com-parison (Anderson, 1998) and colonial advertising generated a comparative frame in which Britishness was articulated as a healthy corporate body. The healthiness of the corporate body of Britain was most clearly materialised in the ways that African commodities were represented to consumers as they filled the growing consumer republic of the 1800s. Sugar, tea, coffee, and tobacco – Africa's 'classic' colonial exports were all presented as medicinal goods: 'attractive additives to the apothecary's shelves' (Walvin, 1997: 118). These mass imperial commodities echoed a symbolism of alimentary nation-alism to be returned to later in order to understand Africa campaigns.

Relatedly – and again in ways that appeal to the concept of biopolitics – the British elite considered its own 'unwashed masses' in ways that ap-proximated the ways that they considered Africans: rendering them 'dark', dangerous, liminal (Bush, 2006: 164, McClintock, 1995), and even consider-ing the possibility of enslaving the irredeemably poor (Rozbicki, 2001). The image of the clean imperial man and the Pears soap bar in the African land-scape and the 'Africanisation' of those Britons that did not fit the bourgeois ideal imaginary were both part of processes of national identity construction through tropes of virtue.

In sum, the point here is that powerful images of consumption emerge and develop from the late eighteenth century. Consumption becomes a social practice that contributes to a consolidation national self identity through the emergence of discerning consumption in which necessity is increasingly accompanied by choice, and within choice aesthetic and moral statements. In regard to the latter, Britishness is built on the associations of consump-tion with Britain's imperial self-esteem. Buying commodities branded in the civilising mission and the 'blackness', 'exoticism', and 'savagery' of Africa, encapsulated a social practice of consumption that was most pivotally narcis-sistic, imperialist, and nationalist.

Consumption and connections

It is important to foreground a point that is only implicit in the section above. This is that consumption is not simply an act, a discrete moment in which money is exchanged for a commodity; rather, it is part of a series of broader circuits of value and material, as Marx argued in more detail and more centrally than anyone else.[6] And, as such, consumption is a social process: not only in the sense that consumption is a refreshing or renewal of production and labour, but also in the sense that it fixes associations between agencies on the consumer chain (Princen, Maniates and Conca, 2002). Consumers connect – albeit in highly mediated fashion – with producers and with remote places and materials. This connection is both material and social; it is mediated and moral.

The argument here is that consumption creates the possibility of association – or more ambitiously of the construction of shared destinies – even if this 'sharing' is enacted over highly uneven social spaces. These associations have proven to be central to the ways in which consumption is endowed with broader political meaning. One early and definitive consumer organisation – the US National Consumers' League – relied on the 'duty of consumers to find out under what conditions the articles they purchase are produced and distributed' (in Wiedenhoft, 2008: 290). Chapter 4 showed how abolitionists created an ethic of consumption in which the fate of slaves was connected with the preference for 'free' or 'slave' sugar. This is one instantiation of a broader implicit proposition embedded in all commodities, one that is made explicit through the ways that commodities are rendered partially as material necessities and – as the previous section argued increasingly so – also as image-rich and morally infused acts of choice or preference.

In the present day, one can see this universally in the rise of fair trade, environmentally friendly, free range, organic, dolphin/bird friendly commodities. Additionally, commodities are increasingly presented as altruistic possibility: the increasingly common practice of highlighting the support of a charity or cause that is embedded in the purchase of a commodity. Indeed, some recent work on the sociology of consumption and advertising has explored the ways in which commodities are presented through 'non-ads', that is, as existential or political statements or questions which bear at best an oblique reference to the product itself (Goldman, 1998: Chapter 7).

Consumer campaigns

Thus far, we have connected consumption, British social identity and Britain's imperial project. This led to the 'domestication' of Africa imagery – a key theme of this book – but it does not yet connect with Africa campaigning. This section will show how abolitionism's campaign politics was both oppositional to prevailing consumer norms but also, in a deeper more immanent sense, affirming a virtuous British consumer ethic.

The campaign to boycott sugar that came from slave plantations emerged in the late 1700s under the broad mantle of abolitionism. Sugar consumer politics was articulated by men through pamphleteering and middle-class women through household consumption. The late 1700s was a period in public culture in which poetry and prose were valid interventions into political discourse, and women both read and produced sentimental stories about the privations of slavery. Within the gendered structure of the time, women asserted a political agency through discretionary purchase.

The boycotting of 'slave sugar' shaped a notion of a moral household: a Christian, lettered, and powerful household. Christian in the sense of displaying due sympathy with the benighted distant others who were often represented in tragic ways best encapsulated in Josiah Wedgwood's iconic 'Am I not a man and a brother' cameo. Lettered in the sense that consumption was progressively framed in intellectual ways: consumption not only as desire and fashion but also as a way of understanding one's place in the world.[7] Buying 'slave sugar' was seen as contributing to the miseries of the plantation system, asserting a complex set of inter-relations across the Atlantic, bringing trade and ethics into the English marketplace. The notion of a powerful household derived from the basic moral argument of the sugar boycott: that consuming slave sugar drove the mass slave labour systems of Caribbean economies. More implicitly but clearly closely connected, this kind of imagery places the middle-class household in a globally pivotal position. It asserts a consumptive connection that was to persist throughout Britain's imperial age: that Britons held the fortunes of distant masses at their discretion. Consider this extract from an anti-slavery pamphlet in the early 1800s:

> It is the duty of the people of England to put an end to ... slavery ... They can, to a certainty, put an end to it, by the rejection of that produce, which forms the chief support and encouragement of slavery, and to abstain from using such produce is therefore their bounden duty. But that, which is the duty of the people of England *collectively*, must, of necessity, be the duty of everyone amongst them *individually* ... I am resolved, for one, to maintain on this point, a conscience void of offence towards God and towards men. (In Sussman, 2000: 37)

Here, we see the evocation of a moralised English identity, a sense of national power, and a Christian notion of rectitude articulated powerfully for the abolitionist cause.

The broad anti-slavery campaign in Britain destabilised the project to associate imperial/national grandeur with the metonym of an alimentary influx of colonial 'nutrients'. Although not explicitly connected with the Society for the Abolition of the Slave Trade, abolitionists developed a powerful public norm towards a consumer boycott of sugar. The key here was to coin the consumption of sugar as an act of pollution rather than imperial health. This required a set of underpinning conflations: national consumption (which rose vertiginously in the late 1700s) with bodily consumption; and of the horror of plantation labour and the content of sugar itself.[8] Most directly, the representation was made that in eating or drinking sugar, one was also ingesting the sweat, blood, and tears of distant African slaves (Kowaleski-Wallace, 1997: 42–51). This was usually – but not always – effected through metaphors. The outcome of this 'anti-saccharite' campaign (Drescher, 1987) was to associate national/bodily health with a purity that was achieved through abstention. The most extreme way of putting this case was rhetorically to associate the consumption of sugar with cannibalism – the colonists' most fantastic and exotic bête noir (Sussman, 2000; Barker, Hulme and Iverson, 1998). Overall, sugar boycotts fitted in with a notion of British nationalism represented through virtuous consumption (Kowaleski-Wallace 1997: 38*ff.*), a trope which was to be mainstreamed into British imperialism in the nineteenth century (Trentmann, 2008; Vernon, 2007: 108*ff.*).

It is worth noting that the sugar boycott was not an anti-consumption campaign. The argument against slave sugar was also an argument to purchase 'free sugar'. In this sense, the sugar boycott cannot be seen as anti-consumption as much as a deepening of the ethical aspects of a growing consumer identity. This was also the case with anti-apartheid, which introduced a 'buycott' as well as a boycott (Chapter 4).

A prominent and more recent public 'thinking through' of the notion of consumption, abnegation, and virtue would be Save the Children Fund's (SCF) 'Skip lunch' campaign. This campaign's underlying aim was to appeal for donations to alleviate famine. The campaign was immensely successful in raising funds and achieving widespread public recognition. The effectiveness of the campaign was partly a result of the tight connections in its framing:[9] to miss a lunch and give the saved money to SCF which would/could use the money to save an African life. The use of a more certain phrasing – not deploying the conditional word *could* – made the campaign clear in terms of action, but very simplistic in terms of how famine happens and how it might be combated. But the connection between an affirmative act of non-consumption and the saving of lives reproduced in a different setting the notion of a nation of wealthy but virtuous citizens. Princess Anne (SCF's Patron) positively affirmed a sense of national good sentiment in her public addresses, and the publicity for the campaign generally appealed to a very broad public (Lidchi, 1993: Chapter 5).

The campaign was contracted to the advertising company Ogilvy and Mathers.[10] In many ways, the way this campaign was run – and its success – sets a precedent for subsequent large public campaigns (not least Make Poverty History as seen in Chapter 8). Ogilvy and Mathers worked concertedly to roll out high-impact and broad-ranging messaging. The discourse within the organisation was a publicity discourse, not a development/poverty one: something which generated constant low-level misunderstanding and even antagonism between the NGO and the advertising company. The target for the campaign was the 'big-hearted *Sun* reader' as well as the politically aware 'knowing' individual. Celebrities were tied in to the campaign, media space won, and the campaign became increasingly one of encouraging everyone in Britain to participate and perhaps wear a T-shirt saying so. In a nutshell, the campaign's success was based on effective marketing which appealed to a feeling of populist British virtue. This aspirational nationalism can be found in all subsequent high-profile campaigns. Throughout the campaign, as Lidchi critically demonstrates, the 'voice' of Africans – any Africans – is entirely absent.

Consumption, identity, brand

On the face of it, charities are brands as much as Guinness, Starbucks and Adidas. (Griffiths, 2005: 121)

Thus far, consumption has been associated with an increasingly rich set of normative and aesthetic possibilities. But this does not bring us squarely into a consideration of an African presence built upon charitable and campaign practices which are only partially to do with consumption. There is a need to broaden out from the Oxfam shops and online retail activities of NGOs and explore a set of campaign and charity activities which, while not about selling commodities are about 'selling' campaigns or indeed the identity of campaign organisations tout court. This is recognised by consultancy and PR firms who see charities as brands, selling 'intangibles' to a consumer market (Saxton, 2008): 'non-profit brands are now being developed deliberately ... not merely as a by-product of other activities' (Ritchie, Swami, and Weinberg, 1999: 26).

The larger NGO/campaign organisations have sold branded commodities for decades. The traditional Oxfam Christmas card is now accompanied by an Oxfam credit card.[11] Oxfam's high street presence makes it rather distinct in comparison with other development NGOs who might sell a small selection of loyalty commodities online. Also, donations to the NGOs can be represented as commodities: for example the purchasing of gifts for poor communities by British individual donors.

There is a difference between the specific consumptive act of donating to a charitable appeal or the politically motivated preference for one set of commodities over another, and the consumption of a campaign. The latter is a more symbolic act of consumption, an identification in which a person acquires an affinity to a certain campaign or charitable organisation. This latter kind of consumption brings us more closely to the interplay between consumption and identity in ways that are broader and richer than an analysis of discrete purchase acts. This form of consumption brings us into perhaps the most salient marker of contemporary consumer culture in Britain: the brand or logo. The argument here is that campaign and charity organisations have come to think of their connections to the British public increasingly within the terms set by the marketing of brands in a consumer society.

Brands are not new, but their pervasiveness is (Klein, 2000). In the marketing journals, a brand is seen as a vital investment for any seller – a form of symbolic capital which serves as a marker for a commodity or set of commodities. In a sense, the brand is the identity of the commodity: it conveys through imagery properties of luxury, trustworthiness, masculinity/femininity, adventurousness, sexuality, exoticism and so on.

As consumption has become such a large and complex part of social life, so the brand has become an increasingly prominent 'grammar' within which people establish aspects of their social identity (Goldman, 1998). The key feature of the brand that allows this connection is its imagery. A brand is not simply a name. Similarly to the way images contain texts, the brand has its own language: it is a set of colours, a symbol, a 'strapline' (short phrase which embodies the brand's identity), a fictional or dramatised character (which might range from a cartoon character to a celebrity or an 'expert'). Commodities frequently come to us garbed in these dense significations of colour, text and voice, and as a result our consumption of the commodity articulates with our sense of ourselves, or our aspirations of what we wish to be, or our desires to be seen in certain ways by others. In short, the purchase of many commodities has become a form of identification or expression, and one facet of this is to display one's emotions in ways that are both declaratory and also to display virtue (Lury, 1997: 73). This kind of expression-form is especially prominent in the 'halo' commodities of campaigns, as Moore shows in her study of 'ribbon culture' (2008): the wearing of a ribbon is a virtuous self-identification achieved through association with a campaign.

Brands are seen by marketing organisations as ways of developing not only preference in the marketplace (buying commodity X over commodity Y) but also of loyalty through identification. This connection between commodities and social identities via the brand has generated a new science of marketing in which public relations and advertising companies – modestly called 'creatives' – work intensively on brand formation and innovation, often relying on data from market research and focus groups.

Campaign branding

Campaign organisations have become increasingly aware of the importance of their institutional image. This self-awareness was partly a result of the increasing 'professionalisation' of NGOs from the late 1980s after the funding boost ushered in by Live Aid and in which the often informal and volunteer-based structures of NGOs were replaced by personnel who had accrued skills in marketing and management and might not have had a history of support for a particular NGO. This meant that NGOs tended to manage themselves in ways that resembled the practices of profit-making organisations.

Oxfam, Christian Aid, CAFOD and others developed stronger images for themselves throughout the 1990s (Stride, 2006: 115). Oxfam has integrated its website, campaign materials, and appeals in the same green colour code; it has its own icon – a crossed white ribbon on a green background; and it has its own strapline 'be humankind'. The use of the phrase strapline comes from marketing practice. It refers to a single sentence attached to a logo which encapsulates in a striking way the identity of the brand. The 'be humankind' strapline has been accompanied by a range of broad and marketable phrases that Oxfam has disseminated throughout the 2000s: 'I'm in' followed shortly after the increased attention to international development bequeathed by Make Poverty History. 'I'm in' also commenced a series of television advertisement campaigns which fully demonstrated Oxfam's ability to make good use of contemporary advertisement techniques, something that was perhaps best demonstrated in the 'be humankind' advertisements which featured sophisticated animation, symbolism, and music. Like many strong advertising campaigns, 'be humankind' employs irony: humankind signals an association with humanitarianism and it also suggests an emotive pull: kindness towards others.

According to one brand marketing agency, Oxfam had a brand value of £172m in 2006, giving it a ranking of the third most lucrative charitable brand.[12] Oxfam might be seen as a leader in much of the branding that has taken place within the campaign sector, but it has been accompanied by many other campaign organisations. Indeed, in the same brand value website, CAFOD and Christian Aid were seen as two of the biggest upward movers. ActionAid's logo contains an inverted 'i' as an exclamation mark which signified its strong campaign remit. The inverted 'i' is also the web icon for ActionAid's website. ActionAid's strapline is 'End poverty. Together'. CAFOD has a similarly 'logofied' name with a global 'O' surrounded by two blue swirls and a strapline 'Just one world'. Christian Aid has a logo of white text embedded in a red envelope/arrow shape which is always strongly foregrounded in their pamphlet and appeal envelopes.

How might we interpret the increasing prominence of logos and straplines in an NGO sector which is the key agency to construct the African presence? How does this increasing prominence specifically relate to issues to do with development and Africa? The literature on marketing sees logos as a device to enhance a firm's or product's standing in an increasingly dense and fluid marketplace. The argument is that the profusion of proximate choices makes price competition less important and consumer loyalty more difficult to maintain. In this context, logos are commodity identities. They try to embody the 'feel' of the commodity or brand: this is why design, colour, font, and image matter so much. NGOs' branding communicates through powerful and simple imagery and text. Collectively, NGOs have generated a branding that evokes a cosmopolitan sensibility: the use of a globe connotes a single space, a shared planetary destiny.[13] NGO brands tend to be based in simple primary colours which communicate a sense of simple and 'pure' values.

NGO logos are attempts to communicate organisational values. These values are both related to the NGO and to the marketplace. The NGO values might involve the political convictions of campaigning (the exclamation mark in ActionAid's logo, or the red background and newsprint urgency of the text in War on Want's logo), the sense of a single humanity (referenced commonly in depictions of a globe), or a spirit of compassion (best encapsulated in Save the Children's arms-outstretched child logo). Additionally, and generically, these logos try to establish an affective presence in the marketplace: as organisations one can trust, as virtuous organisations, as icons of compassion. This is what marketeers and some political analysts call the 'halo effect': the association of virtue with a certain logo or brand.[14]

NGOs have used their brands as key resources to generate public awareness and engagement. This has been most prominent in the electronic media: NGO webpages, YouTube identities, twitter, Facebook, NGO widgets to connect diverse sites together, and sourcing space on other websites.

How has branding affected the modes of representation used by campaign NGOs? In this first place, it is worth noting that brand icons tend to be abstract: they are designed to communicate ideals, feelings, and emotions and therefore they tend not to signify concrete things. Branding does not have much space for an Africa outline (although we will come to see how Africa's outline has become 'logofied' in Chapter 8) or a representation of Africans.[15] One might reasonably expect, then, that the Africanness of campaign organisation branding has been dampened as NGOs have become increasingly professionalised in their marketing activities.

Branding opens up space for a different form of representational practice from the campaign imagery analysed in Chapter 6 because it replaces the emotional relays of sympathy and humanitarianism (associated with disaster and development frames) with a consumer aesthetic. The brand is suggestive and evocative but it is not 'forceful' in the way disaster framing is; nor is it complex in the way that human face framing is. This is something of a general rule in branding and marketing: that brands must appeal to consumers, not accost or challenge consumers with dense messages.

The shift in imaging is adroitly analysed by Chouliaraki (2010) as 'post-humanitarian', that is, driven by a more consumer-centred emotional repertoire in which those who donate or engage with a campaign do so in order to satisfy something in their own utility-seeking selves. Speaking of MPH, Bono declared that 'This is showbusiness; we're creating a drama ... Years ago we were very conscious that in order to prevail on Africa, we would have to get better at dramatising the situation so that we could make Africa less of a burden, more of an adventure' (*Guardian*, 16 June 2005, emphasis added). This opinion reflects the increasing interpolation between Africa campaigning, celebrity, and consumerism. Herein, campaign materials appeal more to the 'contemplation of the self' (Chouliaraki, 2010: 118), evoking a striving to consume and do good – what some have coined as causumerism (Sarna-Wojcicki, 2008). The Oxfam 'Christmas present' ads did this: using the emotionally laden aesthetic of a famine appeal to humorously portray the receiving of unwanted Christmas presents before inviting people to buy presents for distant poor people. Another (more controversial) example would be the Orange ads that were endorsed by MPH during 1995 to be shown at cinemas as part of the ongoing 'Orange Wednesday' theme. In these adverts the Orange executives play an absurd and callous foil to a famine appeal.[16]

The notion of consumer sovereignty is hardly new, but again, there is novelty in the way that consumer sovereignty is articulated. The premise that consumers will only purchase commodities if they seem good quality or value has been overlain with a representation of the consumer as an infantilised, libidinal, and fleetingly discerning agency. Brands are seen as alluring, aspirational vectors; they are not conveying information and do not make expectations of consumers. In some of the marketing literature, brands seem to approximate talismans, full of magical properties that will keep an organisation within the public's awareness and might – through obscure semiotics – engage people in a campaign.

Another aspect of NGOs' 'commoditisation' is the increased use of retail. The best example here is Oxfam: Oxfam has its own online shop. It also has its own 'branded' retail device, Oxfam Unwrapped, which allows people to give gifts on special occasions which are in fact goats and chickens for people in Oxfam project areas. It also has its own eBay site (and has sometimes purchased website banner space from eBay). Oxfam has its own wedding celebration packages. CAFOD has a 'world gifts' website that, like Oxfam, allows people to purchase developmental gifts for people in CAFOD project areas. Perhaps the best-known 'campaign commodity' is the white wristband, of which eight million were sold during 2005. The white wristband became a brand in itself: a signifier of the Make Poverty History campaign coalition. Its brand value was considerably enhanced by numerous celebrity endorsements. But the strong publicity and marketing drive behind the white wristband as commodity and brand did not straightforwardly translate into anything more than a fleeting act of purchase. Surveys of those who were aware of MPH or bought a wristband revealed a strong brand awareness but a far less stable of deep engagement with the issues behind the campaign. Celebrity endorsement provides 'personality' for a commodity but does not introduce campaign issues to consumers.

Celebrity

Join the celebrities by wearing a white band and help end poverty forever. (*Daily Mirror*, 2 February 2005)

Earlier, we argued that Africa campaigning has framed consumption through an association of good politics with good taste. In keeping with a generalised trend in consumer imagery and marketing strategy, campaigns have been increasingly disposed to use celebrity imagery in order to promote their campaigns. As with ethical consumption, this is not entirely new. Larger NGOs have invited prominent personalities (what we might now call celebrities) to endorse campaigns or charitable appeals.

Nevertheless, celebrity association with Africa campaigning experienced a step-change during Live Aid. The dissemination of the famine image was accompanied by the dissemination of the concerned celebrity – arguably a more resounding and persistent image. Live Aid ambitiously brought together almost the full gamut of British pop artists. The Live Aid progeny – Sport Relief, Fashion Relief and so on – have also provided conduits for celebrities to associate themselves with African causes. The central organisation here is Comic Relief.

Comic Relief has become a clearing house for celebrity involvement with appeals for development project funding in Africa and Britain. Comic Relief has the most sophisticated media engagement, the broadest 'address book' of celebrities, and a great deal of cultural resonance within Britain. The latter is based on a populist, humorous, and aspirational appeal to the British to donate money, watch TV, and perform quirky fundraising acts during the biennial Red Nose Day.

What lends the contemporary use of celebrity endorsement its novelty is the broader context of change in consumer identities and the way celebrities are used. In regard to the former, consumer identity has been markedly reshaped through advertisements (which themselves have become increasingly prominent) and the electronic and print media. Campaign NGOs recognise this and have adapted their representational strategies accordingly: Cottle and Nolan (2007: 868) note that since the 1990s 'aid agencies now seek to capture the media spotlight by other means ... to do so they generally seek to engage the media's penchant for celebrity'.

In the vernacular, a celebrity is a person who is famous for being famous. The value of the celebrity is his or her image which connects to, and evokes an identification between a campaign and a personality. Celebrities are portrayed in an almost metaphysical fashion as embodying certain emotional or personality traits: masculinity, trustworthiness, sexuality, empathy, determination, and so on. Chapter 8 will look at Bob Geldof as a prominent campaign celebrity. His personality in the media very much generates an association between Geldof and emotional relays of pragmatism, empathy, and bluntness.

Geldof is not alone. In fact, all campaign NGOs have a list of celebrities who lend their image to an organisation. One can readily see this by looking at NGO websites. Some celebrities have involved relationships with campaigns: Chris Martin in regard to fair trade, Helen Mirren to human rights and arms trade, Mark Thomas to War on Want, and so on. Outside of this relatively restricted circle exist a long list of celebrities whose association with a campaign is very brief and doesn't go beyond an act of endorsement such as a photoshoot or a film clip.[17] Agencies have emerged that try to fit celebrities with the appropriate cause in ways that are based on image promotion and do not require any discussion of 'deep' adherence to a campaign.

But campaigning and Africa's representation have become inexorably 'celebritised' in ways that seem to shift control of representations aimed at issues and fundraising away from NGOs. One phenomenon of the 2000s that illustrates this is the increasing involvement of A-list celebrities and fashion houses in fundraising and cause endorsement. We have seen an example of this in the 'I am Africa' campaign. Another prominent example is the concern expressed by UNICEF as designer labels and associated celebrity models and designers 'got behind' UNICEF, leading to a depletion of UNICEF's own 'brand'. Furthermore – as is often the case with celebrity campaigning (Richey and Ponte, 2011) – the humanitarian appeal is delivered with no appeal to ideas of social justice: fashion houses supporting UNICEF have been linked to textile sweatshops (McDougall, 2006).

This section has outlined the impact of branding on campaign organisations – the increasing prominence of marketing strategies and the rise of celebrity endorsement. The next section looks at representations more closely.

Campaign advertisements

It is not straightforward to explore the ways in which branding has infused Africa campaigns. There are two empirical reference points to explore: the print and electronic media. With regards to the former, one can look at campaign advertisings, and with regard to the latter one can analyse campaign NGO websites. But care needs to be taken concerning the ways the evidence is analysed and the claims that can be made. There are no quantitative claims about the content of websites of the print media. The websites of campaign organisations change daily and cannot be considered as a stable or self-contained 'archive'; the print media constitutes too large a body to encompass and there are limits to the insights provided by some kind of categorisation of advertisements into empirically distinct categories such as 'famine' or 'development'. A more heuristic approach is taken, in which the aim is to discern the key themes of branding and relate them to prominent web and print media imagery.

In order to do this, two bodies of evidence will be used. Firstly, I commissioned a search of a comprehensive advertisement database for any Africa-referenced advertisements in British papers from 2001 to 2008. This was carried out by Billetts Media Monitoring and it yielded 459 separate advertisements. These were filtered down by the author, excluding repeat advertisements and those deemed not appropriate because they did not directly relate to campaigns or charitable appeals (for example 'Rugby World Cup Bike Ride' and 'Wildlife for all Trust'). This yielded 88 advertisements, placed in mainstream national newspapers and magazines.

Secondly, a mapping out of the main campaign websites was done in which home pages were connected to their second-level pages with a particular view to the ways in which images were presented and layered. This was carried out for twelve NGOs in 2009.[18]

Taken as a single body of images and text, advertisements placed by campaign and charity organisations show very clearly that the Africa campaign tradition themes set out in this book are all still present and in a sense vying or cohabiting with each other. Some frames are stronger than others and this generates some tensions within the ways Africa is represented. It is worth stressing the point here that there is no single template for Africa's representation that one can delineate here beyond the simple but cardinal starting point of 'Africa' as a single (racialised) place.

As argued in Chapter 6, the famine image has generally lost its political and moral backing within NGO communities. But, as suggested in Chapter 2, it remains as a secular reference point in Africa's representation. This paradox is the result of the belief by charitable agencies that the famine image works well in eliciting donations during time-sensitive moments. As argued in Chapter 1, it is difficult properly to disentangle cause and effect in this respect: the British public has been so intensely socialised into this image over such a long period of time that it is perhaps the best judgement to say that both charities and publics have accustomed themselves to these images and their signification as moments of giving.

During the time period under scrutiny here, there were three emergency appeals focused on famine or starvation – either as real-time events or as 'precipice' events, that is, catastrophes about to happen. These were the Niger/ West Africa famine, the East Africa mass starvation, and the hunger appeal for southern Africa. It is worth noting here that – as seen with the Ethiopia famine of 1984 – the representation of famine is far from straightforward. The famine in Niger took place in a specific region of that country and was not simply a result of drought and locust plagues as all of the appeals stated. Rather – and in keeping with all famines – exceptional levels of starvation and death were a result of price changes, state action, and broader contexts, both political and environmental. In fact, there was no absolute food shortage in Niger during 2005 (Rubin, 2009). As with the Ethiopian famine of 1984, the famine was framed as a natural disaster in order to enhance the direct and tragic nature of the famine for the purposes of the appeal; the broader political effects on the way Africa is represented were not accounted for.

In each case, the image and text were very similar across a range of agencies. The key textual references were emergency–death–appeal; that is, campaign images presented a humanitarian emergency, posed a potential mass death situation and then made an appeal for money. With one exception (a woman carrying a plastic water drum) all images were of children. The children were mainly in a state of emaciation. The photos were almost always cropped to focus on the face in close-up and always looking upwards towards the camera. In almost all cases, the children were abstract: they were not from a place and didn't have a name. The shock of this kind of image has already been discussed; one can also see that statistics either substitute for or affirm the famine image: 'more than 30 million will need food aid' (Care West Africa appeal), '12 million people face serious food shortages' (Irish Red Cross southern Africa appeal), 'more than 20 million people in Africa urgently need food and water' (British Red Cross, East Africa appeal). Textually, these crises were all narrated as if adult lives were not in peril. No mention of adult men was made and women were only mentioned as mothers and in relation to children.

It is very clear that campaign organisations that also act as relief organisations are still very strongly relying on the kind of famine imagery that was mainstreamed into British culture from Biafra and strongly reaffirmed from Band Aid onwards. Notably, Oxfam has concertedly avoided the famine child image since the 1990s, following its own internal institutional-cultural shift towards positive images. Nevertheless, its West Africa appeal (but not its East Africa appeal) still *textually* evoked the images used by other appeal organisations: 'children are dying as we speak'. Save the Children relied on the same textual evocation of the famine child. Christian Aid also avoided imagery but did not rely on text which evoked famine imagery, instead referring to people and communities rather than children.

The appeal text itself was multiplex: most directly an appeal for help in crisis, but also an appeal to people. This secondary appeal evoked both the ethical virtuousness of the reader and his/her (potential) power. Appeals frequently posed readers as holding the fate of multitudes in their grasp: 'give water, give life' (Water Aid), 'help save children's lives today' (Save the Children). Perhaps the most explicit and powerful example of this trope comes from the World Food Programme (WFP): 'Drought is back in East Africa. How many children will we lose this time? That's up to you.'[19] This text below an extreme close-up of a child's fly-covered face. The child's eyes are closed and – as the text implies – it is possible that the child is nearly dead.

The appeal framing is, of course, an appeal for money. Commonly, in order to elicit donations, appeals offer a kind of 'value for money' calculus in which it is stated that a small donation will have direct, certain, and disproportionately large effects. 'Give water, give life, give £15' (Water Aid) is the most direct example of this. During the East Africa appeal, Save the Children stated that £25 would feed 150 malnourished children which, in the context of a famine appeal, relays a message that £25 will save 150 children's lives. This kind of appeal narrative is based on an equivalence which has pernicious effects. Implicitly, it barters down the price of life (17 pence per life?) in order to make donations seem like very good value. It affirms a certain kind of power that British spectators have over mass life in Africa; something that was also present in the way sugar consumption was framed earlier in the chapter.[20] Less explicitly but significantly, it poses the possibility that the death of Africans is cheaper than the death of a Briton. This might seem like an extreme argument to draw from the famine appeal, but it is not an erratic or isolated point. Looking at war and disaster reporting more generally, it is the case that disasters in Africa get less priority than those in Europe or those involving white or Western people. Can any reader recall any reportage on the wars of the Democratic Republic of Congo from 1995 to 2008? UN estimates put the death toll at over 3 million.[21]

The WFP image noted above – extreme but not exceptional – is very far from the commoditised and marketing-savvy campaign imagery that was discussed earlier. Although one might wish to argue that this kind of schism between emergency appeals and development and campaign work is necessary or not entirely contradictory, it is worth noting that campaign-focused adverts from the same collection seemed to be rebutting emergency appeal framings themselves – in other words battling against assumptions that people make about Africa having been routinely exposed to famine imagery. This was extant in both Christian Aid and Oxfam adverts – unsurprisingly because these are two of the most image-savvy campaign organisations. Thus, Christian Aid poses the text 'dirty low-down spongers' ironically: this epithet seems to be a *vox populi* judgement on Africans – the kind of thing one might say having seen a range of famine appeal adverts. But, subversively, the advert focuses on the ways in which Britain has benefited from Africa ... although the advert's text ends with an appeal to donate juxtaposed to a statistic that 12,000 children will die by tomorrow. *In toto*, this advert both subverts and then, *sotto voce*, reaffirms the famine image.

Oxfam also ran a similar campaign in which *vox populi* statements were contrasted with subversive or thought-provoking commentary. These adverts were presented as a series of 'African Myths', such as 'there's no point in giving to Africa. Everyone's dying of AIDS'. Subsequently, and analogously to the Christian Aid adverts, this series of adverts ends up reaffirming the famine image by taking the same image format and using it for an emergency appeal. Thus, the myth refutation is replaced by 'children are dying as we speak' as the *vox populi* statement; but rather than this being juxtaposed with some kind of counterintuitive statement, instead – and in exactly the same format, the text reads: 'West Africa food crisis. Oxfam is there.'

Both the Christian Aid and Oxfam examples reveal how blurred the boundaries are between campaign and appeal. They also show how aware the larger and more campaign-focused NGOs are of the opinions of the general public and how effective campaigning requires NGOs to use modern and powerful techniques of public communications in order to shape broader public sensibilities.

Website representation

All campaign organisations have become increasingly dedicated to producing a strong web presence. Electronic communications have been proactively mainstreamed into all of the campaign organisations that I interviewed. The major campaign coalition Make Poverty History (MPH, about which more in the next chapter) brought together this prominent interest in 'electronic campaigning': the prognostic framing of MPH was strongly focused on text messaging and online petitions (Sireau, 2009). This section reviews the websites of seven major campaign organisations. It does so by mapping out the image and text content of these organisations' webpages at first (homepage) and second (pages located one click away from the homepage) level during March 2010.

As with the previous section, there is a need to explain the methodological thinking here. As above, the aim is not to generate a quantitative outcome, say, a calculation of the frequency with which certain words were used or the number of hits certain pages received. The aim is rather to draw out from the content a sense of how Africa is represented through text and image. It is important to ensure that all aspects of this representation are dealt with here; but there is no need to be definitive about which images or norms are more prominent than others – although as we saw in the previous section, it became apparent that the famine image was the most prominent.

One of the reasons why the famine image had such prominence was that advertisements in newspapers were seen as the appropriate venue for this representation. Recalling the emotional sense of impact that is required in famine appeals which was discussed in Chapter 1, we realise that newspaper advertisements are a specific kind of media. Spectators have no choice in receiving these images because they are embedded within a newspaper that they have purchased. Furthermore, they are located within news items more generally – perhaps even items about the famine itself if there has been a 'spike' in media interest (Howe, 2009). Websites do not have the unannounced shock impetus that newspaper advertisements do; visitors to a campaign website are already a subset of the British public: those commonly defined by campaign professionals as 'interested'. They have already made a choice to receive images and text from the campaign organisation and will very likely have some idea of what to expect.

This is an important point because it attenuates to some degree the critical points made regarding newspaper advertisements. The web presence of campaign organisations is certainly used for emergency appeals, with weblinks to the Disasters Emergency Committee and famine imagery. But, outside of the crisis moments, campaign organisations are trying to relay more richly their values and to present notions of Africa and Britishness that are sophisticated. The broader aim of campaign webpages is to 'migrate' viewers from 'interested' to 'active' and from there to membership. The hierarchy of responses hopefully elicited from websites was set out clearly by Save the Children: sponsor, donate, act, join.

Before looking at the material in more detail, a couple of points need to be made about the way the material is presented here. Firstly, there are no html references. This is because most of the sites will have changed by the time this chapter is being read. The material is not contentious or difficult to access in any way, so it seems reasonable to leave the reader to trust that these sites were extant during spring 2010. Secondly, although this might seem to suggest that the material here is already dated and therefore redundant, this is not in fact the case. In all of the campaign organisations analysed here, the content of pages has changed, but the formats have not. This relates to the way that webpages are built and managed. Building a website is a capital investment: it requires a substantial payment to a website designer who then provides a structure for the presentation and management of material, the former being visible and the latter invisible and managed by a campaign organisations IT staff. So, after a website is 'live' (available to access universally), campaign staff can renew text and imagery on a daily basis in order to keep the website fresh. But, to change the format – the columns, banners, text boxes and so on – requires more work and has possibly greater repercussions on the way the campaign organisation represents itself. Interestingly, when this section was written in late 2010 the author noticed that the contemporary websites contained a great deal of new text and imagery but largely within the same framework as had been in place during the spring of that year. The point here is simply that the rapid turnover of webpages is not a symptom of endless changes in campaign representation; it is simply a result of the necessity of updating and refreshing existing messages and formats in order to keep an organisation's web presence interesting in the highly fluid and mobile milieu that is cyberspace.

The homepages of the major campaign organisations (Oxfam, Action Aid, Christian Aid, Save the Children, CAFOD) all contain the same key features: a timely and pressing issue as a major headline, subordinate campaign issues presented as a single image and short 'enticing' text, a reference to the organisation's existing activities, and a set of options to engage with a campaign and take action. The images of people on all homepages were pre-dominantly African, but the subjects themselves were presented within the 'human face' idiom set out in Chapter 4: men and women as well as children, people working and studying, people presenting themselves as active, happy, or politically active.

The overall framing of the webpages was very much in the frame of social justice. One can see this in the way these homepages compared with those of the World Development Movement (WDM) and War on Want (WoW), both of which have a more or less awkward relationship with the 'majors' which rely on charitable status, child sponsorship, and in some cases funding from the British government. Unsurprisingly, WoW and WDM's homepages were more explicitly political (enabled by their status as political organisa-tions, not charities). The campaign issues were focused on specific agencies more explicitly: international bankers, the World Bank, and the British gov-ernment. But there was also some overlap. At the time that the websites were mapped out, many homepages were campaigning on poverty in South Africa (tapping into the widespread interest in the World Cup) in similar ways, and issues such as tax evasion and debt were also shared across webpages.

Within the first-level and second-level pages (which are very much inte-grated into each other), a number of key features can be discerned. In regard to imagery, there is a continuing focus on Africans throughout. In second-level pages, Africans are still presented through 'human face' imagery, but also with longer pieces of text, often narrating the experiences of particu-lar subjects: their working life, their hardships, etc. Innovatively, Christian Aid has film clips which have been taken by those involved in Christian Aid projects, which bring the narrative focus closely onto the Africa film-maker. The common print media narrative comes from a white Western interlocutor – an aid worker, UN official, doctor – in ways that edit the way the appeal is presented and reaffirm the voicelessness of Africans. The use of mobile phone-style film clips and (to an extent) vernacular narratives suggests a very distinct subject position for Africans.

The use of film clips chimes with more liberal optimistic renditions of globalisation – theoretically informed by cosmopolitanism – in which we witness a novel form of communication which has the potential to reinscribe the way Africans are represented. The embedded clips in Christian Aid's webpages are mirrored by other organisations with varying degrees of media-tion. Furthermore, all of the major campaign organisations have their own YouTube identities within which various clips are curated. Here, we see the possibility of a diverse range of pretty direct narratives coming from Africa. ActionAid's campaign during February 2010 – Get Lippy – has generated a series of vignettes of women's lives and struggles which are not introduced by a British Action Aid employee, do not come with background music, or any contrived cut-aways. They resemble the video diary format that is common currency in the slew of 'reality' television shows in Britain. They offer a range of 'voices' that are as authentic and articulate as one might see across all genres and spaces. This medium presents a real shift in the way Africans are represented: genuinely novel and working outside of established frames.

However, it is important to calibrate a little here. Firstly, and most obviously, these clips – whether embedded in campaign websites or YouTube accounts – are not widely disseminated. Indeed, the 'Get Lippy' clips had received a few hundred hits when visited by this author. One of the issues here is that YouTube is a lightly mediated space in which there is no thematic identity. Herein lies a dilemma for all campaign organisations between reaching out to people in general through popular media and maintaining strong campaign political identities. This is a constitutive tension within campaign organisations that many interviewees recognised: the sense of compromise between popularity and political conviction in which deeper and more reflective political engagement is seen as the provenance of a 'core' group and easier and more high-impact messaging might get the (sporadic) attention of a wider public. It is within the latter that representations of Africa and Africans remain schematic and most likely to key in with existing framings.

Secondly, the *verite* quality – vernacular language, speaking directly to camera, no cuts – of any clip should not distract from the fact that there will always be some form of mediation in these clips' production. At the very least, talking heads will have been selected; people will have been prepared; locations chosen. These are African voices relayed through the conduit of British campaign NGO priorities. This is not an argument akin to Spivak's argument that the subaltern can never fully represent themselves, which seems to turn on far too exacting a notion of genuine self-representation as to disqualify all humans from speaking. Rather, it is to suggest that the vernaculars of the clips are hybrid: they are both concretely representative and ambitiously globalised. But, mediation and presentation there must be. On the War on Want YouTube site, there exist three clips of 'Stanley' speaking about his cramped conditions of living in Blikkiesdorp, Cape Town. In the first clip, Stanley relays his conditions and 23-year wait for rehousing very directly and spontaneously. He is speaking from his current house, which is poorly lit, and one has the sense of being intimately within Stanley's lifeworld. The second two clips, both of which are short and rather incomplete, seem to suggest trial runs of the video diary. In one clip, Stanley is having a conversation with the camerawoman who clarifies with him how long he has been living in his current house and then reminds him to start with 'My name is Stanley'. His demeanour is of a person needing guidance with the filming; this is not an off-camera scripting, but it does remind us that the clips are produced for campaign purposes through campaign organisations. This is the metanarrative for all of these vernaculars.

In contradistinction, Oxfam and other larger campaign organisations' YouTube clips are more heavily packaged. Oxfam clips are introduced with voiceovers, involve heavier editing, and in some cases have emotionally appropriate musical overdubs. There are fragments of famine appeal intermixed with authenticité in these clips which derive from their higher production values.

The final point which renders the potentially more representative aspects of cyberspace is to note that web clips and second-tier webpages are not the only web presence that campaign organisations have. Additionally, some campaign organisations pay to have banners located on other websites. DEC appeals often locate banners in other websites as part of the effort to disseminate the simple and direct crisis appeal frame. These banners tend to be text-based and an electronic equivalent to the print appeal advertisements which are small, and relay simple text about numbers starving or at risk with a small donation form at the bottom.

Other banners evoke the emaciated child image – interpolated into websites that are not in any way related to issues of Africa campaigning, global poverty or emergency relief. In this fashion, the unanticipated shock impact of the image is very close to that set into a newspaper.

Conclusion

This chapter has brought out the themes that emerge from the increasing comingling of campaigning with appeals to consumers. This has worked in two inter-related ways: both the offering of commodities associated with a campaign and the offering of campaigns as commodities. The latter has involved 'halo' associations based on the use of celebrity and the building up of logos infused with morally virtuous identifications. Each of these tendencies feeds into existing means of communication and also into the growing use of internet communications. The next chapter will consider a specific year within which all of the campaign themes here 'condensed' into a specific and intense campaign, along with the more 'traditional' campaign framings dealt with in earlier chapters.

Notes

1   The conditional here is a result of the claim that George Harrison's Bangladesh concert in 1971 was not only charitable but also political in motivation.

2   Marx, 2004; Smith, 2008; Veblen, 2005.

3   An idiom much used by economic journalists to explain the British economy's per-
    formance, commonly used in a roughly Keynesian way to explain economic stability
    through levels of demand. Indeed, one might imagine Keynes' macroeconomics
    based in demand-side economics as basically a sumptuary model of the economy.

4   For an analysis of the West's longue durée of political colour coding, see Martinot,
    2003.

5   The tension between a virtuous overseas charitable ethic in the context of the priva-
    tions of Victorian urbanisation is brought out keenly in Dicken's novel *Bleak House*
    and the critical term 'telescopic philanthropy' applied to Mrs Jellaby who is indiffer-
    ent to the suffering of her children.

6   Capital I starts with the commodity, and then there is the well-known treatment
    of commodity fetishism. A lucid and historically applied use of Marxist theory to
    understand consumption is Fine, 2007.

7   Indeed, Wedgwood's attitude was to produce goods of discernment, for the wealth-
    ier middle classes.

8   The conflation or association of corporal and national health in consumption has a
    broader genealogy in British national identity – see the fantastic study of national
    identity and free trade in Trentmann, 2008.

9   The effectiveness of very direct connections between issue, action, and motivation is
    exemplified in the disaster frame analysed in Chapter 4.

10 This paragraph is derived from Lidchi, 1993.

11 Perhaps the most infamous Oxfam commodity was the Christmas tree decoration
    with a 'starving baby' image on it (Manzo, 2008: 637).

12 www.intangiblebusiness.com/Reports/The-UKs-Most-Valuable-Charity-Brands-
    2006~379.html, accessed 12 June 2010.

13 Save the Children, Care, CAFOD, and Oxfam have 'global' logos.

14 The halo effect is also used by companies to market their brands through 'ersatz cam-
    paigns' (Hilder et al., 2007: 6). Perhaps the first example of this is Pepsi's attempts to
    tie in their paid celebrity Lionel Richie with USA For Africa (the American equiva-
    lent of Live Aid). See Louise Davis (2010: 99–101).

15 Only the Save the Children logo has an objectification within it – the outstretched-
    arm child.

16 This ad was sprung on the MPH CT very late and was not well received. This was
    not only because there was no time to change the ad – it either had to be run or not
    – but also because the ad strongly suggests that MPH was a charitable appeal.

17 The range of celebrity campaigning can be explored through Dan Brockington's
    blog at http://celebrityanddevelopment.wordpress.com/, accessed 12 June 2010.

18 The NGOs selected were those with a substantial web presence which implies a rich
    set of representations of Africa, and with a headquarters in the UK or with a large
    and active UK subsidiary. This produced the following list: Action Aid, Actions for
    Southern Africa, CAFOD, Christian Aid, Comic relief, One International, Oxfam,
    the Global Coalition for Action Against Poverty (G-CAP, which emerged out of

MPH), War on Want, World Development Movement, Save the Children, and World Vision.

19 Like the *Daily Mirror* headline noted in Chapter 4, the use of 'again' suggests a cyclical or inevitability to Africa's humanitarian crises. This taps into a deep intellectual assumption in the West about Africa's location outside of mainstream or universal history, famously condensed into Hegel's statement that Africa is 'no historical part of the world; it has no movement or development to exhibit' (Hegel, 2004).

20 The life-saving calculus remains prominent in corporate campaigns like RED. See Sarna-Wojcicki (2008: 16).

21 The notion that a formal end to conflict in the form of a peace agreement means an end to violence is convincingly challenged by Autesserre, 2010.

8

The Year of Africa

Can you think of even one African voice or face that has communicated the aspirations, passions, concerns, and expectations of her or his fellow Africans over the last year? (Chukwa-Emeka Chikezie, African Foundation for Development, 2006)

In 2005, the British government hosted the G8 summit which was themed as an intergovernmental meeting that would deal seriously with global poverty. Also during 2005, a major campaign coalition, Make Poverty History (MPH), succeeded in generating mass public awareness of global poverty. The media – especially the BBC – promoted the coverage of Africa throughout the year through its 'Africa Lives' theme and most prominently through its broadcast of Live 8. Finally, the British government, under the leadership of Tony Blair and Gordon Brown, released the Africa Commission report *Our Common Interest* which made a series of bold claims to a solution to poverty in Africa. All in all, 2005 was perhaps the most 'Africa prominent' year in British history – certainly in terms of campaigning. Much of this prominence was driven by MPH, especially as the coalition interacted with other representational organisations. This chapter will look at the 'year of Africa' with a particular focus on MPH and the way Africa was represented.

Framing the global poor

Make Poverty History

MPH was conceived by the NGOs that met in October 2003 as a campaign coalition that would focus on the G8 summit in July 2005. In a letter sent during that period, the embryonic coalition advised (then British Prime Minister) Tony Blair that there would be a concerted mobilisation of public opinion around the G8 in order to make it a 'development summit'. There was, at this stage, no focus on Africa as a campaign image or as deserving special attention. The campaign was focused on poverty as a mass human condition.

Throughout 2004, the strategic planning and organisation building for the campaign took place. In late 2004, the name Make Poverty History was adopted by the coalition, along with the three 'straplines' of debt, aid, and trade. These three policy/issue reference points were the product of a process of negotiation within the coalition in which each participating NGO wished to project its own concerns onto the coalition. The three straplines reflected the main NGO networks that underpinned MPH: the British Overseas NGO Development (BOND, the aid network), the Jubilee Debt Campaign (JDC, the debt network) and the Trade Justice Movement (TJM, the trade network).[1] Thus, throughout 2004, the campaign structured itself through three key issues which were themselves articulated in ways that would seem attractive to a growing coalition of campaign and development agencies. As such, the issues remained generic and transnational, that is, based on broad moral arguments with little reference to specific situations, and with no spatial focus beyond that of the Global South.[2] The arguments were, in essence: remove the illegitimate burden of debt, make international trade fair, and ensure more and better aid.

In addition to the name and the three issues, the coalition's third campaign premise was justice not charity. In other words, MPH aimed to make a strong case that existing international structures of debt, aid, and trade were morally unacceptable. It was not a charitable act that MPH sought, but the righting of a wrong. The premise of the campaign was that any political discussion based in liberal notions of human rights could hardly conclude that existing debt, aid, and trade regimes were just. The campaign planning schedules that MPH devised in 2004 reflected this approach: firstly to make people aware that there was an issue with debt/aid/trade; secondly to make people feel that something was wrong in regard to debt/aid/trade; and finally, that they could influence the G8 to rectify these wrongs.

In 2004, MPH set out its 'asks' (desired outcomes) of the G8. For each of the three policy areas, and with varying degrees of specificity, the coalition stated what would constitute a minimal set of actions significantly to reduce extreme mass poverty.[3] These campaign objectives constituted the core of the lobbying aspect of MPH. They also provided a symbolic reference for the highly successful general outreach that MPH achieved in 2005. The targets on aid increase, debt write-off, and trade regulatory reform provided a moral standard by which to evaluate the G8 summit. As such, the campaign's popular motivation was to force and/or encourage G8 statesmen to adhere to the minimal agenda required to 'make poverty history' which effectively meant make a historically unprecedented effort to reduce extreme mass poverty through commitments on aid, trade, and debt relief.

In sum, by January 2005, MPH had in place a campaign based on a moral argument that extreme mass poverty is unacceptable to anyone with a belief in a shared humanity. The corollary of this was that the focus of the campaign was the extremely poor, the poorest one billion living on less than a dollar a day, and living in the Global South. The campaign agenda was shaped around the three issue/policy straplines of aid, trade, and debt which, for the purposes of mass campaigning, set a standard for the performance of the G8 leaders.[4] Therefore, in terms of civic action, all focus was drawn to Gleneagles and the political will/moral disposition of the heads of states.

Representing poverty

How might we interpret this? In the first place, it is worth noting that there was an explicit attempt not to focus on Africa. The campaign organisations involved in the early shaping of the campaign were all very wary of using 'Africa' to campaign. Individuals in the Coordination Team,[5] and campaign departments within each respective NGO (rightly) held political convictions that Africa had been subjected to a long history of pejorative and negative imagery (Lidchi, 1993). It is to the campaign's merit that from the beginning a conscious effort was made to distance the campaign from the familiar and tired symbolisms of emaciated African children, famine landscapes, or sensationalised violence. These images have a long imperial and post-imperial history, the most recent manifestation of which is the charitable appeals prevalent since the mid-1980s (Harrison and Palmer, 1986). In a sense, 'Africa' as a public image in the UK was judged to be so strongly intertwined with charity that any justice agenda required a different reference, hence the geographically unfixed reference to extreme mass poverty (VSO, 2002).

However, this left a very 'hollow' moral subject to motivate public sensibilities. If making poverty history was the aim of the campaign, there was perhaps surprisingly little imagery or detail from the campaign about 'the poor'. This second distant other – one which would both help identify an injustice framing by posing a subject of moral empathy – was substantially underspecified beyond its property of extreme poverty. This made the initial injustice framing, and any publicity that might emerge from it, rather weak. Instead, campaign publicity was largely focused on the white wristband and various formats of celebrity endorsement for the campaign. These images were underpinned by references to the G8 and the aid/trade/debt triptych.

That this 'hollow other' was not remarked upon by MPH, or even journalists commenting on the campaign, is significant. One reason why this was the case was that most attention was not paid to 'the poor', but to the leaders of the G8 states and especially New Labour, as discussed further later in this chapter. It was in this respect that more personalised and engaged imagery was used. At various stages, satirical but cordial images of the G8 leaders were employed at MPH rallies and by the leading MPH coalition members. For example, Oxfam published a postcard (for supporters to send to Downing Street) with a cartoon of Tony Blair caricatured as a superhero and with a caption referring to trade talks.[6] Because the emotive focus of the campaign was drawn towards the personal motivations and wherewithal of the G8 leaders – and especially Tony Blair – the campaign's relatively unspecific and abstracted categorisation of 'the poor' remained unremarkable: a subject at second remove, whose presence might serve as a means to add more substance to the G8 leaders as the 'passionate' focus of the campaign.

This general hollowness does not, however, give a full account of how the poor were represented. There was also an assumption that coalition members would, under the MPH mantle, generate their own campaigning imagery which would be more detailed, involved, and potentially attempt to explore the possibilities of deeper representations of the poor and potential solidarities with them. And, indeed, this is certainly what happened. The effects of this on MPH were, however, overdetermined by the structure of the campaign itself, and this requires some general comments about the way the MPH coalition worked.

MPH was, *ab initio*, a difficult project not merely because of its scope of ambition, but also because it aspired to draw a diverse coalition of agencies and indeed existing coalitions together. Some agencies would see themselves as campaigners, others as development organisations, religious groups, unions, or charity fund raisers. In one sense or another, all of these groups were private voluntary organisations, but clearly they had very different origins and world views. Perhaps more important than the growing diffuseness of the campaign, as it grew from a handful to 540 members, were the differences between the leading coalition members.

The leading agencies were Oxfam, Christian Aid, Action Aid, CAFOD, War on Want, World Development Movement, and Save the Children. Most of these agencies were represented by one of their senior staff working within the Coordination Team (CT), which was charged with managing the progress of MPH. The CT was not structured as an executive, but as a deliberative co-ordinating body in which decisions would be made through consensus. Each member of the CT had very clear ideas about campaigning and also about the nature of poverty, the G8, and a range of other issues. It was clear very early in the coalition's construction that the campaign – or 'meta campaign' as one CT member put it – would only work if it was loosely coordinated and if each agency would enjoy a good amount of autonomy within the campaign. As a result, MPH itself was actually a rather small institution. It had two posts assigned to it: a 'facilitating' Chair and a Administrative Coordinator. It established a basic consensus regarding general aims, and it coordinated the different commitments of the various agencies to the schedule for 2005 through CT meetings and the various Working Groups. All of this took a great deal of effort, and those on the CT worked phenomenally hard to make MPH a success, but MPH itself had no organisational independence or executive powers.

In essence, MPH served as a rallying point for a diverse coalition and as a co-ordinating body. Contrary to popular perceptions, MPH never acted as an NGO *sui generis,* and it always had a strict one-year lifespan. For sure, a key reason for this – apart from the strategic challenge of managing a diverse coalition – was that existing NGOs did not want to be party to the creation of a 'rival brand' NGO in what is a competitive sector (Griffiths, 2005; Stride, 2006). Thus, MPH provided a powerful issue platform and core image; in other respects – the mobilisation of existing campaigners, the generation of policy analysis and commentary, and campaign imagery – work was done by each agency under the MPH 'franchise'.[7]

The result of this structural pattern to the coalition was that individual NGOs' work on campaign imagery was not part of the work of the CT's weekly strategic meetings. Campaign imagery that focused substantively on poverty was a 'unilateral' affair for each agency. This disconnect becomes all the more significant once it is viewed through the eyes of the public. The general public perception was that MPH was a separate and self-standing campaign organisation. People generally were not aware that MPH was a coalition of campaign agencies, and that without these agencies, MPH would cease to exist. The corollary of this was that, inasmuch as MPH succeeded in mobilising large numbers of 'newly engaged', these people were largely exposed to MPH campaign imagery and not necessarily guided towards the more 'involved' imagery of the separate NGOs. The point is that, the unforeseen consequence of the strategic decision to maintain an abstract or hollow imagery of poverty within MPH and to leave NGOs to develop their own publicity under the MPH mantle was to deliver to the public a very weak image of how one might perceive of the poor. It was within this set of circumstances that a process of 'Africanisation' took place, in effect to 're-fill' the hollowness of poverty imagery and to revive a set of tried-and-tested moral propositions which mobilise people to engage with campaigns on behalf of distant others.

Africanising poverty

> You have to make every story about Africa, about poverty, have an MPH angle. (MPH press campaigner, in Martin *et al.* 2005: 49)

It is certainly the case that MPH steered clear of derivative Africa images. In one instance, the CT had to consider a web clip in which a 'virtual' African child dies of hunger within 30 seconds. At the end of the computer-generated death-image there is a banner stating 'click here to stop this happening'. This clip relies on a proven logic of fund-raising in which a combination of 'shock' and empathy focused on African children provides the emotive 'hook' for engagement. The CT – not without some considerable discussion – decided not to adopt this clip because of its reliance on what one might call the eschatological trope of Africa (cf. Englund, 1998), embedded in public consciousness since Band Aid and Live Aid.

Nevertheless, when one looks at the small number of campaign images of poverty that *were* employed, and when one considers the literatures – spoken and written – of MPH and its spokespeople, it is clear that Africa was the reference point for almost all campaign material. The MPH website had four images of people from the Global South, three of which are African – and all of the three are children.

In regard to written and spoken material, it was the case that most of the examples and human interest stories relayed by MPH coalition members derived from Africa. The booklet, 'Make Poverty History: How You Can Help Defeat Poverty in Seven Easy Steps' (Bedell, 2005), is peppered with statistics and vignettes to convince the reader to take the journey along all seven steps – all of which are from Africa. Throughout 2004 and 2005, a cadre of celebrities/artists was built up, and those who made public statements spoke almost exclusively about Africa, sometimes having been given whistle-stop tours of projects in Africa by specific development agencies. In radio and newspaper interviews, MPH spokespeople would use brief life stories or examples from Africa to make points about access to health care and education.

To clarify the point being made here: it is not that those involved in MPH purposefully (or cynically) employed images of African children to propel the campaign. Rather, the small number of images of the poor used by the campaign were separated from the image work of the individual agencies, with the effect that most people supporting MPH (not a specific NGO) would only be exposed to these images. This enabled an existing disposition towards an injustice diagnostic framing that fixed on Africa specifically as a distant other defined by poverty and evoking empathy.

Poverty, and the Africa campaigning tradition

The campaign also positioned itself within a particular historical lineage. Rather than, say, placing MPH in a tradition of new social movement activism or recent forms of global mobilisation (for example related to the World Social/Regional Forums), MPH gave itself a very 'British' and 'African' historical framing. Let us elaborate further.

Firstly, MPH located itself within an assumed tradition of British civic culture in which Britons hold at heart a global humanitarian impulse, a product of a pragmatic Christian liberalism. The secular reference point for this image of the British civil society is the abolition movement, which MPH evoked as the beginning of a tradition of which it is the most recent manifestation. The second campaign 'moment' that MPH aligns itself with is the anti-apartheid movement, focused on southern Africa, and mainly South Africa. The third campaign moment – which is still active – is the Jubilee Debt Campaign[8] which, although not regionally focused on Africa, is almost exclusively associated with Africa. Jubilee has also relied upon moral arguments and imagery from abolitionism, a reflection of its strong liberal Christian social base and the de facto focus on Africa in regard to severe indebtedness. The Jubilee Debt Campaign's logo is of breaking chain links.

In sum, then, MPH consciously selected a historical narrative (abolition, apartheid, and debt) within which to place itself which was to all intents and purposes 'African', which then became a synonym for poverty. The effect of this was to appeal to (and construct) a specifically British mobilisation regarding Africa based on a liberal Christian humanitarianism which owes its origins to the British empire, from the religious critiques of the slave trade, through the critiques of 'excess' in non-British colonies (especially the Belgian Congo), ending with the Christian/Fabian politics in favour of proper 'trusteeship' of African societies and independence (Grant, 2005; Howe, 1993).

Looking back at 2005, one can readily see that the poverty focus of MPH was accompanied by an implicit/explicit African focus that was expressed not so much through campaign imagery but the literature of the campaign. A cautious judgement at this stage might be that MPH encapsulated an unresolved tension between a weak 'poverty' and a strong 'African' framing. But this does not bring us to recognise the extent of the 'Africanisation' of the campaign which was pretty much absolute by mid-2005. In order to do this, we need to look at the ways in which the campaign expanded beyond expectations and how it interacted with other events during the year. First, however, there is one important counter-position to the portrayal offered in this section that we should engage with.

African poverty and Make Poverty History: a twelve-month challenge?

'It's Africa, stupid!' The pragmatic argument

If the campaign to make poverty history was Africa-focused perhaps that is simply because Africa is poor. Certainly, if we look at World Development Reports we find that the poorest countries are almost entirely African, even if the picture at the level of capita numbers is far less African-centred.[9] And, across a whole range of statistical indicators of poverty, can be discovered an African 'bias': levels of debt, AIDS/HIV seroprevalence and deaths from other poverty-related diseases, literacy rates, infant mortality, life expectancy, and so on. One might then say that MPH campaigners 'intuitively' focused on Africa because that is where the poverty is; more strongly and combatively, one might argue that it might be enjoyable for academics to pick apart campaign discourse, but what really matters is the reality of poverty in Africa and how we might do something to reduce it.

This argument emerged within the MPH campaign. An uncommissioned MPH communication was considered by the Messaging and Communications working group. It was the 'boy' clip[10] mentioned earlier. A debate ensued concerning the extent to which the film clip fed into the famine-image genre (child, face close-up, starvation). One counter-argument was that this clip did capture directly a reality of extreme poverty and should therefore be adopted by MPH. Finally, MPH decided not to endorse the film, but to leave it to individual coalition members whether to use the film.

As noted earlier, the question of the extent to which the MPH agenda actually deals with pervasive and extreme poverty is, in fact, a vexed one which cannot be dealt with properly here. It can certainly be agreed that African economies are exceptionally fragile and that millions of people in Africa endure intolerable lives largely because of their material poverty. But, if we are interested in MPH as a campaign and particularly the ways in which it engaged with and mobilised a broader British public, we should ask how Africa's poverty is accounted for. In other words, how is the prevalence of poverty in Africa explained, or at least presented to a larger public? This is an important question for campaigners precisely because the association of Africa and poverty is hardly a new one; in fact the linking of Africa and poverty brings us directly to the kind of Africa/poverty/charity sensibility that was outlined in Chapter 2 and which the campaign strove to avoid. So, generating a clear narrative on why African economies or peoples are extremely poor becomes very important.

MPH addressed poverty in Africa consistently by referring to the pernicious effects of high levels of indebtedness, low levels of aid, and 'unfair' trade rules. Commendably, there was no 'natural disaster' narrative and no mawk-ish focus on the 'tragedy' of poverty.

For the purposes of mass mobilisation, this understanding of poverty had to be articulated in a highly accessible way: in effect debt/aid/trade became 'headline' wrongs that could be righted. But it is difficult to see how any of these issues could be articulated, developed, and discussed in the public sphere over a period of 12 months. To take the three campaigns that MPH associates with: abolitionism, anti-apartheid, and dropping the debt, each lasted at least ten years in which campaign platforms developed and integrated a range of more complex political perspectives and demands. In each of these cases, an important facet of that year-on-year development was debate and discussion within the campaign group and a readiness to react to changes in circumstances. MPH had made it impossible to do this because it was from the very beginning strictly only going to last for one year.[11] Nor was it possible for MPH to present anything but the most cursory understanding of poverty and its relationship to aid, trade, and debt to the newly engaged within such a short period.

'Eight men in a room'

> You do not, it seems, need to understand the poor in order to save them. (Richard Dowden, *Observer*, 6 January 2008)

The focus on the G8 was presented by MPH in a particular way. In essence, the purpose of the lobbying of the British government, the rally in Gleneagles, and (once they were announced) the Live 8 concerts,[12] was to push the G8 statesmen to agree the requisite aid and debt relief packages to make a significant difference to mass poverty.[13]

This focus generated a particular diagnostic and prognostic framing. If poverty can be 'made history' by the G8 leaders, pushed along by a six-month campaign, poverty ceases to be a structural phenomenon. Any account of poverty based in historical explanation or references to global capitalism is effectively effaced by this representation. One might say that mass campaigns require 'easy' goals or targets, but this does not properly answer the point that if mass poverty is perceived as in some sense 'solved' through a summit, its causes are obscured and trivialised. There were some within leading coalition NGOs who became unhappy working within the coalition because of this.

Furthermore, the focus on the G8 opened space for the re-emergence of aspects of the 'traditional' narrative of African poverty. Seven of the 'eight men' were white, and the theatre of the G8 was set so that 'the poor' or 'Africa' waited in the wings for the outcome which could liberate millions of hardship

(Abugre, 2005). To quote Richard Curtis: 'Eight men who saw that the world was crying out for justice, eight men who realised that suddenly the price of poverty had slipped out of control, eight men who arrived at a hotel in Scotland one day in July and made the greatest decision of our times' (Curtis, 2005: no page).

The 'eight men' became a powerful 'first other' towards which the campaign directed attention, leaving the 'second other' (the African poor) cognitively in a far more remote position. The 'eight men in a room' (first) framing of solutions to African poverty was much more prominent than references to the causes and effects of aid, trade, or debt regimes *vis-à-vis* poverty Africa. The imperatives of campaigning over a very short period and focused on a specific 'window of opportunity' over-rode the desire to represent poverty in a more complex or structural fashion. And, while extremely effective as a means to produce a historical moment of mass mobilisation, this (second) framing produced an image of poverty as African with no prominent explanation as to why this was so. In the absence of an explanation, existing Africa campaign tradition assumptions might easily 'fill the gap'. These assumptions worked perfectly well with the notion that poverty might be alleviated by the decisions of powerful (white) statesmen like Blair. In a soundbite: Africans owned the poverty, Western leaders owned the history.

The argument so far has been that MPH was planned as a global social justice campaign which did not aim to fix poverty to a regional or racial signifier. Nevertheless, because of the decisions made about how the campaign would be rolled out, 'the poor' remained a hollow subject of the campaign, and poverty remained both under-explained and liable to 'Africanisation'.[14] This Africanisation of poverty was always a possibility because of the Africa campaign tradition more generally and especially the legacy of Band Aid: 'when UK consumers[15] think of the developing world, Africa is their starting point ... Sixteen years on, Live Aid, Band Aid and the Ethiopian famine still have a powerful hold on our views of the developing world' (VSO, 2002: 5). The Africanisation of poverty was a result of the lack of MPH-devised imagery of the subjects of injustice or poverty and the near-exclusive focus on Africa for stories of poverty. Furthermore, the short time span and focus on the G8 summit fitted more easily with familiar assumptions about a 'natural' state of poverty in Africa and the external provenance of development solutions. The Africanisation of poverty was both the unintended consequence of strategic campaign decisions and an unfortunate but tolerated effect of a highly effective mass mobilisation around Gleneagles.

The dilemmas of success

The level of popularity of MPH grew beyond the expectations of all those involved in the campaign. In terms of coalition membership, the number of people attending the Gleneagles rally, numbers of text and emails to Blair and Brown, numbers of wristbands sold/worn, and levels of media support, the campaign exceeded all expectations. The runaway success of MPH provided the 'glue' that held together campaign organisations, some of which were increasingly unhappy with the way the campaign was shaping up. It also made the campaign increasingly difficult for the CT to control, and made the campaign a political resource, association with which could provide benefits for others outside the campaign coalition. In other words, as MPH became more popular, it became more liable to 'virtue by association', the 'halo effect' (Hilder et. al, 2007).

This section will consider the articulation of MPH with other agencies which were both engaged with by the campaign coalition and helped make the campaign a success. Within this broader perspective one can readily see how the features of MPH outlined in previous sections – its tension between moralities of social justice and charity/custodianship, its weak imagery of poverty, its textual focus on Africa – enabled a near-complete Africanisation which was at least tolerated by the MPH coalition and which in large degree accounted for the widespread and popular prominence of the campaign.

New Labour

From late 2003, New Labour understood that MPH offered political opportunities, especially for Blair and Brown.[16] Thus, in early 2004, both Blair and Brown had engaged with the campaign, conceiving of it as a political resource and integrating it into their own political strategies. 2005 was seen as an important year for various reasons: it was the year that the UK hosted the G8 and chaired the EU, and it was an election year. For Brown there was a need to maximise his standing both within his party and amongst the general public as the most likely successor to Blair. Regardless of the personal motives of each of them, Make Poverty History mattered because it provided potential political opportunities for both of them. This made Gleneagles a remarkable summit in the extent to which it focused around the 'host' head of state (Payne, 2006).

The coalition's first campaign act (12 November 2003) was to write a letter to Blair, setting out that there would be a strong campaign and lobby movement in 2004/5 focused on the British government's hosting of the G8 and its chairing of the EU. After a while, Blair realised that the government could usefully engage with the campaign, signalling in February 2004 that the G7 and G8 meetings that year would be about Africa.

Perhaps more quickly in the initial stages, Brown engaged with the coalition (*Guardian* 7 January 2004; *New York Times*, 7 February 2005), hosting a workshop for coalition members within the Treasury in February 2004 under the title 'Making Globalisation Work for All – the Challenge of Delivering the Monterrey Consensus'.[17] In early 2004, the global economic justice issues were twofold: trade and financing for development, the latter of which fitted closely with Brown's personal advocacy of the International Finance Facility. The subsequent 'splitting' of development finance into aid and debt reflected the core issues brought into the coalition by different campaign agencies, but it is noteworthy that to some extent the MPH agenda was shaped by the Treasury at this early stage. In early 2005, Brown gave a speech on Africa and development to MPH members at a DFID/UNDP seminar,[18] in which he made historical references to the Marshall Plan which were popularised in the media and some campaign groups as a 'Marshall Plan for Africa' (Gallagher, 2011: 12).

For Blair, the starting point to understand his interest in MPH is his party conference address of 2001, in which he coined the now well-known turn of phrase of Africa as the 'scar on the conscience of the world'. This speech expressed a growing conflation of 'security' with development that has been prevalent since 2001; it also reflected a reinvigorated enthusiasm for international intervention – what one of Blair's advisors at around the same time called a liberal imperialism (Cooper, 2002) – which might 'heal' the violence and poverty in Africa. The prominent place of Africa in this speech provided a counterpoint to Afghanistan and the legitimacy crisis that was growing as a result of the 'war against terrorism'. It did this by foregrounding humanitarianism in a way that military invasion cannot, and by representing intervention as a progressive or liberating project. This speech provides the initiation of a bifurcated foreign policy under Blair from 2001 in which the starkly awful story of the 'war against terrorism' is counterposed by a parallel story of setting out a bold agenda of development for Africa. In the speech, Blair advocates more aid, a version of fair trade largely based on liberalisation, and good governance as the key areas of action (Porteus, 2008: 88–99).

Two years later, and two months after the campaign letters from MPH, Blair was visited by Bob Geldof. Out of this meeting – and as a result of Geldof's initiative by most accounts – Blair agreed to set up an expert panel charged with the task of devising a comprehensive and clear policy agenda to deal with poverty in Africa. The Africa Commission was established in February 2004, and met in March; it was staffed by 16 Commissioners selected by Blair, Geldof, and senior civil servants. The Commission's report was clearly aimed at the British government; it 'does not address an African audience to any significant degree' (Booth, 2005: 494). Furthermore, there is nothing in the Report which might be described as innovative; rather, the Report articulates and frames a policy agenda that has been extant for some years (W. Brown, 2006). It does this in a way that is bold, and it includes some strongly worded statements about the failings and responsibilities of the West.

Blair was strongly associated with the Commission and he strongly endorsed its Report. In the media, the common slippage was to call the Commission the 'Blair Commission'. He spoke of the report as a template for a new policy agenda regarding Africa. Its release in March 2005 integrated into the period in which MPH was really taking off, and focusing increasingly intensely on the G8. The report, *Our Common Interest* (Africa Commission, 2005), was officially presented to the G8 in Gleneagles, and referred to by Blair and Geldof and others in ways that blurred the distinction between MPH and the Commission. Blair and New Labour declared 2005 the 'year of Africa', not the year to end global poverty, again a phrase embraced by the media.

Thus, as MPH was publicly urging Blair to take their demands to the G8, Blair himself was presenting a public profile as a politician seized by the 'Africa problem'. In the media, the 'Blair Commission', the 'year of Africa', and MPH were often spoken of as indistinct. Blair's highly moralised public discourse on Africa, when speaking about *Our Common Interest* or MPH and the G8 led to a strong public shaping of the campaign as one focused on Africa, not poverty.

Equally, Brown – also formally an Africa Commissioner – toured some African countries and connected his domestic policy agenda of child poverty to his Africa agenda. After the Gleneagles MPH rally, Brown addressed Christian Aid in a way that sutured the campaign to the British government: 'We are today seeing Britain at its best, united for one great cause' (in Gorringe and Rosie, 2006: 16).

The assiduous cultivating of a 'now or never' African policy agenda through the Africa Commission Report and the public statements of Blair, Brown, and others[19] made many MPH coalition members uncomfortable. In interviews, members of the CT reflected on the blurring of MPH with New Labour and recognised that the campaign's popularity had proven to be a valuable piece of political capital for Blair and Brown. For some coalition members, this led to a party politicisation of their issues and policies and what was perceived as a fairly cynical opportunism, best manifested in the 'MP chic' of wearing white wristbands.[20]

For those campaign organisations that perceived of their relations with the government as adversarial – most prominently the World Development

Movement, but also Action Aid and War on Want – the fulsome embracing of MPH by New Labour was a symptom of the campaign's weakening and co-option. The justice-based campaign on behalf of the global poor had been 'hijacked' by a humanitarian campaign on behalf of 'Africa'.[21] However, it would be misleading entirely to accept the metaphor of hijacking. Some leading agencies within the coalition saw a close association with New Labour as advantageous to the campaign. These campaign NGOs networked with New Labour, appealed to Blair's liberal Christian world-view, and had no reservations in appealing to New Labour's self-representation as working in Africa's best interests. These NGOs have also developed a certain amount of circulation of personnel into and out of government and rely on British government funding for a sizeable portion of their development activities – facts that led more critical voices within the coalition to perceive of these NGOs as effectively co-opted by New Labour. In sum, then, the Africanisation generated by New Labour was not solely a political device by politicians; it was also a product of leading coalition NGOs believing that positive association with New Labour would benefit the campaign.

Celebrities

The previous section demonstrates how MPH lost some control of its campaign messaging as Blair and Brown positioned themselves as the champions of a new Africa development agenda simultaneously with MPH's focus on them as a target for lobbying and campaigning. This loss of control was manifest in the Africanisation of MPH, which Blair strongly shaped, something that members of the coalition were very aware of, not entirely comfortable with, but willing to concede to for as long as the political profile of the campaign continued to grow so rapidly. But, as 2005 wore on, MPH had also to deal with a range of other agencies which strongly contributed to the building public sensibility about Gleneagles. These agencies might usefully be grouped together as 'cultural producers', that is, those who create cultural products – music, images, publicity – that were either loosely part of MPH or closely associated with it. Here, the role of celebrities will be examined because they came to play a very powerful role in the campaign, especially in terms of public profile.[22]

There is a great deal that might be said about the strong celebrity endorsement of MPH, mainly through the wearing of the white wristband (cf. Richey and Ponte, 2008). It is certainly the general consensus within the coalition that the broad support of celebrities is what gave MPH such high levels of 'brand recognition'; but for those organisations strongly focused on lobbying and more issue-based campaigning, there were real concerns about the ways in which celebrities contributed to a trivialisation or perhaps even a complete forgetting of the issues. However, it is worth considering here two more focused points.

As mentioned in Chapter 7, the catch-all term 'celebrity' needs a little disaggregation. Some celebrities had a long track record of support for a specific NGO – these celebrities were brought in to MPH by an NGO which had briefed them regularly and perhaps taken them to projects in the Global South. Others had come into the campaign during 2004/5, generally to provide a public 'face' for the campaign, with no experience in issues of campaigning or development. A small number, notably Bono and Richard Curtis, were part of an MPH NGO and were therefore working within the coalition. Throughout 2005, there were two celebrities who gained very high public profiles and worked hard on promoting MPH or the Africa Commission and Live 8, focusing on the G8. Both Bono and Geldof came, de facto, to represent MPH in the public eye.

Bono is one of the founders of DATA (Debt Aids Trade Africa), which had a representative on the CT. As such, he was part of the MPH coalition. Because of his high public profile, and his ability to gain the attention of the media, Bono would speak about campaign issues more or less as he wished, although as part of DATA, his announcements fitted within the broad MPH umbrella. He gained his campaign personality especially through his addresses at the New Labour party conference in 2004, and the World Economic Forum at Davos in 2004 (Busby, 2007). Bono's focus throughout 2005 was Africa, reflecting his own personal convictions and the NGO which he founded, funds, and works for. In the preface to Jeffrey Sachs's book *The End of Poverty*, he speaks of Africa as 'an entire continent bursting into flames' (2005: xvi, emphasis in the original). He described his role during 2005 as follows: 'I represent a lot of [African] people who have no voice at all ... They haven't asked me to represent them. It's clearly cheeky but I hope they're glad I do' (in Hume, 2005). Bono's personal focus on Africa, and his public prominence complemented the other processes of Africanisation described above.

Geldof's role was perceived by many organisers of MPH as more problematic. Like Bono, he brought a very high public profile to MPH, but he was less well integrated into MPH. He was not formally linked to MPH at all, having no NGO affiliation. Having established himself as a 'campaign personality' since the mid-1980s, he acted and spoke to his own agenda, which certainly inter-related with MPH but not to a degree that would allow one to say that he was part of the MPH messaging strategy. Furthermore, he had his own connections and projects. He had established an 'inside track' with Blair which he used to promote the idea of the Africa Commission. Geldof assiduously promoted the importance of the Africa Commission – which had no standing beyond its support from Blair, Brown, and Geldof. He spoke about *Our Common Interest* as the defining policy platform for the G8, associating it with MPH which had not aligned itself with the report nor had any involvement with it. For Geldof, the key issue for the G8 was the implementation of the Africa Commission Report, not the meeting of the MPH poverty-related 'asks'.[23]

Geldof's public profile and his popularity with the media lent him an immense presence in 2005. He was perceived by the public as trustworthy and able to 'get things done'. And, more powerfully than Bono, Geldof associated 2005 with Africa. In early 2005, Geldof described himself, in characteristic style, as 'Mr bloody Africa' (*Daily Telegraph*, 4 February 2005). Since Band Aid (see Chapter 4), Geldof has championed African causes. He spoke constantly about Africa in his public statements, published books and produced TV programmes of his experiences in Africa, and – most notably – decided to organise the Live 8 concert in London.[24]

Live 8 was announced by Geldof unilaterally. Although he told members of the CT in camera that he might hold a concert, he did not engage with MPH about the concert and announced the date – which coincided with the G8 rally in Edinburgh – about two months beforehand, despite the fact that the rally had been planned far in advance of Live 8. Live 8 took the public gaze – or at least the English public gaze – from Edinburgh. The messaging of Live 8 was clearly all about Africa, and barely about justice. The Live 8 guitar icon is the African continent, an Ethiopian survivor of the 1984 famine was brought on stage by Madonna, and most of the rather overexcited statements by the musicians on that day related to Africa in one way or another. After the concert, a press release from Live 8 read as follows: 'last Saturday, Live 8 asked for $25bn per annum for Africa to attack the structures of poverty. And today Africa got it. No longer will the lives of the African poor be framed by charity, but rather defined by justice' (in Brown and Kelly, 2005: 25).

This statement illustrates how the MPH policy platform became confused by Live 8 and the Africa Commission, and how the G8 became about Africa when MPH had devised its focus on the G8 around poverty. The 'asking' for $25 billion also elides the charity-justice distinction by using a phrase that frames Live 8 as an appeal for money. Geldof repeated that Live 8 was not about charity, and there was no money raising associated with the concert. Nevertheless, Geldof also associated Live 8 with Live Aid[25] – and this was emotively performed through the use of the Ethiopian woman as a personal story of survival and recovery. A VSO report states that 'the effect of Live 8 ... does not appear to have been a positive one. For many, it has reinforced the fact that little or nothing has changed in the last 20 years, as the images of the event were similar to those in 1985' (Smith, Edge, and Morris, 2006).

The DVD of the concert is also sold as part of a package with Band Aid in a way that presents the two events as part of a single tradition: 'buy charity, get justice free' in the words of the director of one campaign NGO.

Geldof's prominence and independence from MPH generated a fair amount of ill-feeling within the coalition; and Geldof also became angry with some coalition members. The source of the specific tension between Geldof and MPH (which never came into the public realm) was partly his modus operandi and personality, but also his effect on the campaign. He had both promoted MPH as part of his view of 2005, but also confused and conflated MPH with his own Africa advocacy, Live 8, and the Africa Commission.

The tension between Geldof and MPH expressed itself most strongly when it became apparent that Live 8 in London would only host one African artist – Youssou N'Dour (who is a policy advisor for DATA) (see also Bond et. al, 2005). Geldof was steadfast that he would not accommodate any other African artists because he saw the concert's main aim to maximise public popularity and he judged that this would be best done by artists with very high record sales. Many within MPH saw this as morally counter-intuitive to their approach to publicity and messaging.

In sum, then, although many questions have been asked about the role of celebrities generally in campaigning, it is worthwhile taking Bono and Geldof separately because of their engagement with the G8, MPH, and their unique 'celebrity campaigner' public personas. What each of them did was to focus on Africa in their efforts to lobby Blair and to promote awareness of MPH. Geldof's role is especially important here as he was effectively acting independently of MPH, became the most prominent spokesperson during 2005, and because of his organising of Live 8. Live 8, like the Africa Commission, cross-referenced MPH, became associated with MPH by the public, and made the G8 about Africa and the ability of G8 leaders to solve its problems.

The media

MPH was part of a year which experienced a concerted creative effort to put Africa in the public eye. For MPH, this involved a great deal of effort focused on getting the media to propagate their messages; it also involved the use of advertising and public relations firms which, it was felt, would bring skilled and focused imagery to the campaign (Sireau, 2009).

MPH launched itself in the mass public eye with a Christmas special of *The Vicar of Dibley*. This episode was written by Richard Curtis, and starred Dawn French who is a long-standing supporter of Comic Relief and who was married to one of Comic Relief's founders. Dawn French led a delegation of women vicars to present an MPH petition to Downing Street. Curtis – who effectively took a year out during 2005 to dedicate his energies to Comic Relief and MPH – also wrote the drama *The Girl in the Café*, which told a story of how a G8 meeting might deal with global poverty if it had the right intentions. This film included the 'three-second click' reference, which was to become prominent during the build-up to the G8, used at Live 8 around the world and used by MPH until its adverts were withdrawn supposedly for being political. Taken together, the efforts of Comic Relief and Richard Curtis made a great contribution to the reach of MPH throughout the first half of 2005.

Each of these television moments was produced by the BBC. The BBC also had the broadcasting rights to Live 8, and was involved in the production of the event. As a result, each of these programmes had to go through BBC editing before their broadcasting, leading to a certain degree of 'toning down' of the political messaging. For the BBC, these MPH-related programmes fitted well with their 'Africa lives' season which ran throughout 2005 (Smith, Edge, and Morris, 2006: 7–10). This integrated into the G8 build-up, the New Labour 'Year of Africa', and the prominence and dynamism of Comic Relief and Curtis, the latter of which is extremely well networked in the television industry. Comic Relief's involvement with the Global South is solely focused on Africa; the charity was set up after Live Aid as part of that moment in the mid-1980s when cultural producers became aware of Africa and the mass suffering therein. Because Comic Relief handled media relations on behalf of the coalition, there was always going to be a 'bias' towards Africa in the media, who associated MPH with Curtis and Comic Relief.

This programming was packaged as part of a broader cultural moment in which public attention was focused on Africa. In this way, the BBC co-authored the messaging and cultural production of MPH, Blair, and Geldof. Also the electronic media was accompanied by the print media which – by and large – embraced MPH, reported its messages, and in the process helped construct a broad public awareness of Africa, the G8, and the campaign itself.

MPH worked hard to engage the newspapers. The plan was not just to get the message into the broadsheets, and there was an assumption that especially the *Independent* and the *Guardian*, as 'middle-class' papers that had covered debt, trade, and aid in some detail, would be willing to carry pieces related to MPH. MPH also, then, made an effort to get sympathetic coverage from the tabloids, which it did in the *Sun* and *Daily Mirror*, the latter of which editorially aligned itself with MPH.[26] The tabloids' coverage of MPH was strongly skewed towards Africa. For example, a prominent and very supportive article urged readers to attend Live 8 (no mention of the MPH Edinburgh rally) largely through the personality of Bob Geldof (dubbed 'Mr incredible' by the writer): 'He wants this gig to be free and hopes that it will put massive pressure on the G8 leaders to vote to end poverty in Africa' (*Sun*, 7 May 2005). Later in the same article, 'Live 8 will give US President George Bush and Prime Minister Tony Blair a unique opportunity to make the changes that will bring an end to poverty in Africa forever'. The *Sunday Herald* stated that in Edinburgh, the MPH rally would 'draw attention to poverty in Africa', going on to relate the rally to Live Aid and Geldof (8 May 2005). The personalities of Bono and (especially) Geldof were foregrounded in many newspaper stories.

Once the *Daily Mirror* and the *Sun* supported MPH, both found themselves receiving cheques from readers who thought that MPH was a charitable campaign to 'help Africa' (interview with CT member, April 2007). The charitable morality remained prominent throughout 2005 in fact. The prominence of Bob Geldof – who was not part of the MPH campaign but came to play a pivotal role as the G8 summit approached – strongly 'Africanised' the charitable morality that remained within the public realm. This was in the first place a result of his considerable public persona which goes back to his place in the Band Aid/Live Aid campaign of 1984/5 which was focused on Africa. During 2005, Bob Geldof also worked with Tony Blair in the devising of the Africa Commission which – in Geldof's view – was interlinked with MPH. Finally, the Live 8 concerts Africanised MPH by linking closely with the campaign and the G8 and explicitly linking to Africa. The Live 8 guitar was shaped like the continent, and Birhan Woldu, an Ethiopian woman who has survived the famine of 1984, was presented on stage by Madonna, resuscitating the Band Aid association. Furthermore, although all interviewees asserted that MPH was not about Africa, but about poverty, some did recognise that the stories and images that were used were almost entirely based in African case studies. Despite encompassing massive numbers of extremely poor people, India and China did not feature at all.

Collectively, the newspapers, guided by the same motives as the BBC, aimed both to associate themselves and shape a broader public focus on Africa. Particularly guided by a sense of British nationalism that pervades the tabloids in most of its coverage of sport and foreign affairs, reportage helped construct that image of British civic humanitarianism that was at the heart of MPH, the Gleneagles rally, and various lobbying actions. For MPH, the enthusiastic embrace of the campaign by the media was very welcome, and indeed was at the heart of the coalition's strategy, which maintained a very active Media and Messaging Working Group. But the success of the media campaign – much like the success with engaging New Labour – led to a loss of control for MPH. The campaign was promoted and integrated into a broader 'movement' which included Blair's 'year of Africa', the BBC's 'Africa Lives', and a range of different editorial decisions by newspapers to bring Africa, poverty, and the G8 summit indistinctly to public attention.

Africa campaigning and the global social justice movement

This chapter has argued that MPH contained within in it a tension between a desire to set out a case for social justice for the global poor, a failure to set out clearly how (and over what time period) this might be done, and the temptations of familiar – indeed traditional – references to Africa as a moral concern within the British polity and public culture more broadly. The imperial legacy of the African presence in Britain means that any campaign that focuses on this continent will encounter great difficulty escaping tropes of charity, disaster, and salvation which have been the mainstays of Africa campaigns from abolition through to the present day. MPH did not escape these tropes, not simply because of its own design but because its success was closely interlinked with its ability to network into three other agencies that focused on the Gleneagles G8 summit: the New Labour government, celebrity activists, and the media. It would hardly be useful to assign culpability for the way in which MPH lost its social justice message and attained an 'Africa focus', although it bears emphasising that it was very much the 'Africanisation' of the campaign that served to achieve such high levels of public recognition and support, as subsequent surveys have illustrated.[27]

The case of MPH's 2005 campaign suggests that although the 'second other' that Africa represents might be distant and very sketchily configured (black, poor, lacking, etc.), it has immense resonance within British public and political culture which makes it a seductive component of any campaign framing that wishes to attain quick and widespread recognition and response from society generally. As a result, MPH illustrated how difficult it is to frame Africa within a British campaign for global social justice. This was something that many campaign member organisations were well aware of. It would seem that prospective campaigns for social justice will face two key challenges: how to reframe Africa in less distant and traditional imperial ways, and how to challenge rather than work with prevailing assumptions and values within Britain.

MPH encapsulates an internal tension within the Africa campaign tradition, one that has been more prominent in some instances than others. This is between what we have defined as the Africa campaign tradition throughout this book and insurgent tendency, more akin to what is now coined as campaigning for global social justice. This section considers this tension in order to reinforce the message in Chapter 7 that Africa campaigning is currently more multifarious than it has been before and that this is partly as a result of the impacts of globalisation on national identity and the nature of political agency more generally. It also does this to emphasise the limits of the Africa campaign tradition. More positively, this section opens up ways of thinking prospectively about the Africa campaign tradition.

The Africa campaign tradition has always contained a radical thread that has attempted to broaden campaign issues out from the immanent critique of British involvement in Africa and towards something concerned with African social movements, a more profound questioning of the British state, and with more globalised and systemic representations of politics. Within abolitionism, there was a thread of campaigning on the basis of labour solidarity which connected the inequities of British capitalism at home with those over the Atlantic. Anti-colonial movements were in some cases attached to an advocacy of Marxism-Leninism (the Mozambique Angola Committee being the best example). The Anti-Apartheid Movement contained socialist politics emerging from students' involvement. Also, War on Want and the World Development Movement – campaign NGOs that were active within the Jubilee 2000 and MPH coalitions – have also advocated anti-imperialist politics. It was these two NGOs that were least happy with the way that MPH was developing.[28]

To repeat, these currents have been insurgent rather than dominant. As argued throughout the book, Africa campaigns have worked within a historical tradition of affirming a virtuous Britishness, and as a result any globalised/non-nationalist and socialist/revolutionary politics is submerged within layers of campaign framing based in the framing detailed in Chapter 1.

Nevertheless, things change. In the 1990s, a bundle of forms of activism emerged that have been collectively defined as a global social justice movement. Most drastically debuted at the inaugural summit of the World Trade Organisation, these activisms have a shared values aptly summarised as follows:[29] a struggle for labour, environmental,[30] and human rights; a desire to democratise global governance; 'bottom up' structures of authority, global equality in wealth and power; sustainable development. These values generate different frames to those within the Africa tradition. As Sandberg (2006) sets out in an article that uses framing to understand ATTAC Norway, diagnostic framing tends to be set in terms of global structural problems. Prognostic frames are globalised as well: Tobin tax, the abolition of tax havens etc. Motivational framing is based on the evocation of a rising *global* movement (which may or not actually be the case). Thus, the framing of the global social justice movement is both globalised and structural – two facets in contradistinction to the Africa campaign tradition framing. As Brecher *et al.* (2000) argue, the 'us helping them' norm is being replaced by a norm of global common interest.[31]

The presence of global social justice campaigns has affected the Africa campaign tradition in ways that enhance the sense that the tradition is going through unprecedented change. One part of the story of Jubilee 2000 is its transformation from a moderate and Christian campaign towards something more akin to a movement for global social justice. One can get a clear sense of this in the very distinct accounts of Jubilee 2000 from Dent and Peters (1999) and Mayo (2005). After Jubilee 2000, Jubilee South was created as a more 'global social justice' way of attacking debt. An analogous scission took place within MPH. During 2005, global social movement groups and African diaspora groups in the UK[32] were increasingly unhappy about the 'whiteness' of MPH and its political nationalism. There was also some tension generated by the decision by MPH to exclude anti-war groups from the rally in Edinburgh. Associating the wars in Iraq and Afghanistan with global poverty represents the British government as part of the problem rather than part of the solution and this was the key reason for the Stop the War Coalition's exclusion from the protest. As a result of the perceived dominance of British organisation within MPH, the Global Call to Action Against Poverty (G-CAP) was created as a 'Southern' organisation that expounded a more explicitly anti-imperialist approach to global poverty.

It would seem reasonable to suppose that if the global social justice movement persists and perhaps grows, the internal tensions within the Africa campaign tradition will also grow. But, the relationship between the two trends is unlikely to be highly correlated, and this is because of the place of Africa not only within British imperial and post-imperial sensibilities but also Africa's place within the politics of global justice. Outside of South Africa and to a lesser extent Ghana, Kenya, and Zambia, the global social justice movement has only very tenuously managed to engage with social and political organisations in Africa (Larmer, 2007a; 2007b). Geographically, global social justice movements have encapsulated European, North American, Latin American, and South East Asian organisations.[33]

For the global social justice movement, African poverty poses some challenges. Poverty in Africa is generally not a result of labour conditions in a sweatshop or a plantation. Nor has landlessness been a major source of political struggle – although 'land grabs' have increased a great deal since the mid-2000s. Poverty is often the outcome of the conditions of labour and trade within and between low productivity agrarian livelihoods and casual or temporary labour on commercial farms, petty trade, and informal business. The ability of the poor to organise and represent themselves through official organisations is relatively low, and research suggests that poor people tend to advocate their interests through informal, kinship, and religious conduits which are difficult to 'map' into the grand narratives of global social justice.

The 'articulation' of African livelihoods with capital is complex and often indirect – certainly distinct from the scourges of rapid and highly exploitative proletarianisation. There is a lot to unpack here, but for our purposes it is simply to register that global social justice movements have not succeeded in engaging with African poverty, struggle, and exploitation to the degree they have in South Asia, East Asia, or Latin America. As a result, in Britain at least, 'Africa' remains generally within the remit of the Africa campaign tradition.

Conclusion

This chapter has reviewed in some detail a high point in Africa's presence within British public spaces. Between MPH, the government, celebrities, and the media, Africa and its association with poverty became familiar to millions. It has shown how deep aspects of the Africa campaign tradition came to shape the year: the focus on a virtuous Britain/Briton, the sense of an agent-less and indigent Africa as the moral focus of campaigning, and a strong aspirational sense that Britain (or Britain leading the G8) could make heroic differences to global poverty. But, if 2005 was a re-assertion of the Africa campaign tradition, then this was not entirely successful. There emerged out of 2005 a sense of the limitations of MPH's British orientation, but there was also a fair amount of equivocation within the major campaign NGOs.

Campaigners within the MPH coalition were clear on MPH's successes in generating mass public support and indeed maintaining coalition unity in difficult circumstances. But, two major issues led many to reflect cautiously on the fortunes of MPH. In the first instance, the G8 announcements on aid, trade, and debt were disappointing. Although MPH's responses were generally warm towards the G8 declaration, behind the scenes many were very disappointed and even angry. For those who considered MPH's relations with New Labour to be too close, there was a sense of disillusioned vindication. Secondly, MPH's own surveys suggested that popular engagement with MPH had remained shallow and that there had been little success with the 'migration' strategy.[34] As MPH closed, campaigners often felt that they had gained little in terms of new campaign energy. Many local groups who had used MPH as a banner to generate new interest in local activism were very concerned that MPH as a brand (owned by Comic Relief) was now only used as a 'legacy' reference.[35] That is, MPH could not be used in any new active campaigning.[36] In other words, MPH's successes were in part illustrations of its limitations, limitations which can be understood as deriving from the way the Africa campaign tradition frames Africa.

Notes

1 HIV/AIDS was added as a key campaign issue.
2 In fact, because of the effects of the tsunami in early 2005, the main spatial reference in January was to the Indian Ocean basin.
3 It is worth noting the fact that trade reform was always relatively underspecified and unclear in relation to the other two policy areas.
4 MPH aimed to focus on WTO and UN meetings during that year as well, but these attained far less public significance.
5 The Coordination Team constituted the hub of MPH, staffed by 17 representatives of the main campaigning organisations and meeting usually once per week.
6 'Will they be trade heroes or zeros?'
7 During 2005, the MPH logo could be used by coalition members for their own campaigning; thereafter the copyright has been held by Comic Relief and only used occasionally as a 'legacy' reference.
8 Previously Jubilee 2000, and Drop the Debt.
9 South Asia and China together contain the majority of the world's poor. India – with a population of nearly 1 billion, had 44.2 per cent of its population living on less than a dollar a day in 2005. These people barely figured throughout 2005.
10 This shorthand was used by some interviewees.
11 In the event, the campaign struggled to maintain itself after the Gleneagles summit in July.
12 Live 8 was created by Bob Geldof separately from MPH, but was associated with MPH in popular perceptions.
13 The outcomes regarding trade were always more complex, and in any case competence in this area rested mainly with the WTO and the European Commission.
14 Relatedly, Africa is by and large the only spatial assignation within contemporary development nomenclature. See Chambers and Alfini, 2007: 496.
15 Note the nomenclature here. The VSO report was partly a result of a commissioned piece of work by a marketing company. To recall the previous two chapters, we see here an example of how NGOs tend to see the British public as consumers within some kind of marketplace.
16 Relatedly, and more broadly, David Chandler (2007) argues that British government foreign policy has been increasingly articulated as self-image. See also Gallagher, 2009.
17 There is an irony in this title in that the Monterrey agreement stipulates that debt relief should not count against commitments to increase aid, but many G8 countries did this as part of the Gleneagles commitments.
18 The full text of this speech can be found at www.hm-treasury.gov.uk/newsroom_and_speeches/press/2005/press_09_05.cfm, accessed 23 July 2009.
19 It is notable that DFID and Hilary Benn enjoyed a lower profile than might have been expected throughout 2005.
20 These concerns were expressed to journalists during 2005. (Hodkinson, 2005; Quarmby, 2005).
21 Both Blair and Brown routinely anthropomorphised Africa as a single entity, almost

as a single person. See for example Blair's 2001 speech and Brown's article in *New Economy* (2004).

22 A survey commissioned by World Emergency Relief found that 42 per cent of respondents believed that MPH was set up by Bono and Geldof. See WER press release 'G8 will make no difference', September 2005.

23 'We have a doable plan, it is called the Commission for Africa. That is what I have come here [Gleneagles] for, to see that fulfilled ... ' Geldof, at press conference with Blair, 6 July 2005, www.number-10.gov.uk/output/Page7843.asp, accessed 23 July 2009.

24 A sense that Geldof is in some sense globally powerful is softly suggested by Geldof himself and also promoted by the media and other public spokespeople (Clark, 2004; Hewson, 2006: 135). In a letter which was written by Geldof (not for public dissemination) to the producer of the critical documentary *Starsuckers*, Geldof reacts viscerally to the suggestion that he is less than qualified to speak about Africa.

25 And, Bono was a prominent performer in both events.

26 The *Daily Mail* was the least involved tabloid newspaper.

27 A rigorous Public Perceptions of Poverty survey taken throughout 2005 suggested that the 'justice not charity message was not clearly understood by the mass audience, many of whom persisted in believing that MPH was aiming to raise fund for Africa' (Darnton, 2006: 10).

28 And it was from within these two organisations that anonymous interviews were given which argued that MPH had become captured by New Labour.

29 Adapted from Brecher, Costello and Smith, 2000: Chapter 5.

30 The notion that the environment – or a specific ecosystem – has rights is, of course, contested. Normative political theory has enough trouble with the ideal of human rights!

31 This passage is making a point about *framing*, not the actual practices of global social movements. There is enough evidence both of continuing dominance by Western organisations and a certain degree of hyperbole about the current state of global social justice movements to require us to remain cautious about the power and prospects of global social justice movements.

32 This was related to me very strongly by Explo Nani-Kofi, Director of the Nkrumahist African Liberation Support Campaign Network. His organisation was one of those marginalised from MPH because of its declared connection between global poverty and the war in Iraq.

33 This can be seen in the relatively weak presence of Africa references in key global social justice and global civil society books.

34 2.2 per cent of MPH's list of those registered through their website migrated into coalition members' organisations (Hilder *et al.*, 2007: 49).

35 A strongly worded open letter was written to express these concerns. 'The future of Make Poverty History', written by Joanna Brown, Mary Keynes, Ben Margolis, Mahmoud Messkoub, and Bill Phelps: 12 December 2005.

36 The reason for this was that the large NGOs were concerned that if MPH continued it would become a rival brand in an already crowded 'marketplace' of NGO campaign brands. The issue of branding is discussed in Chapter 5.

9

Conclusion

This book has narrated a certain kind of representation of Africa within Britain. It has looked at the Africa campaign tradition as an iterated project: building and modifying a certain kind of framing which is, in essence, about British virtue. It has shown, however, how this tradition is defined as much by change as continuity, and Chapters 7 and 8 have suggested that perhaps in the present day, the Africa campaign tradition is more open, more complex, and more changeable than it has been before. This final chapter will explore some of the possibilities presented by this sense of the present.

Hubris and sadness: campaigns and the print media

During research for this book, I undertook a search of the British broadsheet newspapers for all stories on Africa between 2004 and 2008.[1] This was to get a sense of how public discussions about Africa developed during and after the Year of Africa. The increasing networking between representations of Africa was clear during the 'year of Africa' when campaign organisations assiduously brought the media into their framing. It seemed interesting, therefore, to explore the impact that this engagement might have had on media output after 2005.

It is striking that there are distinct 'moods' generated within the print media text. During 2004 and 2005 – the build-up and events of the Year of Africa – there is a sense of ebullience which was mapped in the previous chapter. After 2005, the mood changes. Discussions about the execution of the 2005 G8 commitments is replete with disillusion concerning the failure to meet targets, or acerbic debate about the political repercussions of this. The sense of 'history' and aspiration is entirely absent. In terms of foreign news reportage, from 2006 to 2008, the topics focused on are: the Darfur conflict, Zimbabwe's electoral violence, Somali pirates, Kenya's fraudulent elections, and war in the Democratic Republic of Congo (DRC). And, within the reportage, a distinct set of normative issues were prominent. These are adumbrated below with some illustrative examples, although no claim is made as to their hierarchy.

There is a frequent invocation of Britain's moral duty *vis-à-vis* Africa. This moral duty was expressed as deriving from both a sense of Britain's power or global leadership, or from its historic interactions with Africa. In regard to Zimbabwe, the notion of moral reasoning for intervention or tougher punitive measures was commonly expressed. A *Times* article states that 'history demands that Britain acts' (31 March 2008). Both of these moral appeals clearly derive from a sense of post-imperial melancholia or nostalgia (Gilroy, 2004; cf. Bush, 2006: 184). The narrative tends to despair of African politics, pose the possibility of British intervention, but equivocate over the consequences of the latter. *The Guardian* even quotes John Gray's statement that Britain suffers from 'post-imperial nostalgia' in regard to Zimbabwe (5 November 2008). This discourse evokes the possibility that Britain has a preternatural mandate to act in the name of a universal code of order, civilisation, or human rights. The implication here is that there was something in Britain's imperial past that was morally upstanding,[2] but that its resuscitation was hard to envisage. Embedded within this discourse, then, is a continued sense of British grandeur – a grandeur that is much needed in the present day because of Africa's[3] continuing crises.

If this aspect of broadsheet media journalism seems moderately confident in Britain's national duty to Africa, much of the rest of the text is not. A strongly argued case is often made that Britain has failed in its moral duty: The *Guardian* accuses the government of a 'failure of moral leadership' (16 December 2008). The indifference of the British government has, it is argued, left Africans in situations of crisis. The language here implies a certain kind of *sotto voce* post-imperial world-view by condemning Britain for 'tolerating' violence in African countries, a phrase that implies that Africa is somehow still under Britain's 'watch'. This is a despairing narrative, not an affirmative one. 'Should we allow Zimbabwe ... to plunge into barbarousness and chaos?' (*Daily Mail*, 26 July 2008).[4]

Another narrative on Britain and Africa questions Britain's right or duty to involve itself in Africa at all. This argument might refer to Britain's questionable abilities or motives. Regarding the former, the point is that Britain does not have the wherewithal to intervene because of resource constraints or because British politicians or military commanders don't have the requisite knowledge of the places into which they might intervene. The *Daily Telegraph* calls this naiveté (2 July 2008). Concerning the latter, Britain's interests are questioned especially by posing examples where Britain seems complicit with African states that have questionable human rights records: 'we've done enough damage' (*Guardian*, 25 June 2008). If this is the case, it is mooted, can Britain be trusted to intervene in the name of rights or justice elsewhere? There is also an associated argument that much of the British government's statements on African problems are the product not of concern for Africans but rather are the outcome of domestic political calculations – something most prominent at the end of 2008 when Blair made his last overseas visit as Prime Minister to Africa.

Thus, a reading of the 'quality' press's Africa coverage reveals a sense of uncertainty. This contrasts with the Africa campaign tradition in which British moral virtue and – as revealed especially in regard to 2005 – an aspirational sense that Britain could in some sense 'rescue' Africa from its poverty and hardship was present. In the cases covered by the print media, the poor are present but more distant: located behind complex social barriers: besieged but assertive sovereignties or confusing and militarised tapestries of clan and faction; at the end of unpredictable causal chains in which acts of intervention might not lead to the best outcomes for the poor and vulnerable.

African sovereignties and campaign representation

This, it seems, is revealing. The broadsheet press have a different remit to campaign organisations. As stated in Chapter 1, campaign organisations are motivated to mobilise and to put their political desiderata boldly on their sleeve. The newspapers have a far less prominent desire to advocate or mobilise (although they can do this, as the *Independent* commonly does). Also, news of Africa is not highly rated by editors compared with domestic news or news from Europe and the USA. Repeatedly, editorial decisions are made that seem to suggest that African crises are valued lower than those from the developed, generally white, and English-speaking world. So, there is far less of an imperative to engage people in Africa as a central point-of-reference; whereas for poverty and development campaigns Africa is the *central* point-of-reference.

The print media offer a distinct representation of Africa to that promulgated by campaign organisations. And, this distinction tells us something about the specific kind of Britishness that the Africa campaign tradition has generally cleaved to.

Normatively, the single issue that all of the newspaper discussion boils down to is the question of African sovereignty: its incompleteness and its persistence. Incompleteness in the sense that interventions take place in spaces of fluid and patchy structures of authority, often associated with what academics call failed states; persistent in that (however substantive internal sovereignty might be) African states can still evoke their territorial claims against intervention (in the way that Zimbabwe and Sudan have done throughout the 2000s). Reports on single-country issues express vexation concerning intervention as foolhardy, incapable, neo-imperialist, or inconsistent. In each case – often for worse rather than better in journalists' views – African sovereignty has created a discussion about proper British action that is vexed by the sovereignty of the state in question.

Within a lot of Africa campaigns tradition, African sovereignty is largely absent. Campaigns are formulated around development issues and a request that the British government act appropriately to (help) solve problems of poverty and underdevelopment. The core connection is issue (diagnosis) and action (prognosis and motivation) in which the role of an African government is largely absent. It is as if NGOs work with people in Britain and people in Africa, the former as good and wealthy citizens, the latter as good and impoverished peoples.

But, as is now well established in the literature on NGOs as agents for development, African states are important gatekeepers, mediators, and brokers of any NGO's operations (Gary, 1996).[5] Furthermore NGOs, and certainly multi- and bi-lateral donors, interact closely with African states, committing funds to projects effected through state institutions (Harrison, 2004). Also, there is plenty of evidence that poverty reduction and development can only take place on a national scale through the infrastructures of states; NGO operations and bilateral/multilateral aid lines can at best provide 'parametric' support to states, the latter of which only become 'developmental' in specific circumstances (Khan, 2010).

The Africa campaign tradition has taken cognisance of African states, but largely within a 'solidarity' trope rather than a development one. The Movement for Colonial Freedom advocated for African sovereignty against British colonialism; the Anti-Apartheid Movement in the UK became increasingly a British advocate for the ANC as government-in-waiting (Klein, 2009: 456); the solidarity campaigns focused on Mozambique, Angola, Western Sahara, and Eritrea were all closely connected with struggles against late or 'internal' colonialism and were also all closely connected with a liberation movement which fought to gain control of the state. Oxfam's development work in the 1960s attained more complex and involved relations with the Tanzanian government, but other examples of representations of sovereignty within the Africa campaign tradition are hard to find.

The media and campaign organisations provide the two most broadcast representations of Africa within British public spaces. It is striking, then, that they should contrast in this specific way: one centrally and anxiously focused on sovereignty and intervention, the other generally not foregrounding sovereignty at all. There are a number of reasons for this contrast which bring us towards a key aspect of the Africa campaign tradition, one which has been immanent throughout the foregoing chapters.

Close framing

Africa campaigns have relied upon a certain kind of framing: a diagnostic prognostic and motivational framing which has been fairly constant throughout the campaign tradition. As Chapter 1 sets out, the diagnostic is commonly based on an absence within Africa, the prognostic focuses on the agency of the British government (or perhaps other British agencies like humanitarian or development NGOs), and the motivational framing relies upon the notion of British public virtue. The strength of this framing derives from its cultural familiarity as a 'layered' legacy of the imperial age. But its strength is also a product of very *close associations* between the three frames, between diagnosis, prognosis, and motivation. This closeness is centrally a product of its Britishness. The introverted nature of this framing derives from its Janus-like quality: speaking about Africa within Britain; reflecting on the nature of British public morality through emergency appeals; considering Britain's place in the world through Africa and the advocacy of British government action therein. Britishness enables a very close association between frames, and this in turn allows campaigns to be more effective: the moves from problem, solution, and agency are easier to make.

The way in which Africa campaigning is framed does not require a strongly figured representation of African sovereignty. Furthermore – unless the campaign diagnostic concerns liberation – this framing would lose some of its strength if it introduced a strong notion of African national sovereignty. As argued in Chapter 1, and as was exemplified in Make Poverty History (Chapter 8), Africa is represented as a very distant other – often aggregated into a single African space (rather than a mosaic of diverging sovereignties and political economies). Any strong formulation of African sovereignty would not only shift the normative location of African sovereignty but it would necessarily disrupt the close, introverted, and nationalist framing that the Africa campaign tradition has cleaved to.

Indeed, this point is best illustrated in the ways that campaigns have dealt with the issue of corruption. African governmental corruption remains a key bugbear for campaigns:[6] during interviews campaigners would often mention corruption as a key concern held by the British public which stymied their propensity to donate or involve themselves with campaigns. Chapter 7 showed how NGOs used a conflation of development, campaigning, and donation appeal based on a series of its own 'vox pops' which were meant to reflect prevailing public attitudes, the key one of which was 'I'm not giving my money to a corrupt leader in Africa'. Campaign organisation surveys have also identified popular concerns with corruption as part of their evaluations as to whether to donate or engage. One of the main criticisms of Jubilee 2000 was that debt relief would reward corrupt governments that had accrued debt through 'white elephants', laundering, and graft.[7]

If governmental corruption has been one of the most 'sticky' issues of campaigns, then its awkwardness derives not only from real (and sometimes legitimate) concerns as to the destination of money or the performance of development projects, but also to the complexifying and destabilising nature of corruption because it introduces African statehood into the framing. How does this affect campaign framing?

Diagnostically, the notion of a (developmental) *absence* remains but is also accompanied by a (political) *presence*: the agency of African states which (for better or worse) profoundly calibrates the efficacy of British intervention. In extremis, corruption can render interventions useless if projects fail because of excessive resource 'skimming'. The sensitivity of this issue can be seen in the remarkably prominent controversy over Martin Plaut's claims that Band Aid relief money was being sequestered by the Tigrayan People's Liberation Front for their guerrilla forces. This led the BBC to make a public apology and it provoked Geldof to make one of his characteristically terse attacks.[8]

Prognostically, British intervention is rendered not as directly beneficial and powerful, but rather as complex and perhaps limited in its scope. African governments, it seems, can deceive, flatter, and obfuscate when faced with interventions from outside in ways that undermine the notion that – should a campaign be successful – intervention will 'work'.[9]

Motivationally, concerns with corruption work against the liberal humani-tarianism that campaigns evoke and draw upon. If these virtuous norms serve as the motivational framing, concerns with corruption introduce a facet of cynicism into the emotional repertoire of the British public: Africa becomes not simply a space in which an absence can be righted through meritworthy intervention but also a space in which African governments might be fraudu-lently undermining the expected connections between concern and action.

In sum, concerns with corruption lend African governments agency. Africa's place as distant other in need remains but is disrupted by a repre-sentation of African statehood as corrupt. The close connections between diagnosis, prognosis, and motivation remain but are loosened by concerns with corruption. One might reasonably speculate that concerns with cor-ruption generate anxieties about British agency (civic or governmental): is intervention ill-conceived or impotent? These kinds of questions – evoked by the corruption issue – bring campaign discourse a lot closer to the broadsheet media reportage. Outside of concerns with corruption, the representation of African sovereignty is almost entirely absent, a feature which ensures that campaign framing remains closely integrated and embedded in a national cultural context.

Liberal and populist

This study will remain with the question of corruption a little longer to develop a second explanation as to why African sovereignties are weakly represented within Africa campaign framing. The basic point here is that, for campaign organisations, the broad normative framework does not endow African state sovereignty with much ontological importance. As noted in Chapter 1, the Africa campaign tradition has been characterised by a moral lineage that has been based on Christian liberal universalism, the former being progressively effaced by the latter, at least discursively. As is well-known in studies of the history of political ideas, liberalism – and many unorthodox forms of Protestantism – have tended to endow many states with an attenuated or conditional sovereignty.[10] This is because the foundational ontology of these traditions starts with the individual as rights bearer or moral being (embodiment of the soul). Subsequently, other collectivities or institutions retain at best secondary status as reflections of a common (and unconstrained) will or protector of rights relations (both freedom to and freedom from).

Concretely, for campaign organisations, this has been reflected in the sense of direct or minimally mediated connections between the British people and the African people via campaign organisations. This is most easily articulated when a campaign's main aim is to liberate Africans from a form of political oppression: slavery or apartheid being key examples, although debt was also portrayed mainly as an external burden upon Africans rather than a series of expenditure items connected to the external accounts of states. In these examples, campaigns were framed prognostically as the freeing of ordinary Africans from unjust political and economic systems. The oppressed African could remain fairly poorly detailed and generic; the British public could be entreated to join a political movement to liberate Africans; and a connection between freedom and rights in Africa and propriety in Britain could be maintained. There is no need for considerations of African state sovereignty within this moral universe.

Campaigning has been both invigorated and possessed by development NGOs since Band Aid. Throughout the 1980s, NGOs presented themselves (and were represented) as grassroots organisations that dealt with 'communities'[11] (Chambers, 1983). This self-portrayal purposefully drew upon an anti-statist and populist discourse of getting resources to the people who needed it and doing bottom-up development. It also merged with the major representational change analysed in Chapter 6, in which NGOs developed positive imagery of Africa by focusing on individual stories and communities rather than children and famine.

The populist turn in NGO discourse reflected in the rise of grassroots development and the shift towards positive campaign and appeal imagery based in life-stories and community projects helped consolidate a representation of campaigning as a direct connection between British supporters and donors and Africans in the sites where NGOs were active; the presence of the state was minimal. This can be seen as an iteration of the moral DNA of the Africa campaign tradition in which the moral focus of campaigns is the individual and the sovereignties within which distant others dwell are negligible or morally ephemeral.

In summary, the contrast between the Africa campaign tradition and the print media appears to be based centrally in different representations of sovereignty. This difference is not incidental; rather, it is a key facet of the close and nationally introspective framing of campaigns. The closeness of the framing results from the sense of agency generated by campaign representations and also from the broader normative structure within which the Africa campaign tradition operates. To reduce it to its bare bones: direct, simple campaign action to free Africans or intervene to deal with a crisis based in lack.

Prospects for the Africa campaign tradition

The brief comparison of campaigning and media representations follows a similar line of argument to the comparison of the Africa campaign tradition and movements for global social justice. Both comparisons tend to highlight the specific boundaries within which the campaign tradition works. Africa campaigns enjoy a long and powerful sense of tradition, but the verso of this strength is that it appears relatively constrained in its framing compared with movements for global social justice and it appears relatively weak in its ability to represent African sovereignties when compared with the (generally more conservative) broadsheet media.

This observation has broader connotations. It is not simply that these comparisons discern some *differentia specifica* of the Africa campaign tradition; it is also that campaigns work within a public space that is now more dense with representation than ever before, and this has had an effect on the African presence more generally. Chapter 8 showed how dense and integrated representations of Africa can become, between campaign organisations, the government, the media, and celebrities. Chapter 7 related how contemporary representation takes place within a more 'commoditised' and globalised context in which Britishness certainly still matters a great deal, but the ways in which it matters are strongly affected by a dynamic and powerful set of global processes.

There is some real novelty here. Patterns in African development and Africa's place in the world are changing, and more interestingly, changing in new ways. Some African countries are growing economically, new or enhanced economic relations with non-Western countries such as China, India, and Brazil have been consolidating themselves.[12] Britain's place in the world continues to change in ways that move it away from its imperial nationalism.

In one sense, Africa's representation has become more banal as it has begun to move into the remit of global circuits of commodity flow. The South African hosting of the football World Cup in 2010 revealed this. The South African government and companies involved with the World Cup made considerable efforts to brand South Africa in ways familiar to mainstream tourism: exotic but in ways that conform to the consumer vision: colourful, enjoyable, accessible. For a while, the vuvuzela horn became a commodity fetishised as African 'spirit'. Cadbury's advertisements at the time relayed fantasies of vibrant townships in the same spirit.

Perhaps the most illustrative exemplar of Africa's 'banalisation' is the film *District 9* (2009). The film uses a thoroughly American genre – the Alien invasion – in a South African context. Almost all major films about Africa that preceded *District 9*[13] implicitly took on a certain kind of moral narrative not dissimilar to the media's liberal vexations: of humanitarian crisis, agonistic responses, and commonly a narrative arc based in Western involvement in Africa. Think of *The Constant Gardener*, or *Blood Diamond*. In contrast, *District 9* can be viewed as an 'alien film', or as a playful engagement with South Africa's unstable post-apartheid negotiations towards nationhood, but it cannot be thought of as an iteration of the liberal dilemma about African absences and Western interventions.

This argument here is not striving to play up Africa's purloining by the global media or international commodity aesthetics. It is simply to recognise that these forms of representation generate different framings of Africa which – when taken together with the media, governments, and celebrity – give a palpable sense of turbulence and complexity to Africa's representation. And this representational prolixity affects the Africa campaign tradition. But, this is not necessarily a 'declinist' argument that 'tradition' is in recess. As we have seen, campaigns can tap into broader cultural and representational currents in order to disseminate messages. They can try to subvert common representations by deploying irony and play. But, there is also a real sense in which campaign organisations need to 'defend' their space in the public gaze if they are to maintain a coherent identity.

This is a tricky balancing act. Campaigns need to maintain a strong identity – often now articulated through the language of branding – and they also need to remain culturally familiar, that is, to be relevant, to connect with people, or to be 'cool' (which is a key reason for the rise of celebrity endorsement). The balance is only made more tricky by a paradox here: the main ways in which identity and cultural familiarity are produced tend also to homogenise campaigns. Branding and celebrity endorsement tend to make campaigns seem like any other 'sign' – as a choice presented to a consumer republic, as another portrayal of lifestyle or emotions amongst those relayed by firms, a variety of cultural producers, and even politicians and parties.[14]

Perhaps one fruitful way to explore these dilemmas and paradoxes is to consider a key argument throughout this book: that Africa campaigns have tended not to generate deep or close connections to African societies. Might it be that a renewed engagement with Africa would both allow campaigns to generate a clear identity in a public realm of signifiers and consumer choices and to revitalise the political aspects of campaigning?

Exploring this question is far from straightforward. The connections – real or desired – between campaign organisations and African associations raise many important issues. These issues go beyond those posed by the previous chapters and which relate to the Africa campaign tradition's imperial provenance, introspection, and nationalism. In a sense, the latter chapters have suggested that these aspects of the tradition are more in flux now than they have been previously. But if there is a window of opportunity for campaign organisations to explore 'African connections' more seriously, there are also issues relating to how these connections might work and especially how African socio-political landscapes relate to the politics of a campaign tradition based in liberal humanitarianism in a thoroughly Western format.

An obvious place to start in an opening-up of this issue lies in the term partnership. Here is the principal modality of political association within any liberal tradition: non-coercive, roughly egalitarian, and interactive. Indeed, as part of their development work, all of the large NGOs have African partner organisations who execute and manage projects. But these partnerships are more complex than the liberal framework allows. Most obviously, partnerships are constructed within a relationship between Western donor NGO and African recipient NGO (Fowler, 1992). There is an unequal material relation that underpins the ostensibly political relation of rough parity.

Furthermore, involvement in a Western NGO's project will change an African NGO: its own organisational structures, scale of operation, sense of priority, and discourse will likely orient towards the (anticipated) preferences of the external funder (Igoe, 2003). This might not be as crude as to produce 'suitcase NGOs' or 'new compradors' (Hearn, 2007), but it does suggest that NGOs depend not only on external funding but also that their values and discourse can be integrated into broader projections of legitimate development work generated by international NGOs.

As campaigns by civil society organisations (CSOs) in Africa gain recognition more broadly, perhaps capturing funding from campaigns in solidarity with the CSO, the deeper patterns of international inequality between Africa and Western campaigns will likely affect the dynamics of partnership. This is the case even at the most basic level of how civil society is defined and funded (Mercer, 2003) The Western and liberal[15] ideals of political action are written into the 'small print' of civil society, even in those forms of partnership that seem most open and equal (Hopgood, 2000).

Another cautionary point might be seen as even more profound: the initial act of 'seeing' an African social organisation cannot be undertaken outside of one's own cultural codes and language. To use the phraseology popularised by James Scott, African organisations would need to be made 'legible' by partner organisations in Britain or elsewhere in the West (Scott, 1998). Even highly articulate and self-reflexive 'solidarity' researchers can find it difficult to feel that they can achieve a full sense of comity with African struggles, and it is highly likely that campaign connections between Britain and Africa would (necessarily) be a great deal more rough and ready. Campaign NGOs in Britain would need to recognise that what they see in terms of African partner campaigns will be deeply conditioned by *how* they see.

This brings us to a closer focus in African politics, one which can only be averred here rather than fully explored. The basic point is that African politics – in all of its contemporary diversity – works within multiple logics, many of which are very different from the kinds of logics that British campaign organisations hold implicitly. Demands for resources, evocations of justice or right, references to metaphysical agencies, and repertoires of collective action can all be embedded in various forms of kin, ethnic, religious community (Kelsall, 2008; Schatzberg, 2002). Nor are these dynamics sealed off from Africa's CSOs and NGOs: on the contrary, hybridity and the layering of different forms of political inter-relation endow African sociability with a sophistication and fluidity that cautions any simple and discrete partnership between a Western campaign and an African partner.

This is not to argue that African politics is simply not 'up to speed' with the currents of campaign organisations, global social justice, or liberal humanitarianism. There are examples of vibrant CSOs throughout the continent and especially in South Africa. But this hardly captures African struggles for accountability, fairness, or assertion of agency. In many contexts, the modern liberal polity is a minority space, and this is so importantly because of the ways in which African political economies have developed. African capitalism is often characterised by hybrid and interstitial social relations: admixtures of trade, wage labour, and agricultural production based in fluid patterns of migration and social interactions. Relatedly, economies are as 'unofficial' as they are 'official'. Indeed, in countries where direct state control has been substantially relinquished, the 'official' economy seems to be something of a minority pursuit, an island of licensed trade and production surrounded by an ocean of partially state-regulated and 'informally' structured economic activity. It is within this context of political economy that hybridity, multiple forms of sociability, and an ability to 'straddle' different social realms is a distinct skill.

In sum, campaign organisations face a range of issues to negotiate if they are to engage with African organisations in ways that are not simply picking an organisation that seems amenable and generating a template within which partnership can be enacted. Representationally this leaves an open field, one in which the common imagery of the Africa campaign tradition seems rather out of place. One needs to start not by asking: 'how should Africa be represented?' but rather 'how might African organisations wish to represent themselves to a British audience and what role might campaign organisations play therein?'

Rethinking frames

The concept of framing has been used throughout this book. It is worth noting that the notion of framing has also been used by campaign organisers when reflecting strategically on the successes and limitations of campaigns. This has become most apparent with the publication of the *Finding Frames* report (Darnton with Kirk, 2011). This report speaks to the Africa campaigning community as a whole as was discussed in a workshop hosted by BOND in spring 2012. This final section considers how a more 'operationalised' approach to framing might be developed from the analyses of this book.

So, what does frame analysis do that is valuable and why is it becoming popular within campaign organisations' own reflections? Framing has been adopted by social movements studies to understand how political issues are represented in ways that define struggle. Frames produce a particular representation of a political issue, a sense of shared values, and a sense of what needs to be done. Frame analysis can be used to look at the ways campaigns set themselves out and try to develop communities with a sense of shared cause. For researchers, this means looking at campaign materials, and interviewing those who have engaged with a movement. For campaigners, frame analysis allows practitioners to reflect on the nature of their identification of issues, their representation of that issue, and its resonance within a broader public.

The diagnostic, prognostic, motivational triad has allowed us to see how Africa has been framed in a way that appeals to and reinforces a sense of public British virtue. But, as a way of understanding how campaigns might change or innovate, frame analysis has its limitations. Here, we come to a dichotomy described in Chapter 6: between broad and shallow campaigns (often based in famine imagery) and narrow and deep campaigns (based in development-rich 'positive' imagery). The focus of frame analysis begs a question: are successful campaigns ones that 'engage' a quite specific group in 'rich' campaigning and imagery; or are they ones that disseminate to a mass audience, expecting single discrete acts of recognition such as a single purchase, text or tweet.

Last year, Oxfam and DFID funded a research project to look at the ways development campaigning was framed which led to the *Finding Frames* report. This was mainly written by Andrew Darnton who had also written an influential evaluation of Make Poverty History, and the results were written up as a report for BOND. The report has a clear argument about framing. It says that development campaigning has generally become broader and shallower since the mid-1980s and perhaps most notably during 2005 when Make Poverty History was rolled out. The use of striking and simple messaging, celebrity endorsement, and the appeal to people as consumers made development campaigning ephemerally popular. But, this kind of framing also produced very limited engagement by those who briefly connected with development campaigning. The report argues that development campaigning needs to shift the balance back towards something more complex, politically infused; something that appeals not to people's sumptuary sensibilities but rather to their humanitarianism.

This sense of two rival motivational frames was drastically posed in a previous publication written for campaign organisations after Make Poverty History: Tom Hampson's *2025: What Next for the Make Poverty History Generation?* which contrasted a future in which campaigners appealed to people through branded appeals to consume, or through a revived Fabian sense of social responsibility. The booklet poses development campaigns as currently in something of a critical juncture – needing to make choices about which overarching frame to run with. *Finding Frames* suggests that this stark choice is pressing and that MPH left a difficult legacy for those who wish to construct deeper representations within Africa campaigns.

Framing dilemmas: deep and narrow, shallow and broad

This anxiety about a successful but 'shallow' form of campaigning has only been sharpened by the publicity attained by the RED branding and its ersatz campaign narrative.[16] Indeed, as different agencies of public address rely on marketing strategies to find a place within people's attention span, commodity producers and advertisers use campaign-like appeals to consumers just as campaign organisations use branding to appeal to potential members.

The use of framing as a way to reflect on the political content of development campaigns is significant. An explicit self-reflection of this kind has not happened since the late 1980s when leading NGOs made conscious decisions not to use famine imagery, but rather to portray Africans through 'human face' imagery. There are some parallels with that period as well. As we saw in Chapter 6, the debate within NGOs in the 1980s was that positive images (of Africans in communities, of Africans doing well on a small-scale basis, of context, of adults, etc.) might be good politics but famine imagery makes good impact, especially in regard to fundraising in emergency situations.

Now, the debate expressed through framing is that deep, politicised, or complex campaign messaging might be good for global social justice, but highly branded and celebrity endorsed campaigns have massive impact and generate high response rates. If there is some resemblance between these two periods (the late 1980s and the post-2005 period) of reflection and deliberation, it is based in a perceived opposition between a simple powerful publicity image which has broad impact, and a complex and less familiar set of images that might well fail to engage the vast majority of people.

But it is worth considering the extent to which this is quite the antinomy that it ostensibly appears. The adoption of codes of representation in the late 1980s did not stop campaign NGOs using famine imagery as and when deemed necessary. Closely related, Action Aid – one of the most explicitly political campaign and lobby NGOs – still has a boldly publicised child sponsorship scheme. Furthermore, all British campaign NGOs – regardless of how radical or strongly put their politics is – has a list of celebrities that associate with the cause.

In essence, then, it is evident that campaign NGOs can disseminate *inconsistent* imagery and that there might emerge moments when campaign managers find that development campaigns have become skewed or out of balance, but that this doesn't necessarily have to lead to a dichotomy, a choice between frames.

Extroversion and history

This is where perhaps an alternative approach might be found by thinking a little more about the strengths and weaknesses of frame analysis as strategy.

As mentioned earlier, frame analysis tends to focus inwards on the values and representations of a campaign community. In this sense, it is difficult to use frame language to understand a campaign organisation that produces incommensurate frames that appeal to different constituencies. But this is the reality for all large campaign organisations.

In this respect, frame analysis would benefit from a better connection with the fact that publics and institutions are both perfectly able to contain within them considerable difference and contradiction. One might imagine that if a development campaign organisation was producing divergent images to a strongly coherent and unified constituency, or a very specific representation to a highly differentiated public, there would be what might stylistically be called noise. But it is much closer to the mark to understand campaign organisations as internally differentiated (between fundraising, campaigning, development education, development projects, and lobbying) and embedded in a diverse and pluralised society. In this context, multiple frames and even inconsistent frames do not necessarily mean bad development campaigning. What matters is a clear strategisation of what kind of appeal frames might have and what expectations one might endow upon them.

The second relatively weak aspect of frame analysis relates to historical context. This matters a great deal in regard to development campaigning and especially in respect to the ways in which Africa is represented and understood within British public culture. There are two crude historical narratives to mention briefly here. One might be called the post-imperial sense of agency: that Britain has a long tradition of intervening for humanitarian and altruistic reasons to save or improve Africa. It is based on an implicit hierarchy in which Britain retains strong agency and Africa retains weak agency as victim or recipient. The second narrative relates to the period since the Biafra secession and is based on a more narrow representation of Africa as a place of extreme poverty, war, and famine. This broad framing is less about British agency and virtue and more about shocking imagery of human suffering.

Surveys repeatedly show how resilient the Africa–famine–extreme poverty association is. And it is an implicit assumption of a great deal of campaign discourse that Britain has a strong potential agency to develop Africa. A very powerful example of this was Make Poverty History in which a lot of the campaigning became a kind of aspirational narrative about the potential for the UK government and the public to eradicate poverty in Africa and elsewhere.

These two historical threads matter because they explain the prevalent public attitudes towards development and Africa in general British public culture. These tropes are extremely resilient. Thinking about mass involvement in campaigning can either mean working with these tropes – and in the process affirming them, or it can mean challenging them. Regarding the latter, one would have to accept that this would put campaign organisations in a position of trying to execute a not insubstantial project of social engineering. The closest example of this that I have found is a series of Oxfam advertisements about debunking myths that start with vox pop attitudes towards corruption, but these were not prominent and seem rather exceptional compared with the majority of campaign publicity. They are certainly outweighed by more familiar humanitarian appeals which resonate closely with the post-imperial and humanitarian frames.

More progressive frames that challenge social values are also part of a broader historical trajectory, associated with the rise of solidarity politics in the late colonial period and maintained through campaigns such as anti-apartheid and important aspects of Drop the Debt. Campaigning here has been consistently politically explicit and focused on political right before popularity. It has always been framed in more adversarial ways than the open and popular framing sketched above. This framing, it seems, is the one that the *Finding Frames* report is arguing should be given greater emphasis.

There are many good reasons for agreeing with this argument: frames based in notions of justice not charity, frames that see poverty as political, frames that allow for richer representations of the distant poor. But, this framing is largely for the 'already engaged', to use the campaigning language. It is a lot less clear how it might be used to engage new people, especially outside of those who are 'cognately engaged' such as those in the global social justice, environmental, or anti-war movements.

Perhaps there are differentiated engagements, associated with different frames. Is it a problem to work on the assumption that a society like Britain's will have radically different forms of engagement? The word 'engagement' needs to be unpacked. There are at least five possible processes at work:

- Vitalising existing memberships of campaigns to re-commit to deep involvement (commitment);
- Appealing to those who have been involved weakly in a campaign organisation to become more involved (migration towards);
- Appealing to those in cognate campaign arenas to bring their existing commitments into a new campaign area (migration across);
- Appealing to specific groups who are currently not involved in any cognate campaigning but who are in some sense civic or charitable to become lightly involved in a campaign organisation (affinity);
- Populist appeals to all to make a single simple discrete act of affinity to a campaign (recognition).

Each of these meanings of engagement connotes different approaches to framing, each of which – if associated with specific engagement goals – is consistent and coherent with development campaigning. Seeing frames as varied and historically and culturally embedded might lead to new and more finely tuned strategising.

This argument is simply a starting point and it might have different implications for different campaign organisations and different campaign issues. These implications are simply part of the uncertainty and politics of development campaigning. A more finely tuned notion of engagement breaks down the moral populism of 'the British nation' and also pares down the expectations of campaigning. But, it also opens up some space outside of the broad/narrow, shallow/deep dilemma.

But there is one significant question begged by this approach. Doesn't this varied framing strategy mean passively accepting the current state of affairs and working within it? Shouldn't development campaigning maintain an optimism of the will against the pessimism of the intellect in which campaigns hope to bring large numbers of people into causes that are often – in their best formulation – extremely difficult to disagree with? In other words, is there a sixth strategy?

- Populist appeals to all to encourage people to think differently about development.

I think that there is a way to answer this question in the affirmative and in a way that is consistent with the approach set out here. Firstly, part of the issue is to be clear on what campaign organisations can do. Campaign organisations are one kind of public address agency amongst many, and they work within an increasingly dense and complex media. This provides many opportunities: some campaign organisations have done fantastically well at innovating within cyberspace for example. But is also means that signals from different public address agencies contest intensively for attention. This simply means that campaign organisations are unlikely to be able to achieve many moments of high prominence and that when they do it is in specific circumstances: namely when campaign organisations work in coalition with each other and with other public address institutions, especially the print and electronic media. After all, those Africa campaigns that succeeded in prosecuting major changes in national values towards African issues did not work alone. Through extended periods of activism, campaigns such as abolition and anti-apartheid succeeded in interjecting their agendas into (parts of) the media and political parties. This also happened in regard to campaigns to drop debt. In closely related campaign areas – for example the campaign to abolish the use of land mines – similar processes have taken place, and have also involved engagement with other states and international organisations. This is the terrain upon which major normative changes are achieved: within coalitions, in a multi-institutional context, international, and over protracted periods.

It is in these specific circumstances that framing possibilities emerge and that the tension identified in the *Finding Frames* report becomes most apposite. In the latter sections of the report, the authors set out what are effectively a set of norms for the production of frames: the adoption of certain words and values over others (justice, mutual support, responsibility, engagements, etc.). The advantage of setting these out is that the report does not identify a code of practice or set of approved and disapproved images but rather a coherent set of coordinates within which to think about those specific moments when campaign framing has to negotiate the tension between popularity and a desire to move social values in a certain direction. This is where the general use of celebrity, high-profile branding, the values of consumption and easy engagement become inconsistent with the nature of the framing and where campaign organisations have as the task at hand the articulation of deep frames (to use the report's language) into a changing and complex society. These normative desiderata also open up possible interactions between the Africa campaign tradition and global social justice frames.

But this does not necessarily have to be a universal move. In other – more usual – circumstances, frames might have more modest consolidating, migrating, affinity, or recognition tasks. As ever, British political culture and indeed the nature of development issues is in a state of flux; having a suitably diverse repertoire of framing strategies seems to fit this situation rather well.

Notes

1 This was done by searching the CD-ROMs for all of the broadsheets in the UK initially using 'Africa' as a search string and then subsequently using finer search words to focus on British attitudes and norms. The search was narrowed by filtering only articles with 'Britain' and then Britain with one or more of the following: 'Britain should', 'Britain must', Britain could', and 'Britain ... moral'. The aim was to capture all normative discourse on Britain-Africa relations. This generated 158 articles. Op-eds were included.

2 Relatedly, two articles evoke one of the most powerful figuratives of the 'high' imperial era, calling Zimbabwe the former 'jewel of Africa' (*Daily Express*, 23 June 2008; *Daily Express*, 30 September 2008), a term used to describe India's centrality to Victorian empire.

3 Although articles commonly focus on a specific country, it is common that each country is 'projected' onto a wider representation of Africa' by speaking about 'countries like Kenya' or making comparisons with other African countries (commonly Rwanda as the archetype of intervention failure and Sierra Leone as the archetype of intervention success).

4 Incidentally, but relevantly, there is a tendency to 'Africanise' specific countries in order to imply general prejudices/assumptions about the nature of Africa, as mentioned elsewhere in the book. Thus the *Independent* speaks of 'countries like Zimbabwe' (28 December 2008) and the *Daily Telegraph* of 'countries like Kenya' (3 January 2008).

5 My own reflections on the nature of African sovereignty can be found in Harrison, 2007.

6 The other is 'compassion fatigue', a phenomenon discussed in Chapter 2. Campaign NGOs have also picked up a public concern that money is wasted on 'bureaucracy' or administration, a result of which is that NGOs very publicly portray the sectoral destination of donations and contributions in ways that visualise 'value for money'.

7 A concern reflected in scholarly concerns about 'moral hazard', i.e. the creation of incentive structures that reward the accrual of bad debt.

8 I spoke with a person centrally involved in Oxfam at the time, and he claimed that most humanitarian organisations knew that 'skimming' of this kind was taking place but made judgements that this was acceptable given the complexity and gravity of the situation. This kind of judgement – and analogous ones made by emergency organisations elsewhere – are discussed in De Waal, 1997.

9 In academic research, this argument has been put most forcefully and convincingly in van de Walle, 2001.

10 A well-known contemporary expression of this is Rawls, 2001.

11 It can be annoying to see every development term being put into inverted commas, but this is simply to signify that the word community can often misrepresent and simplify social collectivities. The term community is a mainstay of NGO work: one might say that 'community' makes African societies legible for international NGO work.

12 India–Africa relations might be described as fairly novel; China–Africa less so. On the latter, see the comprehensive and measured book by Brautigam, 2011.

13 Produced by Peter Jackson, with a South African director Neill Blomkamp.

14 On this scenario, see Hampson, 2006.

15 A quick note on terminology here: I think it is worthwhile now to use the term Western liberalism because – for better or worse – liberalism is no longer simply a Western possession, nor has it been for a good while.

16 There is a large critical literature on RED: Richey and Ponte, 2011; and a special issue of *Journal of Pan African Studies*, 2(6) 2008.

Bibliography

Abrahamsen, R. (2005) 'Blair's Africa: the Politics of Securitization and Fear', *Alternatives*, 30(1): 55–80.

Abugre, C. (2005) 'The G8 Brouhaha: hot air and little substance', *Pambazuka News*, no. 215, www.twnside.org.sg/title2/resurgence/179/cover1.doc, accessed 21 May 2010.

Achebe, C. (1977) 'An Image of Africa: Racism in Conrad's *Heart of Darkness*', *Massachusetts Review* 18: 782–794.

Africa Commission (2005) *Our Common Interest*. London, Africa Commission.

Agamben, G. (1998) *Homo Sacer: Sovereign Power and Bare Life*. Palo Alto, CA, Stanford University Press.

Akinyemi, A. B. (1972) 'The British Press and the Nigerian Civil War', *African Affairs* 71(285): 408–426.

Allen, R. (1986) 'Bob's Not Your Uncle', *Capital and Class*, Winter(30): 31–37.

Amin, A. (2010) 'The Remainders of Race', *Theory, Culture & Society* 27(1): 1–23.

Anderson, B. (1991) *Imagined Communities: Reflections on the Origin and Spread of Nationalism*. London, Verso.

Anderson, B. (1998) *The Spectre of Comparisons*. London, Verso.

Anderson, D. (2006) *Histories of the Hanged*. London, Phoenix.

Anderson, N. (2008) 'Shoppers of the World United: (RED)'s Messaging and Morality in the Fights against AIDS', *Journal of Pan African Studies* 2(6): 32–54.

Anstey, R. (1962) *Britain and the Congo in the 19th Century*. Oxford, Clarendon Press.

Anstey, R. (1975) *The Atlantic Slave Trade and British Abolitionism*. Houndmills, Macmillan.

Anstey, R. (1981) 'Parliamentary Reform, Methodism, and Anti-Slavery Politics, 1929–1833', *Slavery and Abolition* 2(3): 209–226.

Appiah, K. A. (1993) *In My Father's House: Africa in the Philosophy of Culture*. Oxford, Oxford University Press.

Armitage, D. (2002) *The Ideological Origins of the British Empire*. Cambridge, Cambridge University Press.

Austen, R. and W. D. Smith (1969) 'Images of Africa and the British Slave Trade Abolition: the Transition to an Imperialist Ideology 1787–1807', *African Historical Studies* 2(1): 69–83.

Autesserre, S. (2010) *The Trouble with the Congo: Local Violence and the Failure of International Peacebuilding*. Cambridge, Cambridge University Press.

Baaz, M. E. (2001) 'African Identity and the Post-colonial', in M. Baaz and M. Palmberg (eds), *Same and Other: Negotiating African Identity in Cultural Production*. Uppsala, Nordiska Afrikainstituttet, 5–23.

Barker, F., Hulme, P. Iversen, M. (eds) (1998) *Cannibalism and the Colonial World*. Cambridge, Cambridge University Press.

Barnett, A. (2005) '"Me Tarzan. Me save Africa." Jeffrey Sachs, the G8 and Poverty', *Open Democracy*, 4 July.

Barthes, R. (2000) *Camera Lucida*. London, Vintage.

Baudrillard, J. (1981) *For a Critique of the Political Economy of the Sign*. Ann Arbor, MI, Telos Press.

Bayart, J. F. (1993) *The State in Africa: the Politics of the Belly*. London, Heinemann.

Bedell, G. (2005) *Make Poverty History: How You Can Help Defeat Poverty in Seven Easy Steps*. London, Penguin.

Benthall, J. (2010) *Disaster Relief and the Media*. Wantage, Sean Kingston Publishing.

Biccum, A. (2009) *Global Citizenship and the Legacy of Empire: Marketing Development*. London, Routledge.

Black, M. (1992) *A Cause for Our Times. Oxfam: the First Fifty Years*. Oxford, Oxfam.

Blackburn, R. (1988) *The Overthrow of Colonial Slavery 1776–1848*. London, Verso.

Boehmer, E., ed. (2009) *Empire Writing: An Anthology of Colonial Literature 1870–1918*. Oxford, Oxford University Press.

Boltanski, C. (1993) *Distant Suffering: Morality, Media and Politics*. Cambridge, Cambridge University Press.

Bond, P., D. Brutus, and V. Setshedi (2005) 'When Wearing White is not Chic, and Collaboration not Cool', *Foreign Policy in Focus*, 16 June.

Booth, D. (2005) 'The Africa Commission Report: What about the Politics?', *Development Policy Review* 23(4): 493–498.

Brainard, L. and D. Chollett (eds) (2008) *Global Development 2.0*. Washington DC, Brookings Press.

Brantlinger, P. (1985) 'Victorians and Africans: the Genealogy of the Myth of the Dark Continent', *Critical Inquiry* 21(1): 166–203.

Braudel, F. (1993) *A History of Civilizations*, London, Penguin.

Brautigam, D. (2011) *The Dragon's Gift: the Real Story of China in Africa*. Oxford, Oxford University Press.

Brecher, J., T. Costello, and B. Smith (eds) (2000) *Globalisation from Below: the Power of Solidarity*, Cambridge, MA, South End Press.

Brent, R. (1987) *Liberal Anglican Politics: Whiggery, Religion and Reform 1983–1841*. Oxford, Clarendon Press.

British Biafra Society (no date) *Biafra – Britain in the Dock*. London, Goodwin Press.

Brion Davis, D. (1999) *The Problem of Slavery in the Age of Revolution*. Oxford, Oxford University Press.

Brockington, D. (2009) *Celebrity and the Environment: Fame, Wealth and Power in Conservation*. London, Zed Press.

Brookes, H. J. (1995) '"Suit, Tie, and a Touch of Juju." The Ideological Construction of Africa: a Critical Discourse Analysis of News on Africa in the British Press', *Discourse and Society* 6(4): 461–494.

Brown, C. L. (2006) *Moral Capital: Foundations of British Abolitionism*. Chapel Hill, NC, University of North Carolina Press.

Brown, G. (2004) 'The Challenges of 2005: Forging a New Compact for Africa', *New Economy* 11(3): 127–131.

Brown, M. and R. Kelly (eds) (2005) *You're History! How People Make the Difference*. London, Continuum Books.

Brown, S. J. (2008) *Providence and Empire 1815–1914*. Harlow, Pearson Longman.

Brown, W. (2006) 'The Commission for Africa: Results and Prospects for the West's Africa Policy', *Journal of Modern African Studies* 44(3): 349–374.

Burroughs, R. (2009) 'Imperial Eyes or "The Eyes of Another Race"? Roger Casement's Travels in West Africa', *Journal of Imperial and Commonwealth History* 37(3): 383–397.

Busby, J. (2007) 'Bono Made Jesse Helms Cry: Jubilee 2000, Debt Relief, and Moral Action in International Politics', *International Studies Quarterly* 51: 247–275.

Bush, B. (1999) *Imperialism, Race and Resistance*. London, Routledge.

Bush, B. (2006) *Imperialism and Post-colonialism*. London, Longman.

Bush, R. (1988) 'Hunger in the Sudan: the Case of Darfur', *African Affairs* 87 (346): 5–23.

Callaghy, T. (2001) 'Networks of Governance in Africa: Innovation in the Debt Régime', in T. Callaghy, R. Kassimir, and R. Latham (eds), *Intervention and Transnationalism in Africa: Global-Local Networks of Power*. Cambridge, Cambridge University Press: 115–149.

Cannadine, D. (2002) *Ornamentalism: How the British Saw their Empire*. London, Penguin.

Carey, B. (2005) *British Abolitionism and the Rhetoric of Sensibility: Writing, Sentiment and Slavery, 1760–1807*. Houndmills, Palgrave.

Carey, B., M. Ellis, and S. Salhi (eds) (2004) *Discourses of Slavery and Abolition*. Basingstoke, Palgrave Macmillan.

Cell, J. (1989) 'Lord Hailey and the Making of the African Survey', *African Affairs* 88(353): 481–505.

Chabal, P. (1996) 'The African Crisis: Context and Interpretation', in R. Werbner and T. Ranger (eds), *Post-colonial Identities in Africa*. London, Zed Press: 29–45.

Chambers, R. (1983) *Rural Development: Putting the Last First*. London, Prentice Hall.

Chambers, R. and N. Alfini (2007) 'Words Count: Taking a Count of the Changing Language of British Aid', *Development in Practice* 17(4–5): 492–504.

Chandler, D. (2007) 'The Security-Development Nexus and the Rise of "Anti-Foreign Policy"', *Journal of International Relations and Development* 10(3): 362–386.

Cheesman, D. (2009) 'Butskell and the Empire: the House of Commons Prepares for the Scramble from Africa, 1946–56', *Commonwealth and Comparative Politics* 47(3): 248–266.

Chikezie, C. (2006) 'Make Poverty History? Make Migration Easy!', *Open Democracy*, 10 January.

Chouliaraki, L. (2006) *The Spectatorship of Suffering*. London, Sage.

Chouliaraki, L. (2010) 'Post-humanitarianism: Humanitarian Communication beyond the Politics of Pity', *International Journal of Cultural Studies* 13(2): 107–126.

Clark, D. J. (2004) 'The Production of a Contemporary Famine Image: the Image Economy, Indigenous Photographers and the Case of Mekanic Philipos', *Journal of International Development* 16(1): 1–12.

Clarkson, T. (1808) *The History of the Rise, Progress, and Accomplishment of the Abolition of the African Slave-trade by the British Parliament*. London, printed by R. Taylor and Co., for Longman, Hurst, Rees, and Orme.

Cliffe, L. and B. Davidson (1988) *The Long Struggle of Eritrea*. London, Spokesman.

Coen, L. (2003) *The Consumer's Republic: the Politics of Mass Consumption in Postwar America*, New York, Vintage.

Cohen, S. (2001) *States of Denial: Knowing about Atrocities and Suffering*. Cambridge, Polity.

Coleman, D. (2004) 'Henry Smeathman: the Fly-catching Abolitionist', in B. Carey, M. Ellis, and S. Salih (eds), *Discourses of Slavery and Abolition*. Houndmills, Palgrave Macmillan: 141–157.

Colley, L. (2005) *Britons: Forging the Nation 1707–1837*. New Haven, CT, Yale University Press.

Comaroff, J. and J. Comaroff (1997) 'Africa Observed: Discourses of the Imperial Imagination', in R. Grinker and C. Steiner (eds), *Perspectives on Africa*. London, Blackwell: 689–703.

Coombes, A. (1994) *Reinventing Africa: Museums, Material Culture and Popular Imagination*. New Haven, CT, Yale University Press.

Cooper, R. (2002) 'The New Liberal Imperialism', *Guardian*, 7 April.

Coquery-Vidrovitch, C. (1988) *Africa: Endurance and Change South of the Sahara.* Berkeley, CA, California University Press.

Cottle, S. and D. Nolan (2007) 'Global Humanitarianism and the Changing Aid-Media Field', *Journalism Studies* 8(6): 862–878.

Coulter, P. (1989) 'Pretty as a Picture', *New Internationalist* 194(April): 1–4.

Coupland, R. (1933) *The British Anti-Slavery Movement.* London, Thornton Butterworth.

Cowen, N. and R. Shenton (1998) *Doctrines of Development.* London, Routledge.

Crais, C. and P. Scully (2009) *Sara Baartman and the Hottentot Venus.* Princeton, NJ, Princeton University Press.

Crozier, A. (2007) 'Sensationalising Africa: British Medical Impressions of Sub Saharan Africa 1890–1939', *Journal of Imperial and Commonwealth History* 35(3): 393–415.

Curry-Machado, J. (2004) 'How Cuba Burned with the Ghosts of British Slavery: Race, Abolition and the *Escalera*', *Slavery and Abolition* 25(1): 71–93.

Curtin, P. (1964) *The Image of Africa: British Ideas and Action, 1780–1850.* Madison, WI, University of Wisconsin Press.

Curtis, R. (2005) 'Seize the day: a personal message to G8 leaders from Richard Curtis', www.g7.utoronto.ca/scholar/g8summit2005/16g8summit-curtis.pdf.

Darnton, A. (2006) 'Make Poverty History End of Year Notes from Public Perceptions of Poverty Research Programme', manuscript, 25 April.

Darnton, A. with M. Kirk (2011) *Finding Frames: New ways to engage the UK public in global poverty*, http://findingframes.org/report.htm, accessed 23 May 2010.

Dauvergne, P. (2010) *Shadows of Consumption.* Cambridge, MA, MIT Press.

Davidson, B. (1978) *Let Freedom Come.* New York, Little Brown.

Davidson, J. (2007) 'Photographs and Accountability: Cracking the Codes of an NGO', *Accounting, Auditing and Accountability Journal* 20(1): 133–158.

Davis, L. H. (2010) 'Feeding the World a Line?: Celebrity Activism and Ethical Consumer Practices From Live Aid to Product Red', *Nordic Journal of English Studies* 9(3): 89–118.

De Waal, A. (1997) *Famine Crimes: Politics and the Disaster Relief Industry in Africa.* Oxford, James Currey.

de Zengotita, T. (2005) *Mediated: How the Media Shapes Your World and the Way You Live in It*, New York, Bloomsbury.

Denniston, R. (1999) *Trevor Huddleston: a Life.* Basingstoke, Macmillan.

Dent, M. and B. Peters (1999) *The Crisis of Poverty and Debt in the Third World.* Aldershot, Ashgate.

Department for International Development (DFID) (2007) *Public Attitudes Towards Development.* London, DFID.

Devereux, S. (ed.) (2007) *The New Famines: Why Famines Persist in an Era of Globalisation.* London, Routledge.

Diamond, S. (2007) 'Who Killed Biafra?', *Dialectical Anthropology* 31(3): 339–362.

Didi-Huberman, G. (2008) *Images in Spite of All*. Chicago, Chicago University Press.

Donnelly, E. (2007) 'Making the Case for Jubilee: the Catholic Church and the Poor Country Debt Movement', *Ethics and International Affairs* 21(1): 107–133.

Drescher, S. (1987) *Capitalism and Antislavery: British Mobilisation in Perspective*. Oxford, Oxford University Press.

Drescher, S. (1994) 'Whose Abolition? Popular Pressure and the Ending of the British Slave Trade', *Past and Present* 143: 136–166.

Drescher, S. (2002) *The Mighty Experiment: Free Labour versus Slavery in British Emancipation*. Oxford, Oxford University Press.

Duffield, M. (2007) *Development, Security and Unending War*. London, Polity.

Dyer, R. (1997) *White*. London, Routledge.

Edwards, T. (2000) *Contradictions of Consumption*. Buckingham, Open University Press.

Englund, H. (1998) 'Culture, Environment and the Enemies of Complexity', *Review of African Political Economy* 25(76): 179–188.

Equiano, O. (1999) *The Life of Olaudah Equiano*. New York, Dover Publications.

Equiano, O. (2003) *The Interesting Narrative and Other Writings*. London, Penguin.

Escobar, A. (1994) *Encountering Development*. Princeton, NJ, Princeton University Press.

Fenyoe, A. (2005) *Public Perceptions of Poverty. Qualitative Research Findings: Wave 2*, Synovate Research.

Ferguson, N. (2004) *Empire: How Britain Made the Modern World*. London, Penguin.

Fieldhouse, R. (2005) *Anti-Apartheid. A History of the Movement in Britain*. London, Pluto Press.

Fine, B. (2007) *The World of Consumption*. London, Routledge.

Forsyth, F. (1977) *The Making of an African Legend: the Biafra Story*. Harmondsworth, Penguin.

Foucault, M. (1991) *Discipline and Punish: the Birth of the Prison*. London, Penguin.

Foucault, M. (2008) *The Birth of Biopolitics: Lectures at the Collège de France, 1978–1979*. London, Picador.

Fowler, A. (1992) 'Distant Obligations: Speculations on NGO Funding and the Global Market', *Review of African Political Economy* 20(55): 9–29.

Fryer, P. (2010) *Staying Power: the History of Black People in Britain*. London, Pluto Press.

Fulford, T. and T. Kitson (eds) (1998) *Romanticism and Colonialism: Writing and Empire 1780–1830*. Cambridge, Cambridge University Press.

Gallagher, J. (2009) 'Healing the Scar? Idealizing Britain in Africa', *African Affairs* 108(432): 435–451.

Gallagher, J. (2011) *Britain and Africa under Blair*. Manchester, Manchester University Press.

Gallagher, J. and R. Robinson (1953) 'The Imperialism of Free Trade,' *The Economic History Review*, Second series VI(1): 1–15.

Gamson, W. (1995) 'Constructing Social Protest', in H. Johnston and B. Klandermans (eds), *Social Movements and Culture*. London, UCL Press: 85–107.

Gary, I. (1996) 'Confrontation, Co-operation, or Co-optation: NGOs and the Ghanaian State during Structural Adjustment', *Review of African Political Economy* 23(66): 169–195.

Geldof, B. (1986) *Is That It?* London, Penguin.

Giblin, J. and G. Maddox (eds) (1996) *Custodians of the Land. Ecology & Culture in the History of Tanzania*. Oxford, James Currey.

Gilbert, S. (2007) 'Singing Against Apartheid: the ANC Cultural Groups and the International Anti-Apartheid struggle', *Journal of Southern African Studies* 33(2): 421–441.

Gilroy, P. (2004) *After Empire: Melancholia or Convivial Culture?* London, Routledge.

Glennie, J. (2008) *The Trouble with Aid: Why Less Could Mean More for Africa*. London, Zed Press.

Goffman, E. (1986) *Frame Analysis: an Essay on the Organization of Experience*. Boston, MA, Northeast University Press.

Goldman, R. (1998) *Nike Culture: the Sign of the Swoosh*. Thousand Oaks, CA, Sage Press.

Gorringe, H. and M. Rosie (2006) '"Pants to Poverty"? Making Poverty History, Edinburgh 2005', *Sociological Research Online* 11(1).

Gott, R. (2010) 'Shoot to be Sure', in S. Howe (ed.), *The New Imperial Histories Reader*. London, Routledge: 106–115.

Grant, K. (2005) *A Civilised Savagery: Britain and the New Slaveries in Africa, 1884–1926*. London, Routledge.

Gratus, J. (1973) *The Great White Lie: Slavery, Emancipation, and Changing Racial Attitudes*. London, Hutchinson.

Gray, J. (2008) *Black Mass: Apocalyptic Religion and the Death of Utopia*. London, Penguin.

Griffiths, M. (2005) 'Branding and Rebuilding Charity Brands: the Role of Creative Agencies', *Journal of Nonprofit and Voluntary Sector Marketing* 10(2): 121–132.

Grinker, R. and C. Steiner (eds) (1997) *Perspectives on Africa*. London, Blackwell.

Gumbel, N. (2005) *Make Poverty History*. London, Alpha International.

Gurney, C. (2000) '"A Great Cause": the origins of the Anti-Apartheid Movement, June 1959–1960', *Journal of Southern African Studies* 26(1): 123–144.

Gurney, C. (2009) 'The 1970s: the Anti-Apartheid Movement's Difficult Decade', *Journal of Southern African Studies* 35(2): 471–487.

Guyer, J. (2004) *Marginal Gains: Monetary Transactions in Atlantic Africa*. Chicago, Chicago University Press.

Hall, C. (2002) *Civilising Subjects: Metropole and Colony in the English imagination 1830–1867*. Oxford, Polity Press.

Hall, C. and S. Rose (eds) (2006) *At Home with the Empire: Metropolitan Culture and the Imperial World*. Cambridge, Cambridge University Press.

Hammond, D. and A. Jablow (1977) *The Myth of Africa*. New York, Library of Social Science.

Hampson, T. (2006) *2025: What Next for the Make Poverty History Generation?* London, Fabian Society.

Harrison, G. (2004) *The World Bank and Africa: the Construction of Governance States*. London, Routledge.

Harrison, G. (2007) 'Debt, Development and Intervention in Africa: the Contours of a Sovereign Frontier', *Journal of Intervention and State Building* 1(2): 189–209.

Harrison, P. and R. Palmer (1986) *News Out of Africa: Biafra to Band Aid*. London, Hilary Shipman.

Harvey, D. (1990) 'Between Space and Time. Reflections on the Geographic Imagination', *Annals of the Association of American Geographers* 80(3): 418–434.

Hatzfield, J. (2006) *Machete Season: the Killers in Rwanda Speak*. London, Picador.

Hearn, J. (2007) 'African NGOs: the New Compradors?', *Development and Change* 38(6): 1095–1110.

Heerten, L. (2009) 'The Biafran War in Britain: an Odd Alliance of Late 1960s Humanitarian Action', *Journal of the Oxford University History Society* 7: 1–19.

Hegel G. W. F. (2004) *The Philosophy of History*. New York, Dover Publications.

Hewson, P. (2006) '"It's the Politics Stupid": How Neoliberal Politicians, NGOs and Rock Stars Hijacked the Global Justice Movement at Gleneagles ... and How we Let Them', in David Harvie, Keir Milburn, Ben Trott and D. Watts (eds), *Shut Them Down! The G8, Gleneagles 2005 and the Movement of Movements*. London, Autonomedia/Dissent!: 135–149.

Hilder, P., J. Caulier-Grice, and K. Lalore (2007) *Contentious Citizens: Civil Society's Role in Campaigning for Social Change*. London, Young Foundation.

Hilton, B. (2006) *A Mad, Bad, and Dangerous People?: England 1783–1846*. Oxford, Oxford University Press.

Himmelfarb, G. (1991) *Poverty and Compassion: the Moral Imagination of the Late Victorians*. New York, Vintage Books

Himmelman, N. and D. Mupotsa (2008) 'Product (Red): (re) branding Africa?', *Journal of Pan African Studies 2* 6(1–12).

Hintzen, P. (2008) 'Desire and the Enrapture of Capitalist Consumption: Product Red, Africa, and the Crisis of Sustainability', *Journal of Pan African Studies* 2(6): 77–91.

Hobsbawm, E. and T. Ranger (eds) (1992) *The Invention of Tradition*. Cambridge, Cambridge University Press.

Hochschild, A. (1998) *King Leopold's Ghost*. London, Pan

Hochschild, A. (2005) *Bury the Chains: the British Struggle to Abolish Slavery*. Basingstoke, Pan.

Hodkinson, S. (2005) 'Inside the Murky World of Make Poverty History', *Red Pepper*, 28 June.

Hopgood, S. (2000) 'Reading the Small Print in Global Civil Society: the Inexorable Hegemony of the Liberal Self', *Millennium: Journal of International Studies* 29(1): 1–25.

Howe, P. (2009) 'Archetypes of Famine and Response', *Disasters* 34(1): 30–54.

Howe, S. (1993) *Anticolonialism in British Politics*. Oxford, Clarendon Press.

Howe, S. (1998) *Afrocentrism: Mythical Pasts and Imagined Homes*. London, Verso.

Howe, S. (2010) *The New Imperial Histories Reader*. London, Routledge.

Hume, M. (2005) 'It's too Easy for Everybody to Love Live 8', www.spiked-online. com/index.php?/site/article/803/, accessed 9 May 2006.

Igoe, J. (2003) 'Scaling up Civil Society: Donor Money, Ngos and the Pastoralist Land Rights Movement in Tanzania', *Development and Change* 34(5): 863–885.

Irobi, E. (2006) 'A Theatre for Cannibals: Images of Europe in Indigenous African Theatre of the Colonial Period', *New Theatre Quarterly* 22(3): 268–282.

Iweala, U. (2007) 'Stop Trying to "Save" Africa', *Washington Post*, 15 July.

Jackson, R. (1990) *Quasi States: Sovereignty, International Relations and the Third World*. Cambridge, Cambridge University Press.

Jahn, B. (2005a) 'Barbarian Thoughts: Imperialism in the Philosophy of John Stuart Mill', *Review of International Studies* 31(3): 599–618.

Jahn, B. (2005b) 'Kant, Mill, and Illiberal Legacies in International Affairs', *International Organization* 59(1): 177–207.

JanMohamed, A. R. (1985) 'The Economy of Manichean Allegory: the Function of Racial Difference in Colonialist Literature', *Critical Inquiry* 21(1): 39–87.

Jarosz, L. (1992) 'Constructing the Dark Continent: Metaphor as Geographic Representation of Africa', *Geografiska Annaler B* 74(2): 105–115.

Jasper, J. M. and J. Poulsen (1995) 'Recruiting Strangers and Friends: Moral Shocks and Social Networks in Animal Rights and Animal Protest', *Social Problems* 42, 493–312.

Jeal, T. (2001) *Livingstone*, New Haven, CT: Yale University Press.

Jeal, T. (2008) *Stanley: the Impossible Life of Africa's Greatest Explorer*. London, Faber & Faber.

Jennings, J. (2005) 'A Trio of Talented Women: Abolition, Gender and Political Participation 1780–91', *Slavery and Abolition* 26(1): 55–70.

Jennings, M. (2002) '"Almost an Oxfam in Itself": Oxfam and Development in Tanzania in the 1960s and 70s', *African Affairs* 101(405): 509–530

John, N. (2000) 'The Campaign against British Bank Involvement in Apartheid South Africa', *African Affairs* 99(396): 415–433.

Josselin, D. (2007) 'From Transnational Protest to Domestic Political Opportunities: Insights from the Debt Cancellation Campaign', *Social Movement Studies* 6(1): 21–38.

Jungar, K. and E. Salo (2008) 'Shop and Do Good?', in *2 Journal of Pan African Studies* 92(93).

Kaplan, R. (1994) 'The Coming Anarchy: How Scarcity, Crime, Overpopulation, Tribalism, and Disease are Rapidly Destroying the Social Fabric of our Planet', *Atlantic Monthly*, February: 1–16.

Kapoor, I. (2008) *The Postcolonial Politics of Development*. London, Routledge.

Katz-Hyman, M. (2008) 'Doing Good by Doing Well: the Decision to Manufacture products that Supported the Abolition of the Slave Trade and Slavery in Great Britain.' *Slavery and Abolition* 29(2): 219–231.

Kaufmann, C. and R. Pape (1999) 'Explaining Costly International Action: Britain's Sixty-year Campaign Against the Slave Trade', *International Organization* 53(4): 631–668.

Keen, D. (1994) *The Benefits of Famine: a Political Economy of Famine and Relief in Southwestern Sudan, 1983-89*. Princeton, NJ, Princeton University Press.

Keen, D. (2008) *Benefits of Famine: a Political Economy of Famine and Relief in Southwestern Sudan, 1983–9*. Oxford, James Currey.

Keene, E. (2007) 'A Case Study of the Construction of International Hierarchy: British Treaty-Making Against the Slave Trade in the Early Nineteenth Century', *International Organization* 6(3): 311–339.

Kelemen, P. (2007) 'Planning for Africa: the British Labour Party's Colonial Development Policy, 1920–1964', *Journal of Agrarian Change* 7(1): 76–98.

Kelsall, T. (2008) 'Going with the Grain in African Development?', *Development Policy Review* 26(6): 627–655.

Khan, M. (2010) 'Political Settlements and the Governance of Growth-Enhancing Institutions', *SOAS Working Paper*. London.

Kim, E. (2002) 'Race Sells: Racialised Trade Cards in 18th Century Britain', *Journal of Material Culture* 7(2): 137–165.

Klein, G. (2009) 'The British Anti-Apartheid Movement and Political Prisoner Campaigns, 1973–1980', *Journal of Southern African Studies* 35(2): 455–470.

Klein, N. (2000) *No Logo*. London, Flamingo.

Kohn, M. and D. O'Neill (2006) 'A Tale of Two Indias: Burke and Mill on Empire and Slavery in the West Indies and America', *Political Theory* 34(2): 192–228.

Koivunen, L. (2009) *Visualising Africa in Nineteenth-Century British Travel Accounts*. London, Routledge.

Korten, D. (1984) *People-Centered Development: Contributions Toward Theory and Planning Frameworks*. Herndon, VA, Kumarian Press.

Kothari, U. (2006) 'An Agenda for Thinking about "Race" in Development', *Progress in Development Studies* 6(1): 9–23.

Kowaleski-Wallace, E. (1997) *Consuming Subjects: Women, Shopping, and Business in the Eighteenth Century*. New York, Columbia University Press.

Kroen, S. (2004) 'A Political History of the Consumer', *The Historical Journal* 47(3): 709–736.

Landau, P. (2002) 'Empires of the Visual: Photography and Colonial Administration in Africa' in P. Landau and D. Kaspin (eds), *Images and Empires: Visuality in Colonial and Post-colonial Africa*. Berkeley, CA, University of California Press: 141–171.

Landau, P. and D. Kaspin (eds) (2002) *Images and Empires: Visuality in Colonial and Post-colonial Africa*. Berkeley, CA, University of California Press.

Larmer, M. (2007a) 'Southern African Social Movements at the World Social Forum in Nairobi', European Sociological Association.

Larmer, M. (2007b) 'More Fire Next Time?', *Journal of African and Asian Studies* 42(1): 25–37.

Lester, A. (2010) 'Imperial Networks: Creating Identities in Nineteenth Century South Africa and Britain', in S. Howe (ed.), *The New Imperial Histories Reader*. London, Routledge: 139–147.

Lidchi, H. (1993) *'All in the Choosing Eye': Charity, Representation and Developing World*. Milton Keynes, Open University.

Linebaugh, P. and M. Redicker (2002) *The Many-Headed Hydra: the Hidden History of the Revolutionary Atlantic*. London, Verso.

Linfield, S. (2010) *The Cruel Radiance: Photography and Political Violence*. Chicago, Chicago University Press.

Lissner, J. (1981) 'Merchants of Misery', *New Internationalist* 100: 23–25.

Lockwood, M. (2005) 'Will a Marshall Plan for Africa Make Poverty History?', *Journal of International Development* 17: 775–789.

Lonsdale, J. (2005) 'How to Study Africa: from Victimhood to Agency', *Open Democracy,* 1 September.

Lovejoy, P. (2006) 'Autobiography and Memory: Gustavas Vassa, alias Olauda Equiano, the African', *Slavery and Abolition* 27(3): 317–247.

Luetchford, M. and P. Burns (2003) *Waging the War on Want. 50 Years of Campaigning Against World Poverty*. London, War on Want.

Luke, D. (2007) 'African Presence in the Early History of the British Isles and Scandinavia', in I. Sertima (ed.), *African Presence in Early Europe*. New Brunswick, NJ, Transaction Publishers: 223–244.

Lury, C. (1997) *Consumer Culture*. Toronto, Rutgers University Press.

Macey, D. (2009) 'Rethinking Biopolitics: Race and Power in the Wake of Foucault', *Theory, Culture & Society* 26(6): 186–205.

MacKenzie, J. (ed.) (1986) *Imperialism and Popular Culture*. Manchester, Manchester University Press.

Macrae, J., A. Zwi, M. R. Duffield, H. Slim (eds) (1994) *War and Hunger: Rethinking International Responses to Complex Emergencies*. London, Zed Press.

Magubane, Z. (2008) 'The (Product) Red Man's Burden: Charity, Celebrity, and the Contradictions of Coevalness', *Journal of Pan African Studies* 2(6): 1–25.

Mahoney, J. and K. Thelen (eds) (2010) *Explaining Institutional Change: Ambiguity, Agency and Power*. Cambridge, Cambridge University Press.

Manzo, K. (2006) 'An Extension of Colonialism? Development Education, Images and the Media.' *The Development Education Journal* 12(2): 9–12.

Manzo, K. (2008) 'Imaging Humanitarianism: NGO Identity and the Iconography of Childhood', *Antipode* 40(4): 632–657.

Marcuse, H. (2002) *One-Dimensional Man: Studies in the Ideology of Advanced Industrial Society*. London, Routledge.

Martin, A., C. Culey, S. Evans (2005) *Make Poverty History 2005 Campaign Evaluation*. London, Firetail.

Martinot, S. (2003) *The Rule of Racialisation: Class, Identity, Governance*. Philadelphia, PA, Temple University Press.

Marx, K. (2004) *Capital: Critique of Political Economy v. 1*. London, Penguin.

Mawdsley, E. (2008) 'Fu Manchu versus Dr Livingstone in the Dark Continent? Representing China, Africa, and the West in British Broadsheet Newspapers', *Political Geography* 27(5): 509–529.

Maxwell, D. (2011) 'Photography and the Religious Encounter: Ambiguity and Aesthetics in Missionary Representations of the Luba of South East Belgian Congo', *Comparative Studies in Society and History* 53(1): 38–74.

Mayer, R. (2002) *Artificial Africas: Colonial Images in the Times of Globalization*. Dartmouth, University Press of New England.

Mayo, M. (2005) *Global Citizens: Social Movements and the Challenge of Globalisation*. London, Zed Press.

Mbembe, A. (2001) *On the Postcolony*. Berkeley, CA, University of California Press.

McCaskie, T. (1999) 'Cultural Encounters: Britain and Africa in the Nineteenth Century', in A. Porter (ed.), *The Nineteenth Century*. Oxford, Oxford University Press: 644–690.

McClintock, A. (1995) *Imperial Leather: Gender Race and Sexuality in the Colonial Contest*. London, Routledge.

McDougall, D. (2006) 'Now Charity Staff Hit at Cult of Celebrity', *Observer*, 26 November.

McLynn, F. (1992) *Hearts of Darkness: the European Exploration of Africa*. London, Pimlico.

Mehta, U. S. (1999) *Liberalism and Empire: a Study in Nineteenth-century British Liberal Thought*. Chicago, Chicago University Press.

Mercer, C. (2003) 'Performing Partnership: Civil Society and the Illusions of Good Governance in Tanzania', *Political Geography* 22(7): 741–763.

Moeller, S. (1999) *Compassion Fatigue. How the Media sell Disease, Famine, War and Death*. London, Routledge.

Moore, S. (2008) *Ribbon Culture: Charity, Compassion and Public Awareness*. Houndmills, Palgrave.

Morrison, T. (1992) *Playing in the Dark: Whiteness and the Literary Imagination*. Cambridge, MA, Harvard University Press.

Morton, S. and S. Bygrave (eds) (2008) *Foucault in an Age of Terror: Essays on Biopolitics and the Defence of Society*. Houndmills, Palgrave.

Mudimbe, V. Y. (1988) *The Invention of Africa: Gnosis, Philosophy, and the Order of Knowledge*. Bloomington, IN, Indiana University Press.

Mudimbe, V. Y. (1992) *The Surreptitious Speech: Presence Africaine and the Politics of Otherness 1947–1987*. Chicago, University of Chicago Press.

Muthu, S. (2003) *Enlightenment against Empire*. Princeton, NJ, Princeton University Press.

Nederveen Pieterse, J. (1992) *White on Black: Images of Africa in Western Popular Culture*. New Haven, CT, Yale University Press.

Neitzsche, F. (2003) *Twilight of the Idols and the Anti-Christ*. London, Penguin.

nfp Synergy (no date) 'What are the Barriers to Charities' Campaigning?', manuscript.

Nkrumah, K. (1965) *Neocolonialism: the Last Stage of Imperialism*. London, Thomas Nelson.

Norrell, A. (no date) 'Bridging Gaps of a Bridge Too Far? The Management of Advocacy within Service Providing NGOs in the UK', *CVO International Working Paper, No. 3*.

Nussbam, M. (2001) *Upheavals of Thought: the Intelligence of Emotions*. Cambridge, Cambridge University Press.

Okri, B. (2009) 'Introduction', *Ten Years of the Caine Prize for African Writing*. London, New Internationalist.

Oldfield, J. R. (1998) *Popular Politics and British Anti-Slavery: the Mobilisation of Public Opinion Against the Slave Trade 1787–1807*. London, Frank Cass.

Oliver, P. and H. Johnston (2000) 'What a Good Idea! Ideologies and Frames in Social Movement Research', *Mobilisation: an International Journal* 4(1): 37–54.

Palmberg, M. (2001) 'A Continent without Culture?', in M. Baaz and M. Palmberg (eds), *Same and Other: Negotiating African Identity in Cultural Production*. Uppsala, Nordiska Afrikainstituttet, 197–209.

Palmer, R. (1987) 'Africa in the Media', *African Affairs* 86(343): 241–247.

Papaioannou, T., H. Yanakopoulos, and Z. Aksoy (2009) 'Global Justice: From Theory to Development Action', *IKD Working Paper* 44.

Park, M. (2002 [1816]) *Travels in the Interior Districts of Africa: Performed in the Years 1795, 1796, and 1797*. Ware, Wordsworth Editions.

Payne, A. (2006) 'Blair, Brown and the Gleneagles Agenda: Making Poverty History, or Confronting the Global Politics of Unequal Development?', *International Affairs* 82(5): 917–935.

Pettigrew, W. (2007) 'Free to Enslave: Politics and the Escalation of Britain's Transatlantic Slave Trade 1688–1714', *William and Mary Quarterly* 64(1): 3–38.

Philo, G. (1993) 'From Buerk to Band Aid: the Media and the 1984 Ethiopian Famine', in J. Eldridge, *Getting the Message: News Truth and Power*. London, Routledge: 104–126.

Philo, G. (n.d.) *Television and the Ethiopian Famine. From Buerk to Band Aid.* UNESCO.

Pitts, J. (2005) *A turn to Empire: the Rise of Liberal Imperialism in Britain and France.* Princeton, NJ, Princeton University Press.

Porter, B. (2008) *Critics of Empire: British Radicals and the Imperial Challenge.* London, I. B. Tauris.

Porteus, T. (2008) *Britain in Africa.* London, Zed Press.

Prashad, V. (2007) *The Darker Nations.* New York, New Press.

Pratt, M. (1992) *Imperial Eyes: Travel Writing and Transculturation.* London, Routledge.

Price, R. (2006) 'One Big Thing: Britain, Its Empire, and Their Imperial Culture', *Journal of British Studies* 45(3): 602–627.

Price, R. (2008) *Making Empire: Colonial Encounters and the Creation of Imperial Rule in Nineteenth-Century Africa.* Cambridge, Cambridge University Press.

Princen, T., M. Maniates, K. Conca (eds) (2002) *Confronting Consumption.* Cambridge, MA, MIT Press.

Quarmby, K. (2005) 'Why Oxfam is Failing Africa', *New Statesman*, 30 May 2005.

Raikes, P. (1989) *Modernizing Hunger.* London, James Currey.

Ramamurthy, A. (2003) *Imperial Persuaders: Images of Africa and Asia in British Advertising.* Manchester, Manchester University Press.

Ranciere, J. (2009) *The Future of the Image.* London, Verso.

Ranger, T. (1995) 'The Invention of Tradition in Colonial Africa', in E. Hobsbawm and T. Ranger (eds), *The Invention of Tradition.* Cambridge, Canto: 211–263.

Rawls, J. (2001) *The Law of Peoples.* Cambridge, MA, Harvard University Press.

Reddy, S. (1999) 'AAM and UN: Partners in the International Campaign against Apartheid', *The Anti-Apartheid Movement: a 40-Year Perspective.* Anti-Apartheid Movement, Oxford, manuscript: 40–49.

Reno, W. (2011) *Warfare in Independent Africa.* Cambridge, Cambridge University Press.

Richardson, D. (2005) 'Slavery and Bristol's "Golden Age"', *Slavery and Abolition* 26(1): 35–54.

Richey, L. and S. Ponte (2008) 'Better (Red) than Dead? Celebrities, Consumption, and International Aid', *Third World Quarterly* 29(4): 711–729.

Richey, L. A. and S. Ponte (2011) *Brand Aid. Shopping Well to Save the World.* Minneapolis, MN, Minnesota University Press.

Ritchie, R., S. Swami, and C. Weinberg (1999) 'A Brand New World for Non-Profits', *International Journal of Nonprofit and Voluntary Sector Marketing* 4(1): 26–42.

Robinson, R. and J. Gallagher (1961) *Africa and the Victorians: the Official mind of Imperialism.* Basingstoke, Macmillan.

Rootes, C. and C. Saunders (2005) 'Development of the Global Justice Movement in Britain', *ACI Conference on Genealogies of the Global Justice Movement*, Paris, France, 30 September–1 October 2005.

Rose, N. (1990) *Governing the Soul: the Shaping of the Private Self.* London, Routledge.

Rose, N. (2001) 'The Politics of Life Itself', *Theory Culture and Society* 18(6): 1–30.

Rozbicki, M. (2001) 'To Save Them From Themselves: Proposals to Enslave the British Poor, 1698–1755', *Slavery and Abolition* 22(2): 29–50.

Rubin, O. (2009) 'The Niger Famine: a Collapse in Entitlements and Democratic Responsiveness', *Journal of Asian and African Studies* 44(3): 279–298.

Ryan, J. (1997) *Picturing Empire: Photography and the Visualisation of the British Empire.* London, Reaktion Books.

Sachs, J. (2005) *The End of Poverty. How We Can Make it Happen in Our Lifetime.* London, Penguin.

Said, E. (2005) *Orientalism.* London, Penguin.

Samman, E., E. Mc Auliffe, and M. MacLachlan (2009) 'The Role of Celebrity in Endorsing Poverty Reduction Through International Aid', *International Journal of Nonprofit and Voluntary Sector Marketing* 14(2): 137–148.

Sandberg, S. (2006) 'Fighting Neoliberalism with Neoliberal Discourse: ATTAC Norway, Foucault, and Collective Action Framing', *Social Movement Studies* 5(3): 209–227.

Sarna-Wojcicki, M. (2008) 'Refigu(red): Talking Africa and Aids in "Causumer" Culture', *Journal of Pan African Studies* 2(6): 14–31.

Saxton, J. (2008) *A Strong Charity Brand Comes from Strong Beliefs and Values.* London, nfp Synergy.

Schatzberg, M. (2002) *Political Legitimacy in Middle Africa: Father, Family, Food.* Bloomington, IN, Indiana University Press.

Scott, J. C. (1998) *Seeing Like a State: How Certain Schemes to Improve the Human Condition Have Failed.* New Haven, CT, Yale University Press.

Sebe, B. (2009) 'Heroes of the British and French Empires, 1850–1914', in R. Clarke (ed.), *Celebrity Colonialism.* Cambridge, Cambridge Scholars Publishing: 37–55.

Sen, A. (1983) *Poverty and Famines: an Essay on Entitlement and Deprivation.* Oxford, Oxford University Press.

Sennett, R. (2004) *Respect in a World of Inequality.* New York, W. W. Norton.

Sertima, J. (ed.) (2007) *African Presence in Early Europe.* New Brunswick, NJ, Transaction Publishers.

Sherwood, M. (2001) 'Race, Empire and Education: Teaching Racism', *Race and Class* 42(3): 1–28.

Sherwood, M. (2004) 'Britain, the Slave Trade and Slavery 1808–1843', *Race and Class* 46(2): 54–77.

Sireau, N. (2009) *Make Poverty History: Political Communication in Action.* Basingstoke, Palgrave Macmillan.

Skinner, R. (2009) 'The Moral Foundations of British Anti-Apartheid Activism, 1946–1960', *Journal of Southern African Studies* 35(2): 399–416.

Smillie, I. (1995) *The Alms Bazaar: Altruism Under Fire: Non-Profit Organisations and International Development*. London, IT Publications.

Smith, A. (2008) *Wealth of Nations: a Selected Edition*. London, Penguin.

Smith, A. (2009) *The Theory of Moral Sentiments*. London, Penguin.

Smith, J., L. Edge, and V. Morris (2006) *Reflecting the Real World? How British TV portrayed Developing Countries in 2005*. VSO.

Snow, D. and R. Benford (1988) 'Ideology, Frame Resonance and Participant Mobilisation', in B. Klandermans, H. Kriesi and S. Tarrow (eds), *International Social Movement Research 1*. London, JAI Press: 197–217.

Snow, D. and R. Benford (1992) 'Master Frames and Cycles of Protest', in A. Morris and C. McClurg Mueller (eds),*Frontiers in Social Movement Theory*. New Haven, CT, Yale University Press: 133–155.

Snow, D., E. Burke Rochford, Jr., S. K. Worden, and R. D. Benford (1986) 'Frame Alignment Processes, Micromobilization, and Movement Participation', *American Sociological Review* 51(4): 464–481.

Sontag, S. (2004) *Regarding the Pain of Others*. London, Penguin.

Stockwell, S. (2008) 'Splendidly Leading the Way? Archbishop Fisher and Decolonisation in British Colonial Africa', *Journal of Imperial and Commonwealth History* 36(3): 545–564.

Stoler, L. A. (1995) *Race and the Education of Desire: Foucault's "History of Sexuality" and the Colonial Order of Things*. Durham, NC, Duke University Press.

Stoler, L. A. (2002) *Carnal Knowledge and Imperial Power: Race and the Intimate in Colonial Rule*. Berkeley, CA, University of California Press.

Street, J. (2002) 'Bob, Bono and Tony B: the Popular Artist as Politician', *Media Culture and Society* 24(3): 433–441.

Stride, H. (2006) 'An Investigation into the Values of Branding: Implications for the Charity Sector', *Journal of Nonprofit and Voluntary Sector Marketing* 11(2): 115–124.

Stuart, J. (2008) 'Overseas Mission, Voluntary Service and Aid to Africa: Max Warren, the Church Missionary Society and Kenya, 1945–63', *Journal of Imperial and Commonwealth History* 36(3): 527–543.

Sussman, C. (2000) *Consuming Anxieties: Consumer Protest, Gender, and British Slavery, 1713–1833*. Stanford, CA, Stanford University Press.

Tarrow, S. (1998) *Power in Movement: Social Movements and Contentious Politics*. Cambridge, Cambridge University Press.

Tarrow, S. (2005) *The New Transnational Activism*. Cambridge, Cambridge University Press.

Temperley, H. (1977) 'Capitalism, Slavery and Ideology', *Past and Present* 75(1): 94–118.

Thompson, A. (2005) *The Empire Strikes Back: the Impact of Imperialism on Britain from the Mid-nineteenth Century*. London, Longman.

Thörn, H. (2006) 'Solidarity Across Borders: the Transnational Anti-Apartheid Movement', *Voluntas* 17: 285–301.

Thörn, H. (2009) *Anti-Apartheid and the Emergence of a Global Civil Society*. Basingstoke, Palgrave Macmillan.

Thornton, J. (1998) *Africa and Africans in the Making of the Atlantic World, 1400–1800*. Cambridge, Cambridge University Press.

Tibbles, A. (2008) 'Facing Slavery's Past: the Bicentenary of the Abolition of the British Slave Trade', *Slavery and Abolition* 29(2): 293–303.

Time Magazine (1968) 'Nigeria's Civil War: Hate, Hunger and the Will to Survive', www.time.com/time/magazine/article/0,9171,838607,00.html, 23 August.

Trentmann, F. (2008) *Free Trade Nation. Commerce, Consumption, and Civil Society in Modern Britain*. Oxford, Oxford University Press.

Turner, M. (2005) '"Setting the captive free": Thomas Perronet Thompson, British radicalism, and the West Indies, 1820s–1860s', *Slavery and Abolition* 26(1): 115–132.

Vallely, P. (no date) 'Was 2005 the Year of Africa?', http://webarchive.nationalarchives. gov.uk/20100823124637/developments.org.uk/articles/was-2005-the-year-of-africa, accessed 13 March 2010.

van de Walle, N. (2001) *African Economies and the Politics of Permanent Crisis 1979–1999*. Cambridge, Cambridge University Press.

van der Gaag, N. and C. Nash (1987) *Images of Africa. The UK Report*. Oxfam Report.

Vansina, J. (1991) *Paths in the Rainforests: Towards a History of Political Tradition in Equatorial Africa*. London, James Currey.

Veblen, T. (2005) *Conspicuous Consumption*. London, Penguin.

Vernon, J. (2007) *Hunger*. Cambridge, MA, Harvard University Press.

Vickers, R. (2011) *The Labour Party and the World. Vol. 2: Labour's Foreign Policy since 1951*. Manchester, Manchester University Press.

VSO (2002) *The Live Aid Legacy: the developing World Through British Eyes*, VSO, www. vso.org.uk/Images/liveaid_legacy_tcm8–784.pdf, accessed 13 March 2010.

Wainaina, B. (2005) 'How to Write about Africa', *Granta* 92(Winter), www.granta. com/Archive/92/How-to-Write-about-Africa/Page-1, accessed 13 March 2010.

Walker, R. B. W. (1992) *Inside/Outside: International Relations as Political Theory*. Cambridge, Cambridge University Press.

Wallace, T., L. Bornstein, and J. Chapman (1999) *The Aid Chain: Coercion and Commitment in Development NGOs*. London, ITDG Publishing.

Walvin, J. (1997) *Fruits of Empire: Exotic Produce and British Taste, 1660–1800*. Houndmills, Macmillan.

Walzer, M. (1996) *Thick and Thin: Moral Argument at Home and Abroad*. Notre Dame, IN, Notre Dame University Press.

Ward, S. (ed.) (2001) *British Culture and the End of Empire*. Manchester, Manchester University Press.

Waterton, E. and R. Wilson (2009) 'Talking the Talk: Policy, Popular and Media Responses to the Bicentenary of the Abolition of the Slave Trade using the 'Abolition Discourse', *Discourse and Society* 20(3): 381–399.

Waugh, A. and S. Cronje (1969) *Biafra: Britain's Shame*. London, Michael Joseph.

Webster, W. (2005) *Englishness and Empire 1939–1965*. Oxford, Oxford University Press.

Wenar, L. (2006) 'Accountability in International Development Aid', *Ethics and International Affairs* 20(1): 1–23.

Westley, F. (1991) 'Bob Geldof and Live Aid: the Affective Side of Global Social Innovation', *Human Relations* 44(10): 1011–1036.

Wiedenhoft, W. (2008) 'An Analytical Framework for Studying the Politics of Consumption: the Case of the National Consumers' League', *Social Movement Studies* 7(3): 281–303.

Wilson, K. (ed.) (2003) *The Island Race: Englishness, Empire and Gender in the Eighteenth Century*. London, Routledge.

Woods, M. (2008) 'Atlantic Slavery and Traumatic Representation in Museums: the National Great Blacks in Wax Museum as a Test Case', *Slavery and Abolition* 29(2): 151–171.

World Emergency Relief (2005) 'G8 will Make Little or no Difference. New Research Reveals low Public Confidence in G8 Results', manuscript.

Wright, G. (1997) *The Destruction of a Nation*. London, Pluto Press

Wright-Mills, C. (1997) *The Racial Contract*. Ithaca, NY, Cornell University Press.

Yates, A. and L. Chester (2006) *The Troublemaker: Michael Scott and his Lonely Struggle against Injustice*. London, Arurum.

Young, C. (2004) 'The End of the Post-colonial State in Africa? Reflections on Changing African Political Dynamics', *African Affairs* 103 (410): 23-49.

Index

Note: 'n' after a page reference indicates the number of a note on that page.

Fabian Colonial Bureau 7, 48
Finding Frames 195–196, 199, 201

G8 62, 67, 89–90, 92–96, 159–162,
    167–171, 173–181, 182n17,
    183n22, 184
Geldof, B. 67, 70n11, 70n19, 70n20,
    106, 113, 126n12, 147, 170–171,
    173–177, 182n12, 183n22, 183n23,
    182n24, 189
Gill, P. 112–113, 117
Gleneagles 67, 92, 161, 167–172, 177–
    178, 182n11, 182n17, 183n23

Huddlestone, T. 74, 85, 98n29

Innocence 27–29, 116

Jubilee 2000 6, 56n21, 70n21, 71, 74,
    88–90, 99n35, 99n36, 102, 179,
    180, 182n8, 189

Live 8 67, 70n19, 92, 99n43, 99n45, 106,
    167, 173–177, 182n12
Livingstone, D. 17n16, 43–45
London Missionary Society 43–45, 49,
    56n9

Mandela, N. 64, 72, 85–87, 90–91, 97n1,
    130
Movement for Colonial Freedom 7, 49,
    76, 83–84
Quakers 55n6, 78, 97n4

Rhodes, C. 47, 56n16, 84
Royal Geographical Society 43
Rwanda 32, 102, 210n3

Save the Children 7, 119, 140, 144, 150,
    153, 157n13, 158n18, 162
Sharp, G. 41, 55n6, 78, 82
Sierra Leone 18, 53, 102, 116, 201
Somalia 29, 68, 116
Stanley, H. M. 17n16, 44–45
Sudan 19–23, 27, 35–36, 56n22, 68, 115,
    187

Tigrayan People's Liberation Front 111,
    189
Trade Justice Movement 160

War on Want 7, 11, 98n27, 144, 147,
    154–155, 158n18, 162, 172, 179
Wedgwood, J. 58, 81–82, 139, 157n7
Wilberforce, W. 78, 82, 85, 88, 97n9

Year of Africa 15, 125, 159, 171, 176–
    177, 184